Options Trading for Beginners

© **Copyright 2022 NFT Publishing - All rights reserved.**

This document is geared towards providing exact and reliable information regarding the topic and issue covered. The publication is sold with the idea that the publisher is not required to render accounting, officially permitted or otherwise qualified services. If advice is necessary, legal or professional, a practised individual in the profession should be ordered from a Declaration of Principles which was accepted and approved equally by a Committee of the American Bar Association and a Committee of Publishers and Associations.

In no way is it legal to reproduce, duplicate, or transmit any part of this document in either electronic means or printed format. Recording this publication is strictly prohibited, and any storage of this document is not allowed unless with written permission from the publisher. All rights reserved.

The information provided herein is stated to be truthful and consistent in that any liability, in terms of inattention or otherwise, by any usage or abuse of any policies, processes, or directions contained within is the solitary and utter responsibility of the recipient reader. Under no circumstances will any legal responsibility or blame be held against the publisher for any reparation, damages, or monetary loss due to the information herein, either directly or indirectly.

Want to receive exclusive updates, promotions, and bonus content related to this book and others, plus the chance to win free books? Look no further! Simply scan the QR code above and enter your email address on the landing page to join our email list.

As a member of our email list, you'll receive:

- Insider information and behind-the-scenes insights
- Special promotions and discounts on future purchases
- Early notification of future book releases

- The chance to win free books through our monthly sweepstakes

Don't wait - scan the QR code and join our email list today for your chance to win!

Table of content

Chapter 1: Call Options — 13

Chapter 2: Put Options — 18

Chapter 3: Intrinsic Value & How to Calculate it — 23

Chapter 4: Extrinsic Value — 27

Chapter 5: Option Premium — 33

Chapter 6: Strike Price — 39

Chapter 7: Options - OTM vs ITM — 45

Chapter 8: Expiration of Options — 51

Chapter 9: Selling Options — 57

Chapter 10: Option Direction — 62

Chapter 11: Option Spreads — 68

Chapter 12: Leverage — 75

Chapter 13: Notional Value — 81

Chapter 14: Cost Basis Reduction	87

Chapter 15: Getting Options Filled	93

Chapter 16: Number of Occurrences	99

Chapter 17: Volume & Open Interest	105

Chapter 18: Bid-Ask Spread	111

Chapter 19: What is the Importance of Liquidity in Options Trading?	117

Chapter 20: Options Assignment Understanding Assignment for Trading Options	123

Chapter 21: Options Assignment Risk	128

Chapter 22: Probability of Profit	134

Chapter 23: Break-Even Price	139

Chapter 24: Return on Capital	144

Chapter 25: Implied Volatility: Historic vs Implied	148

Chapter 26: How Does Implied Volatility Impact Option Pricing	153

Chapter 27: Implied Volatility Rank vs Implied Volatility Percentile	159

Chapter 28: Standard Deviation	168

Chapter 29: Implied Volatility & Standard Deviation 173

Chapter 30: Understanding Market Trends and Sentiment 178

Chapter 31: Volatility Skew 183

Chapter 32: Contrarian Mindset 189

Chapter 33: Implied Volatility Mean Reversion Explained 193

Chapter 34: Market Awareness Explained: Understanding the Importance 199

Chapter 35: What is Options Delta & How to Trade it? 208

Chapter 36: Delta & Directional Assumption Explained 212

Chapter 37: Gamma Explained: What is it & How to Trade it 219

Chapter 38: Theta Explained: What is it & How to Trade it 227

Chapter 39: Vega: What is it & How to Trade it 231

Chapter 40: Vega's Impact On Longer-Dated Options 238

Chapter 41: Portfolio Management: Short Delta & Short Vega Explained   243

Chapter 42: Day Trading Using SPY Explained   248

Chapter 43: Stock Correlation Explained   252

Chapter 44: Beta Explained: What is it & How to Trade it   256

Chapter 45: Four Factors for Measuring Risk: Delta, Gamma, Theta, and Vega   262

Chapter 46: Rolling an options trade explained   269

Chapter 47: Keeping Track of Rolled Options Explained   274

Chapter 48: Locking in Profit by Purchasing Options   279

Chapter 49: Option Spread Differences   283

Chapter 50: Defined Risk Spreads Explained   287

Chapter 51: Trade Entry Checklist   292

Chapter 52: Trading Options In A Small Account   299

Chapter 53: Credit Strategies For Earnings   303

Chapter 54: What Is A Covered Call & How Do I Trade It? 310

Chapter 55: How to Trade Covered Puts 318

Chapter 56: Covered Put Trading Strategies 324

Chapter 57: How to Trade Vertical Debit Spreads 330

Chapter 58: Comparing Bullish Option Strategies 336

Chapter 59: Bullish Strategy Adjustments: PMCC: Poor Man's Covered Call 343

Chapter 60: Buy Debit Spreads For Less Than Intrinsic Value 347

Chapter 61: Why & How to Finance Spreads in Options Trading 353

Chapter 62: How to Trade a Poor Man's Covered Call 359

Chapter 63: What is a Covered Put & How to Trade it? 365

Chapter 64: Short Put Adjustments Explained 369

Chapter 65: How to Trade a Short Naked Call 374

Chapter 66: What is a Short Strangle & How do I Trade it? 380

Chapter 67: Short Strangle Trading Tutorial 384

Chapter 68: Best Short Strangle Adjustments: 3 Short Strangles 388

Chapter 69: What is a Short Straddle 395

Chapter 70: How to Trade a Short Straddle Strategy 399

Chapter 71: Vertical Put Credit Spread Tutorial 405

Chapter 72: What is the Iron Condor Strategy? 411

Chapter 73: How to Trade the Iron Condor Strategy 415

Chapter 74: Chicken Iron Condor Strategy Tutorial 422

Chapter 75: How to Trade Earnings Announcements 428

Chapter 76: Iron Condor Adjustments Tutorial 435

Chapter 77: What is a Dynamic Iron Condor? 440

Chapter 78: Different Types of Iron Condors 447

Chapter 79: What is a Broken Wing Butterfly? 453

Chapter 80: How to Close a Broken Wing Butterfly 459

Chapter 81: Broken Wing Put Butterfly Tutorial 466

Chapter 82: What is a Poor Man's Covered Put? 470

Chapter 83: How to Trade a Poor Man's Covered Put 476

Chapter 84: What are Calendar Spread Strategies? 484

Chapter 85: How to Create a Put Calendar Spread 489

Chapter 86: How to Trade Call Calendar Spreads 496

Chapter 87: How to Manage Calendar Spreads 501

Chapter 88: What is a Butterfly Spread? 506

Chapter 89: How to Trade a Butterfly Spread 512

11

Chapter 90: How to Manage Butterfly Spreads 516

Chapter 91: What is a Condor Spread? 522

Chapter 92: How to Trade a Condor Spread 526

Chapter 93: How to Manage Condor Spreads 533

Chapter 94: What is a Diagonal Spread? 540

Chapter 95: How to Trade a Diagonal Spread 546

Chapter 96: How to Manage Diagonal Spreads 552

Chapter 97: How to Trade Options on Volatility 558

Chapter 98: Risk Management for Options Trading 563

Chapter 99: How to Create a Trading Plan 569

Chapter 100: Conclusion 576

Chapter 1: Call Options

Options trading can be a complex and intimidating endeavor for many investors. However, with a solid understanding of the basics and a willingness to learn, anyone can become a successful options trader. In this book, we will guide you through the ins and outs of options trading, starting with the most basic and essential of all options: call options.

Definition of Call Options

A call option is a type of financial contract that gives the holder the right, but not the obligation, to buy an underlying asset at a specific price (strike price) on or before a specific date (expiration date). The holder of the call option is betting that the price of the underlying asset will increase, while the seller of the call option is betting that the price of the underlying asset will stay the same or decrease.

Call options are often used as a way to speculate on the future price of an asset, such as a stock, commodity, or currency. They can also be used as a form of risk management, allowing traders to limit their potential losses while still participating in potential gains.

How Call Options Work

When buying a call option, the buyer pays a premium to the seller for the right to purchase the underlying asset at the strike price on or before the expiration date. The premium is essentially an insurance policy for the buyer, as it guarantees that they can buy the underlying asset at the strike price, regardless of what the market price is.

If the price of the underlying asset rises above the strike price before the expiration date, the buyer can exercise their option and buy the underlying asset at the strike price. They can then sell the underlying asset at the higher market price, resulting in a profit.

For example, if a trader buys a call option on a stock with a strike price of $50 and a premium of $2, and the stock price rises to $60 before the expiration date, the trader can exercise their option and buy the stock at $50. They can then sell the stock at $60, resulting in a profit of $8 ($60 - $50 - $2 premium).

The Mechanics of Buying and Selling Call Options

Buying a call option is a relatively straightforward process. The buyer simply pays the premium to the seller and receives the option contract. The contract will specify the strike price, expiration date, and underlying asset.

Selling a call option, also known as writing a call option, is a bit more complex. When selling a call option, the seller is essentially agreeing to sell the underlying asset at the strike price if the buyer chooses to exercise the option. This means that the seller must be willing and able to sell the underlying asset at the strike price.

The Potential Benefits and Risks of Call Options Trading

Call options trading can be a great way to profit from rising prices of underlying assets. However, as with any form of trading, it comes with its own set of risks.

One of the main benefits of call options trading is the ability to limit potential losses. Since the buyer only pays the premium for the option, their potential loss is limited to the premium paid. This is in contrast to traditional stock trading, where the potential loss is unlimited.

Another benefit of call options trading is leverage. Because options trading allows traders to control a large amount of underlying assets with a relatively small investment, it can be a great way to amplify potential gains.

However, there are also risks associated with call options trading. One of the main risks is time decay. As the expiration date of the option approaches, the option's value decreases, regardless of the price of the underlying asset. This means that a trader who buys a call option and sees the price of the underlying asset rise, but not enough to cover the time decay, may still end up with a loss.

Another risk is volatility. If the price of the underlying asset is highly volatile, the premium on the call option may increase, making it more expensive to buy. This can also increase the risk of a loss if the price of the underlying asset does not rise enough to cover the increased premium.

Finally, there is the risk of a gap. A gap is a sudden and unexpected change in the price of the underlying asset, which can occur due to a variety of factors such as an earnings release or a natural disaster. If a gap occurs, the trader may be forced to exercise the option at a loss or may not be able to exercise the option at all.

In summary, call options trading can be a great way to profit from rising prices of underlying assets while limiting potential losses. However, it is important to understand the risks, including time decay, volatility, and gaps, and to have a solid risk management plan in place. With a solid understanding of the basics and a willingness to learn, anyone can become a successful options trader.

Chapter 2: Put Options

In chapter one, we introduced the basics of call options and how they can be used to profit from rising prices of underlying assets. In this chapter, we will dive deeper into the world of options trading and explore the other side of the coin: put options.

Definition of Put Options

A put option is a type of financial contract that gives the holder the right, but not the obligation, to sell an underlying asset at a specific price (strike price) on or before a specific date (expiration date). The holder of the put option is betting that the price of the underlying asset will decrease, while the seller of the put option is betting that the price of the underlying asset will stay the same or increase.

Put options are often used as a way to speculate on the future price of an asset, such as a stock, commodity, or currency. They can also be used as a form of risk management, allowing traders to limit their potential losses while still participating in potential gains.

How Put Options Work

When buying a put option, the buyer pays a premium to the seller for the right to sell the underlying asset at the strike price on or before the expiration date. The premium is essentially an insurance policy for the buyer, as it guarantees that they can sell the underlying asset at the strike price, regardless of what the market price is.

If the price of the underlying asset falls below the strike price before the expiration date, the buyer can exercise their option and sell the underlying asset at the strike price. They can then buy the underlying asset at the lower market price, resulting in a profit.

For example, if a trader buys a put option on a stock with a strike price of $50 and a premium of $2, and the stock price falls to $40 before the expiration date, the trader can exercise their option and sell the stock at $50. They can then buy the stock at $40, resulting in a profit of $8 ($50 - $40 + $2 premium).

The Mechanics of Buying and Selling Put Options

Buying a put option is a relatively straightforward process. The buyer simply pays the premium to the seller and receives the option contract. The contract will specify the strike price, expiration date, and underlying asset.

Selling a put option, also known as writing a put option, is a bit more complex. When selling a put option, the seller is essentially agreeing to buy the underlying asset at the strike price if the buyer chooses to exercise the option. This means that the seller must be willing and able to buy the underlying asset at the strike price.

The Potential Benefits and Risks of Put Options Trading

Put options trading can be a great way to profit from falling prices of underlying assets.

However, as with any form of trading, it comes with its own set of risks.

One of the main benefits of put options trading is the ability to limit potential losses. Since the buyer only pays the premium for the option, their potential loss is limited to the premium paid.

This is in contrast to traditional short selling, where the potential loss is unlimited.

Another benefit of put options trading is the ability to profit from a market downturn. While traditional stock investors may have to wait for the market to recover to see gains, put options traders can profit from a falling market by exercising their options.

However, there are also risks associated with put options trading. One of the main risks is time decay, just like in call options. As the expiration date of the option approaches, the option's value decreases, regardless of the price of the underlying asset. This means that a trader who buys a put option and sees the price of the underlying asset fall, but not enough to cover the time decay, may still end up with a loss.

Another risk is volatility. If the price of the underlying asset is highly volatile, the premium on the put option may increase, making it more expensive to buy. This can also increase the risk of a loss if the price of the underlying asset does not fall enough to cover the increased premium.

Finally, there is the risk of a gap. A gap is a sudden and unexpected change in the price of the underlying asset, which can occur due to a variety of factors such as an earnings release or a natural disaster. If a gap occurs, the trader may be forced to exercise the option at a loss or may not be able to exercise the option at all.

In summary, put options trading can be a great way to profit from falling prices of underlying assets while limiting potential losses. However, it is important to understand the risks, including time decay, volatility, and gaps, and to have a solid risk management plan in place. With a solid understanding of the basics and a willingness to learn, anyone can become a successful options trader.

Chapter 3: Intrinsic Value & How to Calculate it

In the previous chapters, we introduced the basics of call and put options and how they can be used to profit from rising or falling prices of underlying assets. In this chapter, we will delve deeper into the concept of intrinsic value and how it affects the value of options.

Definition of Intrinsic Value

Intrinsic value is the inherent value of an option contract, based on the underlying asset's price in relation to the strike price. The intrinsic value of a call option is the difference between the underlying asset's price and the strike price, while the intrinsic value of a put option is the difference between the strike price and the underlying asset's price.

For example, if a stock is currently trading at $50 and a call option has a strike price of $45, the intrinsic value of the call option is $5 ($50 - $45). Similarly, if a put option has a strike price of $55 and the stock is currently trading at $50, the intrinsic value of the put option is $5 ($55 - $50).

How Intrinsic Value Affects the Value of Options

The intrinsic value of an option contract is one of the main factors that determine the value of the option. The intrinsic value represents the inherent worth of the option contract and is a key component in determining the value of an option.

For example, if a call option has an intrinsic value of $5 and a premium of $2, the total value of the option would be $7 ($5 intrinsic value + $2 premium). However, if the same option had an intrinsic value of $0 and a premium of $2, the total value of the option would be $2 ($0 intrinsic value + $2 premium).

It's important to note that an option can also have an extrinsic value, which represents the value of the option beyond its intrinsic value. The extrinsic value is also known as the time value or the volatility premium and it represents the time remaining until the expiration of the option and the volatility of the underlying asset.

How to Calculate Intrinsic Value

Calculating intrinsic value is relatively straightforward. To calculate the intrinsic value of a call option, simply subtract the strike price from the current market price of the underlying asset. To calculate the intrinsic value of a put option, simply subtract the current market price of the underlying asset from the strike price.

For example, if a stock is currently trading at $50 and a call option has a strike price of $45, the intrinsic value of the call option would be $5 ($50 - $45). Similarly, if a put option has a strike price of $55 and the stock is currently trading at $50, the intrinsic value of the put option would be $5 ($55 - $50). It's important to note that intrinsic value can only be calculated for in-the-money options (options that have intrinsic value) and not for out-of-the-money options (options that have no intrinsic value).

To teach readers how to calculate intrinsic value, one strategy could be to provide them with a list of stocks and their current prices, as well as a list of call and put options with their strike prices. The readers can then practice calculating the intrinsic value of each option. Another strategy could be to provide a step-by-step guide on how to calculate intrinsic value, including examples and exercises for the readers to practice.

It's also important to note that intrinsic value is only one aspect of an option's value. Extrinsic value, or the time value, also plays a role in the overall value of an option. This will be discussed in more detail in the next chapter. Understanding the concept of intrinsic value is crucial for any options trader as it helps in determining the potential profitability of an option trade. It also helps in understanding the risk involved in trading options. Mastering the ability to calculate intrinsic value will give traders a better understanding of the options market and allow them to make more informed trades.

Chapter 4: Extrinsic Value

In the options trading world, intrinsic value is a well-known concept but extrinsic value is not as widely understood. Extrinsic value is the value that an option has beyond its intrinsic value. It is also known as time value or implied volatility. Extrinsic value is an important concept for options traders to understand, as it affects options pricing and can be used to make trades that are more profitable and less risky. In this chapter, we will define extrinsic value, explain how it affects options pricing, discuss the importance of extrinsic value in options trading, and provide strategies for using extrinsic value to make trades.

Definition of Extrinsic Value

Extrinsic value is the value that an option has beyond its intrinsic value. It is the difference between the price of an option and its intrinsic value. Extrinsic value is also known as time value or implied volatility. It represents the amount of money that an option holder can make if the option is held until expiration and the underlying asset's price moves in the holder's favor. Extrinsic value is important because it affects options pricing.

How Extrinsic Value Affects Options Pricing

Extrinsic value affects options pricing because it represents the potential for the underlying asset's price to move in the holder's favor. The more time an option has until expiration, the more potential there is for the underlying asset's price to move in the holder's favor. As a result, options with more time until expiration have more extrinsic value and are therefore more expensive.

Options traders can use extrinsic value to identify options that are overpriced. When an option's price is higher than its intrinsic value, it is considered to be overpriced. This means that the option is not a good value and should not be purchased. By understanding extrinsic value, options traders can avoid overpriced options and make trades that are more profitable and less risky.

Importance of Extrinsic Value in Options Trading

Extrinsic value is an important concept for options traders to understand, as it affects options pricing and can be used to make trades that are more profitable and less risky. When an option has a high extrinsic value, it represents a high potential for the underlying asset's price to move in the holder's favor. This means that options traders can use extrinsic value to identify options that have the potential to be profitable and make trades accordingly.

Extrinsic value is also important because it can be used to identify options that are overpriced. When an option's price is higher than its intrinsic value, it is considered to be overpriced. This means that the option is not a good value and should not be purchased. By understanding extrinsic value, options traders can avoid overpriced options and make trades that are more profitable and less risky.

Strategies for Using Extrinsic Value to Make Trades

There are several strategies that options traders can use to make trades that are more profitable and less risky using extrinsic value. These strategies include:

1. Buying options with high extrinsic value: When an option has a high extrinsic value, it represents a high potential for the underlying asset's price to move in the holder's favor. Options traders can use extrinsic value to identify options that have the potential to be profitable and make trades accordingly.
2. Selling options with low extrinsic value: When an option has a low extrinsic value, it represents a low potential for the underlying asset's price to move in the holder's favor. Options traders can use extrinsic value to identify options that have a low potential for profit and sell them for a profit.
3. Buying options with high implied volatility: Implied volatility is a measure of the expected volatility of the underlying asset's price. Options with high implied volatility have high

extrinsic value and represent a high potential for the underlying asset's price to move in the holder's favor. Options traders can use implied volatility to identify options that have the potential to be profitable and make trades accordingly.
4. Selling options with low implied volatility: When an option has a low implied volatility, it represents a low potential for the underlying asset's price to move in the holder's favor. Options traders can use implied volatility to identify options that have a low potential for profit and sell them for a profit.
5. Hedging: Options traders can use extrinsic value to hedge their positions by purchasing options with high extrinsic value in case the underlying asset's price moves in an unfavorable direction.

In conclusion, extrinsic value is an important concept for options traders to understand. It represents the potential for the underlying asset's price to move in the holder's favor, and it affects options pricing. By understanding extrinsic value, options traders can identify options that have the potential to be profitable and make trades accordingly. By using the strategies outlined in this chapter, options traders can make trades that are more profitable and less risky. It's important to note that extrinsic value is just one aspect to consider when making trades, and traders should also consider other factors such as volatility, time to expiration, and market conditions.

Chapter 5: Option Premium

Option premium is a term that is commonly used in the world of options trading. It is the price that an option holder pays to purchase an option. The option premium is made up of two components: intrinsic value and extrinsic value. Intrinsic value is the inherent value of an option, while extrinsic value is the value that an option has beyond its intrinsic value. In this chapter, we will define option premium, explain how it is calculated, discuss the importance of option premium in options trading, and provide strategies for using option premium to make trades.

Definition of Option Premium

Option premium is the price that an option holder pays to purchase an option. It is made up of two components: intrinsic value and extrinsic value. Intrinsic value is the inherent value of an option, while extrinsic value is the value that an option has beyond its intrinsic value. The option premium represents the total value of an option and is used to determine the price at which an option is bought or sold.

How Option Premium is Calculated

Option premium is calculated by adding the intrinsic value and extrinsic value of an option. The intrinsic value of an option is determined by the difference between the underlying asset's price and the strike price, while the extrinsic value of an option is determined by the amount of time until expiration and the implied volatility of the underlying asset's price.

To calculate the option premium, you need to know the intrinsic value and extrinsic value of an option. You can find this information on most financial websites or through your brokerage account. Once you have this information, you can use the following formula to calculate the option premium:

Option Premium = Intrinsic Value + Extrinsic Value

Importance of Option Premium in Options Trading

Option premium is an important concept for options traders to understand, as it affects options pricing and can be used to make trades that are more profitable and less risky. When an option has a high option premium, it represents a high potential for the underlying asset's price to move in the holder's favor. This means that options traders can use option premium to identify options that have the potential to be profitable and make trades accordingly.

Option premium is also important because it can be used to identify options that are overpriced. When an option's price is higher than its intrinsic value, it is considered to be overpriced. This means that the option is not a good value and should not be purchased. By understanding option premium, options traders can avoid overpriced options and make trades that are more profitable and less risky.

Strategies for Using Option Premium to Make Trades

There are several strategies that options traders can use to make trades that are more profitable and less risky using option premium. These strategies include:

1. Buying options with high option premium: When an option has a high option premium, it represents a high potential for the underlying asset's price to move in the holder's favor. Options traders can use option premium to identify options that have the potential to be profitable and make trades accordingly.
2. Selling options with low option premium: When an option has a low option premium, it represents a low potential for the underlying asset's price to move in the holder's favor. Options traders can use option premium to identify options that have a low potential for profit and sell them for a profit.
3. Buying options with high intrinsic value: When an option has a high intrinsic value, it represents a high potential for the underlying asset's price to move in the holder's favor. Options traders can use intrinsic value to identify options that

have the potential to be profitable and make trades accordingly.
4. Selling options with low extrinsic value: When an option has a low extrinsic value, it represents a low potential for the underlying asset's price to move in the holder's favor. Options traders can use extrinsic value to identify options that have a low potential for profit and sell them for a profit.
5. Hedging: Options traders can use option premium to hedge their positions by purchasing options with high option premium in case the underlying asset's price moves in an unfavorable direction.
6. Combining strategies: Options traders can combine strategies to make trades that are more profitable and less risky. For example, they can buy options with high option premium and sell options with low option premium at the same time.

In conclusion, option premium is an important concept for options traders to understand. It represents the total value of an option and affects options pricing. By understanding option premium, options traders can identify options that have the potential to be profitable and make trades accordingly. By using the strategies outlined in this chapter, options traders can make trades that are more profitable and less risky. It's important to note that option premium is just one aspect to consider when making trades, and traders should also consider other factors such as volatility, time to expiration, and market conditions.

Chapter 6: Strike Price

The strike price, also known as the exercise price, is a crucial aspect of options trading. It is the price at which an option holder has the right to buy or sell the underlying asset. The strike price is used to determine the intrinsic value of an option, which is a key factor in options pricing. In this chapter, we will define strike price, explain how it affects options pricing, discuss the importance of strike price in options trading, and provide strategies for using strike price to make trades.

Definition of Strike Price

The strike price, also known as the exercise price, is the price at which an option holder has the right to buy or sell the underlying asset. It is the price at which the option can be exercised. The strike price is determined at the time the option is created and remains fixed throughout the life of the option. It is a key factor in options pricing and is used to determine the intrinsic value of an option.

39

How Strike Price Affects Options Pricing

The strike price affects options pricing by determining the intrinsic value of an option. The intrinsic value of an option is the difference between the underlying asset's price and the strike price. The intrinsic value represents the potential for the underlying asset's price to move in the holder's favor. When the underlying asset's price is above the strike price, the option has intrinsic value. When the underlying asset's price is below the strike price, the option has no intrinsic value.

Options traders can use the strike price to identify options that have the potential to be profitable. When an option's strike price is lower than the underlying asset's price, it represents a high potential for the underlying asset's price to move in the holder's favor. This means that options traders can use the strike price to identify options that have the potential to be profitable and make trades accordingly.

Importance of Strike Price in Options Trading

The strike price is an important concept for options traders to understand, as it affects options pricing and can be used to make trades that are more profitable and less risky. When an option's strike price is lower than the underlying asset's price, it represents a high potential for the underlying asset's price to move in the holder's favor. This means that options traders can use the strike price to identify options that have the potential to be profitable and make trades accordingly.

The strike price is also important because it can be used to identify options that are overpriced. When an option's strike price is higher than the underlying asset's price, it is considered to be overpriced. This means that the option is not a good value and should not be purchased. By understanding the strike price, options traders can avoid overpriced options and make trades that are more profitable and less risky.

Strategies for Using Strike Price to Make Trades

There are several strategies that options traders can use to make trades that are more profitable and less risky using the strike price. These strategies include:

1. Buying options with low strike price: When an option's strike price is lower than the underlying asset's price, it represents a high potential for the underlying asset's price to move in the holder's favor. Options traders can use the strike price to identify options that have the potential to be profitable and make trades accordingly.
2. Selling options with high strike price: When an option's strike price is higher than the underlying asset's price, it represents a low potential for the underlying asset's price to move in the holder's favor. Options traders can use the strike price to identify options that have a low potential for profit and sell them for a profit.
3. Buying in-the-money options: In-the-money options are options with a strike price that is lower than the underlying asset's price. These options have intrinsic value and represent a high

potential for the underlying asset's price to move in the holder's favor. Options traders can use the strike price to identify in-the-money options and make trades accordingly.
4. Selling out-of-the-money options: Out-of-the-money options are options with a strike price that is higher than the underlying asset's price. These options have no intrinsic value and represent a low potential for the underlying asset's price to move in the holder's favor. Options traders can use the strike price to identify out-of-the-money options and sell them for a profit.
5. Buying options with high implied volatility: Implied volatility is a measure of the expected volatility of the underlying asset's price. Options with high implied volatility and low strike price have high potential for the underlying asset's price to move in the holder's favor. Options traders can use implied volatility and strike price together to identify options that have the potential to be profitable and make trades accordingly.

6. Hedging: Options traders can use the strike price to hedge their positions by purchasing options with low strike price in case the underlying asset's price moves in an unfavorable direction.

In conclusion, strike price is an important concept for options traders to understand. It affects options pricing and can be used to make trades that are more profitable and less risky. By understanding the strike price, options traders can identify options that have the potential to be profitable and make trades accordingly. By using the strategies outlined in this chapter, options traders can make trades that are more profitable and less risky. It's important to note that strike price is just one aspect to consider when making trades, and traders should also consider other factors such as volatility, time to expiration, and market conditions.

Chapter 7: Options - OTM vs ITM

In options trading, options are classified as either out-of-the-money (OTM) or in-the-money (ITM) based on their intrinsic value. OTM options have a strike price that is higher than the current underlying asset's price, while ITM options have a strike price that is lower than the current underlying asset's price. In this chapter, we will define OTM and ITM options, explain how they differ in terms of intrinsic value and extrinsic value, discuss the importance of OTM and ITM options in options trading, and provide strategies for using OTM and ITM options to make trades.

Definition of OTM and ITM Options

OTM options are options with a strike price that is higher than the current underlying asset's price. These options have no intrinsic value and represent a low potential for the underlying asset's price to move in the holder's favor. OTM options are often used by options traders to generate income through the sale of options.

ITM options are options with a strike price that is lower than the current underlying asset's price. These options have intrinsic value and represent a high potential for the underlying asset's price to move in the holder's favor. ITM options are often used by options traders to speculate on the price movement of an underlying asset.

How OTM and ITM options differ in terms of intrinsic value and extrinsic value

OTM options have no intrinsic value and their value is entirely made up of extrinsic value. The extrinsic value of an OTM option is determined by the amount of time until expiration and the implied volatility of the underlying asset's price. OTM options have a low potential for the underlying asset's price to move in the holder's favor.

ITM options have intrinsic value and their value is made up of both intrinsic value and extrinsic value. The intrinsic value of an ITM option is determined by the difference between the underlying asset's price and the strike price. The extrinsic value of an ITM option is determined by the amount of time until expiration and the implied volatility of the underlying asset's price. ITM options have a high potential for the underlying asset's price to move in the holder's favor.

Importance of OTM and ITM options in options trading

OTM and ITM options are important in options trading because they represent different levels of potential for the underlying asset's price to move in the holder's favor. OTM options are often used by options traders to generate income through the sale of options, while ITM options are often used by options traders to speculate on the price movement of an underlying asset.

OTM options are also important in options trading because they have a lower potential for the underlying asset's price to move in the holder's favor. This makes them less risky than ITM options. On the other hand, ITM options are important in options trading because they have a higher potential for the underlying asset's price to move in the holder's favor. This makes them more risky than OTM options.

Strategies for using OTM and ITM options to make trades

There are several strategies that options traders can use to make trades using OTM and ITM options. These strategies include:

1. Selling OTM options: When an option's strike price is higher than the underlying asset's price, it represents a low potential for the underlying asset's price to move in the holder's favor. Options traders can use OTM options to generate income by selling them for a profit.
2. Buying ITM options: When an option's strike price is lower than the underlying asset's price, it represents a high potential for the underlying asset's price to move in the holder's favor. Options traders can use ITM options to speculate on the price movement of an underlying asset.

3. Writing covered calls: A covered call is a strategy in which an options trader sells call options on a stock they already own. The trader receives income from the sale of the call options, but also limits their potential profit on the stock. This strategy can be used to generate income using OTM options.
4. Buying protective puts: A protective put is a strategy in which an options trader buys put options on a stock they own. The trader receives insurance against a decline in the stock's price, but also limits their potential profit on the stock. This strategy can be used to protect a position using ITM options.
5. Combining strategies: Options traders can combine strategies to make trades that are more profitable and less risky. For example, they can sell OTM options and buy ITM options at the same time.

In conclusion, OTM and ITM options are important concepts for options traders to understand. They represent different levels of potential for the underlying asset's price to move in the holder's favor. OTM options are less risky and often used for income generation, while ITM options are more risky and often used for speculation. By understanding the difference between OTM and ITM options, options traders can make trades that are more profitable and less risky. As always, it is important to be aware of the risks involved in options trading and to always seek professional advice before making any trades.

Chapter 8: Expiration of Options

Options expiration is an important aspect of options trading. It is the date on which an option contract expires and the holder loses the right to exercise the option. The expiration date is determined at the time the option is created and is a key factor in options pricing. In this chapter, we will define option expiration, explain how it affects options pricing, discuss the importance of option expiration in options trading, and provide strategies for using option expiration to make trades.

Definition of Option Expiration

Option expiration is the date on which an option contract expires and the holder loses the right to exercise the option. The expiration date is determined at the time the option is created and remains fixed throughout the life of the option. Options expiration is a key factor in options pricing, as the closer an option is to expiration, the less time there is for the underlying asset's price to move in the holder's favor.

How Option Expiration Affects Options Pricing

Option expiration affects options pricing by determining the time remaining for the underlying asset's price to move in the holder's favor. The closer an option is to expiration, the less time there is for the underlying asset's price to move in the holder's favor. This means that options that are closer to expiration have less potential for profit and are therefore less valuable.

Options traders can use expiration to identify options that have the potential to be profitable. When an option has a long time until expiration, it represents a high potential for the underlying asset's price to move in the holder's favor. This means that options traders can use expiration to identify options that have the potential to be profitable and make trades accordingly.

Importance of Option Expiration in Options Trading

Option expiration is an important concept for options traders to understand, as it affects options pricing and can be used to make trades that are more profitable and less risky. The closer an option is to expiration, the less time there is for the underlying asset's price to move in the holder's favor. This means that options that are closer to expiration have less potential for profit and are therefore less valuable.

Option expiration is also important because it can be used to identify options that are overpriced. When an option is close to expiration, it is considered to be overpriced. This means that the option is not a good value and should not be purchased. By understanding option expiration, options traders can avoid overpriced options and make trades that are more profitable and less risky.

Strategies for Using Option Expiration to Make Trades

There are several strategies that options traders can use to make trades using option expiration. These strategies include:

1. Buying options with long time until expiration: When an option has a long time until expiration, it represents a high potential for the underlying asset's price to move in the holder's favor. Options traders can use expiration to identify options that have the potential to be profitable and make trades accordingly.
2. Selling options with short time until expiration: When an option is close to expiration, it represents a low potential for the underlying asset's price to move in the holder's favor. Options traders can use expiration to identify options that have a low potential for profit and sell them for a profit.
3. Buying options with high implied volatility: Implied volatility is a measure of the expected volatility of the underlying asset's price. Options with high implied volatility and long time until expiration have high potential for the underlying asset's price to move in the holder's favor. Options traders can use implied volatility and expiration together to identify options that have the

potential to be profitable and make trades accordingly.
4. Selling options with low implied volatility: Implied volatility is a measure of the expected volatility of the underlying asset's price. Options with low implied volatility and short time until expiration have low potential for the underlying asset's price to move in the holder's favor. Options traders can use implied volatility and expiration together to identify options that have a low potential for profit and sell them for a profit.
5. Hedging: Options traders can use option expiration to hedge their positions by purchasing options with long time until expiration in case the underlying asset's price moves in an unfavorable direction.

In conclusion, option expiration is an important concept for options traders to understand.
It affects options pricing and can be used to make trades that are more profitable and less risky. By understanding option expiration, options traders can identify options that have

the potential to be profitable and avoid overpriced options. Additionally, by using the strategies outlined in this chapter, options traders can improve their chances of success in the options market. However, it's important to remember that option expiration is just one aspect to consider when making trades, and traders should also consider other factors such as strike price, volatility, and market conditions. As always, it is important to be aware of the risks involved in options trading and to always seek professional advice before making any trades.

In the end, understanding option expiration is crucial for options traders to make trades that are more profitable and less risky. It is a key factor in options pricing, and can be used to identify options that have the potential to be profitable and avoid overpriced options. By understanding option expiration and using the strategies outlined in this book, options traders can improve their chances of success in the options market. However, it's important to remember that options trading carries risk and professional advice should always be sought before making any trades.

Chapter 9: Selling Options

Selling options is a popular strategy in options trading that can be used to generate income. It is the process of selling an option contract to another trader in exchange for a premium. In this chapter, we will define selling options, explain how it can be used to generate income, discuss the risks associated with selling options, and provide strategies for selling options to make trades.

Definition of Selling Options

Selling options is the process of selling an option contract to another trader in exchange for a premium. The option contract gives the buyer the right, but not the obligation, to buy or sell the underlying asset at a specified price on or before the expiration date. When an options trader sells an option, they receive the premium from the buyer and are obligated to sell or buy the underlying asset at the specified price if the option is exercised.

How Selling Options Can Be Used to Generate Income

Selling options can be used to generate income by collecting the premium from the option buyer. The premium is the amount that the buyer pays to the seller for the option contract. The seller collects the premium up front and can keep it regardless of whether the option is exercised or expires.

The seller can generate income by selling options in two ways:

1. Selling call options: This is when the seller receives a premium in exchange for the right to sell the underlying asset at a specific price.
2. Selling put options: This is when the seller receives a premium in exchange for the right to buy the underlying asset at a specific price.

Risks Associated with Selling Options

There are several risks associated with selling options, including:

1. Unlimited risk: When selling options, the seller is obligated to sell or buy the underlying asset at the specified price if the option is exercised. This means that the seller has unlimited risk if the underlying asset's price moves in an unfavorable direction.
2. Time decay: The value of an option decreases as it approaches expiration. This means that the seller may not be able to sell the option for a profit if it is close to expiration.
3. Volatility: The price of an option is affected by the volatility of the underlying asset's price. If the underlying asset's price becomes more volatile, the option will become more valuable, and the seller may not be able to sell the option for a profit.

Strategies for Selling Options to Make Trades

There are several strategies that options traders can use to sell options to make trades. These strategies include:

1. Selling covered calls: A covered call is a strategy in which an options trader sells call options on a stock they already own. The trader receives income from the sale of the call options, but also limits their potential profit on the stock.
2. Selling cash-secured puts: A cash-secured put is a strategy in which an options trader sells put options and has the cash on hand to buy the underlying asset if the option is exercised.
3. Selling naked options: A naked option is a strategy in which an options trader sells an option without owning the underlying asset. This strategy is considered to be high-risk and is not recommended for novice traders.
4. Combining strategies: Options traders can combine strategies to make trades that are more profitable and less risky.

For example, they can sell covered calls and cash-secured puts at the same time.

It is important to remember that selling options is a high-risk strategy and not recommended for novice traders. Additionally, it's important to be aware of the risks associated with selling options, such as unlimited risk, time decay, and volatility. Before making any trades, traders should seek professional advice and have a comprehensive understanding of the risks and strategies involved in selling options.

In conclusion, selling options is a popular strategy in options trading that can be used to generate income. By understanding the definition, benefits, risks and strategies of selling options, traders can make trades that are more profitable and less risky. However, it's important to remember that options trading carries risk and professional advice should always be sought before making any trades.

Chapter 10: Option Direction

Option direction is an important aspect of options trading. It refers to the direction in which the underlying asset's price is expected to move. In this chapter, we will define option direction, explain how it affects options pricing, discuss the importance of option direction in options trading, and provide strategies for using option direction to make trades. We will also include a use case study to illustrate the concepts discussed in this chapter.

Definition of Option Direction

Option direction refers to the direction in which the underlying asset's price is expected to move. In options trading, there are two types of option direction: call options and put options.

Call options are options that give the holder the right, but not the obligation, to buy the underlying asset at a specified price on or before the expiration date. These options are used when the underlying asset's price is expected to increase.

Put options are options that give the holder the right, but not the obligation, to sell the underlying asset at a specified price on or before the expiration date. These options are used when the underlying asset's price is expected to decrease.

How Option Direction Affects Options Pricing

Option direction affects options pricing by determining the potential for the underlying asset's price to move in the holder's favor. Call options have a higher potential for profit when the underlying asset's price is expected to increase, while put options have a higher potential for profit when the underlying asset's price is expected to decrease.

For example, if an options trader believes that the stock price of XYZ company will increase, they would buy call options. If the stock price of XYZ company does indeed increase, the value of the call options will also increase, and the trader can make a profit.

Importance of Option Direction in Options Trading

Option direction is an important concept for options traders to understand, as it affects options pricing and can be used to make trades that are more profitable and less risky. By understanding option direction, options traders can identify options that have the potential to be profitable and make trades accordingly.

For example, if an options trader believes that the stock price of XYZ company will decrease, they would buy put options. If the stock price of XYZ company does indeed decrease, the value of the put options will increase, and the trader can make a profit.

Strategies for Using Option Direction to Make Trades

There are several strategies that options traders can use to make trades using option direction. These strategies include:

1. Buying call options: When an options trader believes that the underlying asset's

price will increase, they can buy call options to profit from the price increase.
2. Buying put options: When an options trader believes that the underlying asset's price will decrease, they can buy put options to profit from the price decrease.
3. Combining strategies: Options traders can combine strategies to make trades that are more profitable and less risky. For example, they can buy call options and put options at the same time to hedge their position and limit their potential losses.
4. Using technical analysis: Options traders can use technical analysis to identify trends in the underlying asset's price and make trades accordingly. For example, if a stock's price has been consistently trending upward, the trader may choose to buy call options.

Use Case Study

An options trader named John is interested in trading the stock of XYZ company. John conducts research and finds that the stock price of XYZ company has been consistently trending upward for the past few months. Based on this information, John decides to buy call options on the stock of XYZ company.

John buys call options with a strike price of $50 and an expiration date in three months. The premium for the call options is $2 per share. John believes that the stock price of XYZ company will increase to $55 in three months.

Three months later, the stock price of XYZ company has indeed increased to $55. The value of John's call options has also increased to $5 per share. John can then sell the call options for a profit of $3 per share.

In this example, John used option direction and technical analysis to make a profitable trade. By understanding the potential for the underlying asset's price to increase, John was able to identify call options that had the potential to be profitable and make a trade accordingly.

In conclusion, option direction is an important aspect of options trading. It refers to the direction in which the underlying asset's price is expected to move and affects options pricing. By understanding option direction, options traders can identify options that have the potential to be profitable and make trades accordingly. Additionally, by using the strategies outlined in this chapter, options traders can improve their chances of success in the options market. However, it's important to remember that options trading carries risk and professional advice should always be sought before making any trades.

Chapter 11: Option Spreads

Option spreads are a popular strategy in options trading that can be used to reduce risk. They involve the simultaneous buying and selling of options with different strike prices and expiration dates. In this chapter, we will define option spreads, explain how they can be used to reduce risk, discuss the different types of option spreads, and provide strategies for using option spreads to make trades. We will also include a case study to illustrate the concepts discussed in this chapter.

Definition of Option Spreads

An option spread is a strategy in which an options trader simultaneously buys and sells options with different strike prices and expiration dates. The goal of an option spread is to reduce risk by offsetting the cost of the bought option with the income from the sold option.

There are two types of option spreads: debit spreads and credit spreads. A debit spread is when the cost of the bought option is greater than the income from the sold option, while a credit spread is when the income from the sold option is greater than the cost of the bought option.

How Option Spreads Can Be Used to Reduce Risk

Option spreads can be used to reduce risk by offsetting the cost of the bought option with the income from the sold option. This means that the trader's potential loss is limited to the difference between the strike prices of the options.

Additionally, option spreads can be used to take advantage of different market conditions. For example, a trader might use a call spread if they believe the market will go up, or a put spread if they believe the market will go down.

Types of Option Spreads

1. Call spreads: A call spread is a strategy in which a trader buys a call option with a lower strike price and sells a call option with a higher strike price. This strategy is used when the trader believes the underlying asset's price will increase.
2. Put spreads: A put spread is a strategy in which a trader buys a put option with a higher strike price and sells a put option with a lower strike price. This strategy is used when the trader believes the underlying asset's price will decrease.
3. Calendar spreads: A calendar spread is a strategy in which a trader buys a call or put option with a long-term expiration date and sells a call or put option with a short-term expiration date. This strategy is used when the trader believes the underlying asset's price will change over time.
4. Butterfly spreads: A butterfly spread is a strategy in which a trader buys a call or put option at the middle strike price and sells two call or put options at the higher and lower strike prices. This strategy is used when the trader believes the

underlying asset's price will stay relatively stable.

Strategies for Using Option Spreads to Make Trades

There are several strategies that options traders can use to make trades using option spreads. These strategies include:

1. Using call spreads to take advantage of an upward market: When an options trader believes that the underlying asset's price will increase, they can use a call spread strategy to profit from the price increase. This can be done by buying a call option with a lower strike price and selling a call option with a higher strike price.
2. Using put spreads to take advantage of a downward market: When an options trader believes that the underlying asset's price will decrease, they can use a put spread strategy to profit from the price decrease. This can be done by buying a put option with a higher strike price and

selling a put option with a lower strike price.
3. Using calendar spreads to take advantage of changing market conditions: When an options trader believes that the underlying asset's price will change over time, they can use a calendar spread strategy. This can be done by buying a call or put option with a long-term expiration date and selling a call or put option with a short-term expiration date.
4. Using butterfly spreads to take advantage of stable market conditions: When an options trader believes that the underlying asset's price will stay relatively stable, they can use a butterfly spread strategy. This can be done by buying a call or put option at the middle strike price and selling two call or put options at the higher and lower strike prices.

Case Study

An options trader named Sarah is interested in trading the stock of ABC company. Sarah conducts research and finds that the stock price of ABC company has been relatively stable for the past few months. Based on this information, Sarah decides to use a butterfly spread strategy.

Sarah buys a call option with a strike price of $50 and an expiration date in six months. She also sells two call options, one with a strike price of $55 and another with a strike price of $45. This creates a butterfly spread, where Sarah is betting that the stock price of ABC company will stay relatively stable and close to the $50 strike price.

Six months later, the stock price of ABC company has indeed stayed relatively stable, closing at $52. The value of Sarah's call option at the $50 strike price has increased to $2 per share, while the value of the call options at the $55 and $45 strike prices have decreased to $0.50 and $0.20 per share, respectively. This means Sarah has made a profit of $1.30 per share on the butterfly spread.

In this example, Sarah used the butterfly spread strategy to take advantage of the stable market conditions of the stock of ABC company. By understanding the potential for the underlying asset's price to stay relatively stable, Sarah was able to create a spread that had the potential to be profitable and make a trade accordingly.

In conclusion, option spreads are a popular strategy in options trading that can be used to reduce risk. They involve the simultaneous buying and selling of options with different strike prices and expiration dates. By understanding the different types of option spreads and how they can be used to take advantage of different market conditions, options traders can make trades that are more profitable and less risky. Additionally, by using the strategies outlined in this chapter, options traders can improve their chances of success in the options market. However, it's important to remember that options trading carries risk and professional advice should always be sought before making any trades.

Chapter 12: Leverage

Leverage is an important concept in options trading that can be used to increase potential profits and losses. It refers to the use of borrowed money to increase the buying power of an investment. In this chapter, we will define leverage, explain how it affects options trading, discuss the importance of leverage in options trading, and provide strategies for using leverage to make trades. We will also include a case study to illustrate the concepts discussed in this chapter.

Definition of Leverage

Leverage refers to the use of borrowed money to increase the buying power of an investment. In options trading, leverage is used to increase the potential profits and losses of a trade. This is done by using a small amount of capital to control a larger amount of the underlying asset.

For example, if an options trader has $1,000 and wants to buy a call option on a stock that is trading at $50 per share, they would only be able to buy 20 shares. However, if they used leverage, they could borrow $9,000 and buy 180 shares of the stock. This would increase the potential profits and losses of the trade.

How Leverage Affects Options Trading

Leverage affects options trading by increasing the potential profits and losses of a trade. This can be beneficial for options traders who are looking to make a large profit from a small investment. However, leverage also increases the risk of a trade, as the potential losses can also be larger.

For example, if an options trader uses leverage to buy a call option on a stock that is trading at $50 per share, they would have the potential to make a large profit if the stock price increases. However, if the stock price decreases, the trader would also have the potential to make a large loss.

Importance of Leverage in Options Trading

Leverage is an important concept in options trading because it can be used to increase potential profits and losses. This can be beneficial for options traders who are looking to make a large profit from a small investment. However, it's important for traders to understand the risks associated with leverage, as the potential losses can also be larger.

For example, if an options trader uses leverage to buy a put option on a stock that is trading at $50 per share, they would have the potential to make a large profit if the stock price decreases. However, if the stock price increases, the trader would also have the potential to make a large loss.

Strategies for Using Leverage to Make Trades

There are several strategies that options traders can use to make trades using leverage. These strategies include:

1. Using leverage to increase the potential profits and losses of a trade: When an options trader wants to make a large profit from a small investment, they can

use leverage to increase the potential profits and losses of a trade.
2. Using leverage to hedge against a potential loss: When an options trader wants to hedge against a potential loss, they can use leverage to offset the cost of the bought option with the income from the sold option.
3. Using leverage to take advantage of different market conditions: When an options trader wants to take advantage of different market conditions, they can use leverage to increase their buying power. For example, if the trader believes the market will go up, they can use leverage to buy more call options, and if they believe the market will go down, they can use leverage to buy more put options.
4. Using leverage with caution: While leverage can increase potential profits, it is important for traders to use it with caution. Traders should be aware of the risks associated with leverage and only use it if they are comfortable with the potential losses.

Case Study

An options trader named David is interested in trading the stock of XYZ company. David conducts research and finds that the stock price of XYZ company has been consistently trending upward for the past few months. Based on this information, David decides to use leverage to increase the potential profits of his trade.

David has $5,000 to invest in the stock of XYZ company. He uses leverage to borrow $20,000 and buys call options on the stock of XYZ company. The strike price of the options is $50, and the expiration date is in three months. The premium for the call options is $2 per share. David believes that the stock price of XYZ company will increase to $60 in three months.

Three months later, the stock price of XYZ company has indeed increased to $60. The value of David's call options has also increased to $10 per share. David can then sell the call options for a profit of $8 per share.

In this example, David used leverage to increase the potential profits of his trade. By understanding the potential for the underlying asset's price to increase, David was able to use leverage to buy more call options, which led to a higher profit. However, it's important to note that David also had the potential for a higher loss, as the use of leverage can also increase the potential losses of a trade.

In conclusion, leverage is an important concept in options trading that can be used to increase potential profits and losses. It is important for options traders to understand the risks associated with leverage and use it with caution. Additionally, by using the strategies outlined in this chapter, options traders can improve their chances of success in the options market. However, it's important to remember that options trading carries risk and professional advice should always be sought before making any trades.

Chapter 13: Notional Value

Notional value is an important concept in options trading that refers to the value of the underlying asset in a trade. It is used to calculate the total cost of an options trade and can affect the pricing of options. In this chapter, we will define notional value, explain how it affects options pricing, discuss the importance of notional value in options trading, and provide strategies for using notional value to make trades. We will also include a case study to illustrate the concepts discussed in this chapter.

Definition of Notional Value

Notional value refers to the value of the underlying asset in a trade. It is used to calculate the total cost of an options trade and can affect the pricing of options. For example, if an options trader wants to buy a call option on a stock that is trading at $50 per share, the notional value of the trade would be $50 per share.

How Notional Value Affects Options Pricing

Notional value affects options pricing by determining the total cost of an options trade. The notional value of a trade is used to calculate the intrinsic value and extrinsic value of an option. For example, if an options trader wants to buy a call option on a stock that is trading at $50 per share and the strike price of the option is $45 per share, the intrinsic value of the option would be $5 per share.

Importance of Notional Value in Options Trading

Notional value is an important concept in options trading because it is used to calculate the total cost of an options trade and can affect the pricing of options. Understanding the notional value of a trade can help options traders make more informed decisions and increase their chances of success in the options market.

For example, if an options trader wants to buy a put option on a stock that is trading at $50 per share, they would need to understand the notional value of the trade in order to calculate the intrinsic value and extrinsic value of the option. This information would then help the trader determine if the option is overvalued or undervalued, and make a decision on whether to buy the option or not.

Strategies for Using Notional Value to Make Trades

There are several strategies that options traders can use to make trades using notional value. These strategies include:

1. Using notional value to calculate intrinsic value: When an options trader wants to determine if an option is overvalued or undervalued, they can use the notional value of the trade to calculate the intrinsic value of the option.
2. Using notional value to determine the total cost of a trade: When an options trader wants to determine the total cost of a trade, they can use the notional value of the trade to calculate the

intrinsic value and extrinsic value of the option.
3. Using notional value to take advantage of different market conditions: When an options trader wants to take advantage of different market conditions, they can use the notional value of the trade to determine if the option is overvalued or undervalued. For example, if the trader believes the market will go up, they can use the notional value to determine if a call option is undervalued and therefore a good buy.
4. Using notional value to make informed decisions: When an options trader wants to make an informed decision, they can use the notional value of the trade to determine the intrinsic value and extrinsic value of the option. This can help the trader determine if the option is overvalued or undervalued and make a decision on whether to buy the option or not.

Case Study

An options trader named John is interested in trading the stock of DEF company. John conducts research and finds that the stock price of DEF company has been consistently trending downward for the past few months. Based on this information, John decides to use notional value to determine if a put option on DEF company is undervalued.

John wants to buy a put option on DEF company with a strike price of $50 per share and an expiration date in three months. The current stock price of DEF company is $45 per share. John uses the notional value of the trade to calculate the intrinsic value of the option. The intrinsic value of the option is $5 per share, which is the difference between the strike price and the current stock price.

John then determines that the put option is undervalued and decides to buy the option. Three months later, the stock price of DEF company has indeed decreased to $40 per share. The value of John's put option has also increased to $10 per share. John can then sell the put option for a profit of $5 per share.

In this example, John used notional value to determine if a put option on DEF company was undervalued. By understanding the notional value of the trade and the intrinsic value of the option, John was able to make an informed decision and buy the option, which led to a profit. Additionally, by using the notional value, John was able to take advantage of the downward trend in DEF company's stock price.

In conclusion, notional value is an important concept in options trading that is used to calculate the total cost of an options trade and can affect the pricing of options. Understanding the notional value of a trade can help options traders make more informed decisions and increase their chances of success in the options market. By using the strategies outlined in this chapter, options traders can improve their chances of success in the options market. However, it's important to remember that options trading carries risk and professional advice should always be sought before making any trades.

Chapter 14: Cost Basis Reduction

Cost basis reduction is an important concept in options trading that refers to the process of minimizing losses by adjusting the cost of an investment. It can be used to reduce the potential losses of a trade and increase the chances of success in the options market. In this chapter, we will define cost basis reduction, explain how it can be used to minimize losses, discuss the importance of cost basis reduction in options trading, and provide strategies for using cost basis reduction to make trades. We will also include a case study to illustrate the concepts discussed in this chapter.

Definition of Cost Basis Reduction

Cost basis reduction refers to the process of minimizing losses by adjusting the cost of an investment. In options trading, cost basis reduction can be used to reduce the potential losses of a trade by adjusting the strike price of an option or by using option spreads.

How Cost Basis Reduction Can be Used to Minimize Losses

Cost basis reduction can be used to minimize losses by adjusting the strike price of an option or by using option spreads. By adjusting the strike price of an option, an options trader can reduce the potential losses of a trade by decreasing the difference between the strike price and the current stock price. For example, if an options trader wants to buy a put option on a stock that is trading at $50 per share, they can adjust the strike price to $45 per share, which would reduce the potential losses of the trade.

Option spreads can also be used to minimize losses by reducing the potential losses of a trade. For example, if an options trader wants to buy a call option on a stock that is trading at $50 per share, they can use a call spread to reduce the potential losses of the trade. A call spread is an options trading strategy in which an options trader buys a call option with a strike price that is lower than the current stock price, and sells a call option with a strike price that is higher than the current stock price. This creates a spread between the two options, which reduces the potential losses of the trade.

Importance of Cost Basis Reduction in Options Trading

Cost basis reduction is an important concept in options trading because it can be used to minimize losses and increase the chances of success in the options market. By adjusting the strike price of an option or by using option spreads, options traders can reduce the potential losses of a trade and increase the chances of making a profit. Additionally, cost basis reduction can also be used to manage risk and protect profits by adjusting the strike price or using option spreads to lock in gains.

Strategies for Using Cost Basis Reduction to Make Trades

There are several strategies that options traders can use to make trades using cost basis reduction. These strategies include:

1. Adjusting the strike price of an option: By adjusting the strike price of an option,

an options trader can reduce the potential losses of a trade.
2. Using option spreads: By using option spreads, an options trader can reduce the potential losses of a trade by creating a spread between two options.
3. Locking in gains: By adjusting the strike price or using option spreads, an options trader can lock in gains and protect profits.
4. Managing risk: By adjusting the strike price or using option spreads, an options trader can manage risk and reduce the potential losses of a trade.

Case Study

An options trader named Sarah is interested in trading the stock of GHI company. Sarah conducts research and finds that the stock price of GHI company has been consistently trending upward for the past few months. Based on this information, Sarah decides to use cost basis reduction to minimize losses.

Sarah wants to buy a call option on GHI company with a strike price of $50 per share and an expiration date in three months. The current stock price of GHI company is $45 per share. Sarah decides to use a call spread to reduce the potential losses of the trade. Sarah buys a call option with a strike price of $45 per share and sells a call option with a strike price of $55 per share.

Three months later, the stock price of GHI company has indeed increased to $55 per share. The value of Sarah's call options has also increased. Sarah can then sell the call options for a profit while minimizing her potential losses.

In this example, Sarah used cost basis reduction to minimize losses by using a call spread. By understanding the potential for the underlying asset's price to increase, Sarah was able to reduce the potential losses of the trade and increase her chances of making a profit. Additionally, by using cost basis reduction, Sarah was able to manage her risk and protect her profits.

In conclusion, cost basis reduction is an important concept in options trading that can be used to minimize losses and increase the chances of success in the options market. It is important for options traders to understand the concept of cost basis reduction and use it to make trades. Additionally, by using the strategies outlined in this chapter, options traders can improve their chances of success in the options market while minimizing losses. However, it's important to remember that options trading carries risk and professional advice should always be sought before making any trades. It's also important to note that cost basis reduction is not a guarantee of success, but rather a way to manage risk and increase the chances of success in the options market. As always, it's important to conduct proper research and use a well thought out strategy before making any trades.

Chapter 15: Getting Options Filled

Getting options filled is an important aspect of options trading that refers to the process of ensuring that options trades are executed at the desired price. In this chapter, we will define getting options filled, explain how to ensure that options trades are filled at the desired price, discuss the importance of getting options filled in options trading, and provide strategies for getting options filled such as using limit orders, market orders, and stop-loss orders. We will also include a case study to illustrate the concepts discussed in this chapter.

Definition of Getting Options Filled

Getting options filled refers to the process of ensuring that options trades are executed at the desired price. This means that when an options trader places an order to buy or sell an option, the trade is executed at the price that the trader specified.

How to Ensure That Options Trades are Filled at the Desired Price

There are several ways to ensure that options trades are filled at the desired price. These include:

1. Using limit orders: A limit order is an order to buy or sell an option at a specific price or better. By using a limit order, an options trader can ensure that the trade is executed at the desired price or better.
2. Using market orders: A market order is an order to buy or sell an option at the current market price. By using a market order, an options trader can ensure that the trade is executed at the current market price.
3. Using stop-loss orders: A stop-loss order is an order to buy or sell an option when the price reaches a certain level. By using a stop-loss order, an options trader can ensure that the trade is executed at the desired price or better.

Importance of Getting Options Filled in Options Trading

Getting options filled is an important aspect of options trading because it ensures that trades are executed at the desired price. This is important because it can affect the profitability of a trade. If a trade is executed at a price that is not the desired price, the profitability of the trade may be affected. Additionally, getting options filled can also be used to manage risk by ensuring that trades are executed at the desired price or better.

Strategies for Getting Options Filled

There are several strategies that options traders can use to get options filled. These include:

1. Using limit orders: By using a limit order, an options trader can ensure that the trade is executed at the desired price or better.
2. Using market orders: By using a market order, an options trader can ensure that the trade is executed at the current market price.

3. Using stop-loss orders: By using a stop-loss order, an options trader can ensure that the trade is executed at the desired price or better.

Case Study

An options trader named Jake is interested in trading the stock of JKL company. Jake conducts research and finds that the stock price of JKL company has been consistently trending upward for the past few months. Based on this information, Jake decides to buy a call option on JKL company with a strike price of $50 per share and an expiration date in three months.

Jake wants to ensure that the trade is executed at the desired price, so he uses a limit order to buy the option. He specifies that he wants to buy the option at a price of $2 per share or better. This means that if the option is trading at a price of $2 per share or lower, his order will be filled. If the option is trading at a price higher than $2 per share, his order will not be filled.

Jake's order is filled at a price of $2 per share, and he buys the option at the desired price. Three months later, the stock price of JKL company has indeed increased to $55 per share. The value of Jake's call option has also increased, and he can then sell the option for a profit.

In this example, Jake used a limit order to ensure that his trade was executed at the desired price. By using a limit order, Jake was able to buy the option at a price that he was comfortable with, which increased the chances of profitability for his trade. Additionally, by getting his option filled at the desired price, Jake was able to manage his risk and protect his profits.

In conclusion, getting options filled is an important aspect of options trading that ensures that trades are executed at the desired price. By using strategies such as limit orders, market orders, and stop-loss orders, options traders can increase the chances of getting their trades filled at the desired price. Additionally, by getting options filled at the desired price, options traders can manage risk and protect profits.

However, it's important to remember that options trading carries risk and professional advice should always be sought before making any trades.

Chapter 16: Number of Occurrences

The number of occurrences is an important concept in options trading that refers to the number of times that an option can be exercised. In this chapter, we will define the number of occurrences, explain how it affects options pricing, discuss the importance of number of occurrences in options trading, and provide strategies for using number of occurrences to make trades. We will also include a case study to illustrate the concepts discussed in this chapter.

Definition of Number of Occurrences

The number of occurrences refers to the number of times that an option can be exercised. Options can be either American style or European style. American-style options can be exercised at any time before the expiration date, while European-style options can only be exercised on the expiration date. The number of

99

occurrences is important because it affects the price of an option.

How Number of Occurrences Affects Options Pricing

The number of occurrences affects options pricing because it affects the value of an option. American-style options are generally more expensive than European-style options because they can be exercised at any time before the expiration date. This means that the value of an American-style option is generally higher than the value of a European-style option.

Importance of Number of Occurrences in Options Trading

The number of occurrences is an important concept in options trading because it affects the price of an option. By understanding the number of occurrences, options traders can make more informed decisions about buying and selling options. Additionally, the number of occurrences can be used to manage risk by choosing options with a higher number of occurrences, which are generally more expensive.

Strategies for Using Number of Occurrences to Make Trades

There are several strategies that options traders can use to make trades using the number of occurrences. These strategies include:

1. Buying American-style options: By buying American-style options, an options trader can take advantage of the fact that they can be exercised at any time before the expiration date.
2. Buying European-style options: By buying European-style options, an options trader can take advantage of the fact that they are generally less expensive than American-style options.
3. Managing risk: By choosing options with a higher number of occurrences, an options trader can manage risk and protect profits.

Case Study

An options trader named Alex is interested in trading the stock of XYZ company. Alex conducts research and finds that the stock price of XYZ company has been consistently trending upward for the past few months. Based on this information, Alex decides to buy a call option on XYZ company with an expiration date in three months.

Alex has the option to choose between an American-style option or a European-style option. The American-style option has a higher number of occurrences, which means it can be exercised at any time before the expiration date. The European-style option can only be exercised on the expiration date.

Alex decides to buy the American-style option because it has a higher number of occurrences and can be exercised at any time before the expiration date. This allows Alex to take advantage of any short-term price fluctuations in the stock of XYZ company.

Three months later, the stock price of XYZ company has indeed increased. Alex can then exercise the option and sell the stock for a profit.

In this example, Alex used the number of occurrences to make a trade by choosing the American-style option. By understanding the number of occurrences and how it affects the price of an option, Alex was able to make a more informed decision and take advantage of the fact that the American-style option could be exercised at any time before the expiration date. Additionally, by choosing the American-style option, Alex was able to manage his risk and protect his profits.

In conclusion, the number of occurrences is an important concept in options trading that affects the price of an option. By understanding the number of occurrences, options traders can make more informed decisions about buying and selling options. Additionally, the number of occurrences can be used to manage risk by choosing options with a higher number of occurrences, which are generally more expensive. However, it's important to remember that options trading carries risk and professional advice should always be sought before making any trades.

Chapter 17: Volume & Open Interest

Volume and open interest are two important concepts in options trading that refer to the number of options contracts that are traded and the number of options contracts that are held by traders, respectively. In this chapter, we will define volume and open interest, explain how they affect options pricing, discuss the importance of volume and open interest in options trading, and provide strategies for using volume and open interest to make trades. We will also include a case study to illustrate the concepts discussed in this chapter.

Definition of Volume & Open Interest

Volume refers to the number of options contracts that are traded on a given day. It is a measure of the activity in the options market and can be used to gauge the level of interest in a particular stock or option.

Open interest refers to the number of options contracts that are held by traders. It is a measure of the total number of options contracts that are currently outstanding and can be used to gauge the level of interest in a particular stock or option.

How Volume & Open Interest Affect Options Pricing

Volume and open interest affect options pricing because they are indicators of the level of interest in a particular stock or option. A high volume of trading activity and a high level of open interest can indicate that there is a lot of interest in the stock or option, which can drive up the price. Conversely, a low volume of trading activity and a low level of open interest can indicate that there is little interest in the stock or option, which can drive down the price.

Importance of Volume & Open Interest in Options Trading

Volume and open interest are important concepts in options trading because they are indicators of the level of interest in a particular stock or option. By understanding the volume and open interest, options traders can make more informed decisions about buying and selling options. Additionally, volume and open interest can be used to manage risk by choosing options with a high volume and open interest, which are generally considered to be more liquid and less risky.

Strategies for Using Volume & Open Interest to Make Trades

There are several strategies that options traders can use to make trades using volume and open interest. These strategies include:

1. Buying options with high volume: By buying options with high volume, an options trader can take advantage of the fact that there is a lot of interest in the stock or option, which can drive up the price.
2. Selling options with low volume: By selling options with low volume, an options trader can take advantage of the fact that there is little interest in the stock

or option, which can drive down the price.
3. Buying options with high open interest: By buying options with high open interest, an options trader can take advantage of the fact that there are a lot of options contracts held by traders, which can indicate a high level of interest in the stock or option.
4. Selling options with low open interest: By selling options with low open interest, an options trader can take advantage of the fact that there are few options contracts held by traders, which can indicate a low level of interest in the stock or option.

Case Study

An options trader named Sarah is interested in trading the stock of ABC company. Sarah conducts research and finds that the volume of trading activity in the options market for ABC company has been consistently high over the past few months. Additionally, the level of open interest in the options for ABC company is also high. Based on this information, Sarah decides to buy a call option on ABC company with an expiration date in three months.

Sarah's research and analysis of the volume and open interest of the options for ABC company indicates that there is a high level of interest in the stock, which can drive up the price. Additionally, the high volume and open interest of the options for ABC company indicate that the options are liquid and less risky.

Three months later, the stock price of ABC company has indeed increased. Sarah can then exercise the option and sell the stock for a profit.

In this example, Sarah used the volume and open interest to make a trade by buying an option with a high volume and open interest. By understanding the volume and open interest and how they affect the price of an option, Sarah was able to make a more informed decision and take advantage of the high level of interest in the stock of ABC company. Additionally, by choosing an option with a high volume and open interest, Sarah was able to manage her risk and protect her profits.

In conclusion, volume and open interest are important concepts in options trading that affect the price of an option. By understanding the volume and open interest, options traders can make more informed decisions about buying and selling options. Additionally, volume and open interest can be used to manage risk by choosing options with a high volume and open interest, which are generally considered to be more liquid and less risky. However, it's important to remember that options trading carries risk and professional advice should always be sought before making any trades.

Chapter 18: Bid-Ask Spread

The bid-ask spread is an important concept in options trading that refers to the difference between the highest price that a buyer is willing to pay for an option (the bid) and the lowest price that a seller is willing to accept for an option (the ask). In this chapter, we will define the bid-ask spread, explain how it affects options pricing, discuss the importance of the bid-ask spread in options trading, and provide strategies for using the bid-ask spread to make trades. We will also include a case study to illustrate the concepts discussed in this chapter.

Definition of Bid-Ask Spread

The bid-ask spread is the difference between the highest price that a buyer is willing to pay for an option (the bid) and the lowest price that a seller is willing to accept for an option (the ask). The bid-ask spread is a measure of the liquidity of the options market and can be used to gauge the level of demand for a particular stock or option.

How Bid-Ask Spread Affects Options Pricing

The bid-ask spread affects options pricing because it is a measure of the liquidity of the options market. A narrow bid-ask spread can indicate that there is a high level of demand for the stock or option, which can drive up the price. Conversely, a wide bid-ask spread can indicate that there is little demand for the stock or option, which can drive down the price.

Importance of Bid-Ask Spread in Options Trading

The bid-ask spread is important in options trading because it is a measure of the liquidity of the options market. By understanding the bid-ask spread, options traders can make more informed decisions about buying and selling options. Additionally, the bid-ask spread can be used to manage risk by choosing options with a narrow bid-ask spread, which are generally considered to be more liquid and less risky.

Strategies for Using Bid-Ask Spread to Make Trades

There are several strategies that options traders can use to make trades using the bid-ask spread. These strategies include:

1. Buying options with a narrow bid-ask spread: By buying options with a narrow bid-ask spread, an options trader can take advantage of the high level of demand for the stock or option, which can drive up the price.
2. Selling options with a wide bid-ask spread: By selling options with a wide bid-ask spread, an options trader can take advantage of the low level of demand for the stock or option, which can drive down the price.
3. Buying options with a narrow bid-ask spread and selling options with a wide bid-ask spread: By buying options with a narrow bid-ask spread and selling options with a wide bid-ask spread, an options trader can take advantage of the difference in demand for the stock or option and make a profit.

Case Study

An options trader named John is interested in trading the stock of XYZ company. John conducts research and finds that the bid-ask spread for the options of XYZ company is very narrow. Additionally, the volume of trading activity in the options market for XYZ company is also high. Based on this information, John decides to buy a call option on XYZ company with an expiration date in three months.

John's research and analysis of the bid-ask spread and volume of trading activity of the options for XYZ company indicates that there is a high level of demand for the stock, which can drive up the price. Additionally, the narrow bid-ask spread and high volume of trading activity of the options for XYZ company indicate that the options are liquid and less risky.

Three months later, the stock price of XYZ company has indeed increased. John can then exercise the option and sell the stock for a profit.

In this example, John used the bid-ask spread and volume of trading activity to make a trade by buying an option with a narrow bid-ask spread and high volume of trading activity. By understanding the bid-ask spread and how it affects the price of an option, John was able to make a more informed decision and take advantage of the high level of demand for the stock of XYZ company. Additionally, by choosing an option with a narrow bid-ask spread and high volume of trading activity, John was able to manage his risk and protect his profits.

In conclusion, the bid-ask spread is an important concept in options trading that affects the price of an option. By understanding the bid-ask spread, options traders can make more informed decisions about buying and selling options. Additionally, the bid-ask spread can be used to manage risk by choosing options with a narrow bid-ask spread, which are generally considered to be more liquid and less risky. However, it's important to remember that options trading carries risk and professional advice should always be sought before making any trades. Additionally, it's important to keep an eye on the volume of trading activity, as this can also affect the liquidity and risk associated with an option.

Chapter 19: What is the Importance of Liquidity in Options Trading?

Liquidity is a key concept in options trading that refers to the ease with which an option can be bought or sold at a given price. In this chapter, we will define liquidity in options trading, explain how it affects options pricing, discuss the importance of liquidity in options trading, and provide strategies for finding liquidity in options trading. We will also include a case study to illustrate the concepts discussed in this chapter.

Definition of Liquidity in Options Trading

Liquidity in options trading refers to the ease with which an option can be bought or sold at a given price. A liquid option is one that can be easily bought or sold at a fair price, while an illiquid option is one that is difficult to trade at a fair price.

How Liquidity Affects Options Pricing

Liquidity affects options pricing because it is a measure of the demand for the stock or option. A liquid option will have a lower bid-ask spread, indicating that there is a high level of demand for the stock or option, which can drive up the price. Conversely, an illiquid option will have a wider bid-ask spread, indicating that there is little demand for the stock or option, which can drive down the price.

Importance of Liquidity in Options Trading

Liquidity is important in options trading because it allows options traders to buy or sell an option at a fair price. A liquid option is less risky than an illiquid option because it can be easily bought or sold at a fair price. Additionally, liquidity can be used to manage risk by choosing options with a high level of liquidity, which are generally considered to be less risky.

Strategies for Finding Liquidity in Options Trading

There are several strategies that options traders can use to find liquidity in options trading. These strategies include:

1. Choosing options with a high volume of trading activity: By choosing options with a high volume of trading activity, an options trader can take advantage of the high level of demand for the stock or option, which can drive up the price.
2. Choosing options with a narrow bid-ask spread: By choosing options with a narrow bid-ask spread, an options trader can take advantage of the high level of demand for the stock or option, which can drive up the price. A narrow bid-ask spread also indicates a high level of liquidity, making it easier for the trader to buy or sell the option at a fair price.
3. Researching the underlying stock or asset: By researching the underlying stock or asset, an options trader can gain a better understanding of the factors that affect the demand for the stock or option. This can help the trader identify options with a high level of liquidity.

4. Monitoring implied volatility: Implied volatility is a measure of the level of volatility in the options market. A high level of implied volatility can indicate that there is a high level of demand for the stock or option, which can drive up the price. An options trader can use this information to find options with a high level of liquidity.

Case Study

An options trader named Jane is interested in trading the stock of ABC company. Jane conducts research and finds that the volume of trading activity in the options market for ABC company is high. Additionally, the bid-ask spread for the options of ABC company is also narrow. Based on this information, Jane decides to buy a call option on ABC company with an expiration date in six months.

Jane's research and analysis of the volume of trading activity and bid-ask spread of the options for ABC company indicates that there is a high level of liquidity in the options market.

Additionally, the high volume of trading activity and narrow bid-ask spread of the options for ABC company indicate that the options are less risky.

Six months later, the stock price of ABC company has indeed increased. Jane can then exercise the option and sell the stock for a profit.

In this example, Jane used the volume of trading activity and bid-ask spread to find liquidity in the options market. By understanding the importance of liquidity in options trading, Jane was able to make a more informed decision and take advantage of the high level of demand for the stock of ABC company. Additionally, by choosing an option with a high volume of trading activity and narrow bid-ask spread, Jane was able to manage her risk and protect her profits.

In conclusion, liquidity is an important concept in options trading that affects the price of an option. By understanding liquidity, options traders can make more informed decisions about buying and selling options. Additionally, liquidity can be used to manage risk by choosing options with a high level of liquidity, which are generally considered to be less risky. However, it's important to remember that options trading carries risk and professional advice should always be sought before making any trades.

Chapter 20: Options Assignment Understanding Assignment for Trading Options

Options assignment is a key concept in options trading that refers to the process of a call option holder being assigned shares of the underlying stock or a put option holder being required to sell shares of the underlying stock. In this chapter, we will define options assignment, explain how it affects options trading, discuss the importance of understanding options assignment in options trading, and provide strategies for managing options assignment risk. We will also include a case study to illustrate the concepts discussed in this chapter.

Definition of Options Assignment

Options assignment is the process of a call option holder being assigned shares of the underlying stock or a put option holder being required to sell shares of the underlying stock.

This occurs when the holder of the option decides to exercise the option.

How Options Assignment Affects Options Trading

Options assignment affects options trading because it can have a significant impact on the price of the option. When a call option is assigned, the holder of the option is required to buy shares of the underlying stock at the strike price. This can drive up the price of the option. Conversely, when a put option is assigned, the holder of the option is required to sell shares of the underlying stock at the strike price. This can drive down the price of the option.

Importance of Understanding Options Assignment in Options Trading

Understanding options assignment is important in options trading because it allows options traders to manage their risk and make more informed decisions about buying and selling options. By understanding how options assignment affects the price of an option, options traders can make more informed decisions about when to exercise an option and when to let it expire.

Strategies for Managing Options Assignment Risk

There are several strategies that options traders can use to manage the risk associated with options assignment. These strategies include:

1. Choosing options with a high level of liquidity: By choosing options with a high level of liquidity, an options trader can reduce the risk of the option being assigned at an unfavorable price.
2. Using stop-loss orders: By using stop-loss orders, an options trader can limit their losses if the option is assigned at an unfavorable price.
3. Using options spreads: By using options spreads, an options trader can reduce the risk of the option being assigned at an unfavorable price.

Case Study

An options trader named Michael is interested in trading the stock of XYZ company. Michael buys a call option on XYZ company with an expiration date in six months. Michael's analysis of the stock and the options market indicates that the stock is likely to increase in value.

However, Michael is concerned about the risk of options assignment. To manage this risk, Michael chooses an option with a high level of liquidity and uses a stop-loss order to limit his losses if the option is assigned at an unfavorable price.

Six months later, the stock price of XYZ company has indeed increased. However, Michael's option is not assigned and he is able to exercise the option and sell the stock for a profit.

In this example, Michael used strategies such as choosing options with a high level of liquidity and using stop-loss orders to manage the risk of options assignment. By understanding the importance of options assignment in options trading, Michael was able to make more informed decisions and protect his profits.

In conclusion, options assignment is a key concept in options trading that can have a significant impact on the price of an option. It is important for options traders to understand how options assignment affects options trading and to have strategies in place to manage the risk associated with options assignment. By understanding options assignment and managing risk, options traders can make more informed decisions about buying and selling options and protect their profits. However, it's important to remember that options trading carries risk and professional advice should always be sought before making any trades. Additionally, It's also important to keep in mind the expiration date of the option and to act accordingly, because if the option expires unexercised, the holder will lose the premium paid for the option.

Chapter 21: Options Assignment Risk

Options assignment risk is a key concept in options trading that refers to the risk associated with the process of a call option holder being assigned shares of the underlying stock or a put option holder being required to sell shares of the underlying stock. In this chapter, we will define options assignment risk, explain how it affects options trading, discuss the importance of managing options assignment risk in options trading, and provide strategies for managing options assignment risk. We will also include a case study to illustrate the concepts discussed in this chapter.

Definition of Options Assignment Risk

Options assignment risk is the risk associated with the process of a call option holder being assigned shares of the underlying stock or a put option holder being required to sell shares of the underlying stock. This risk can arise if the holder of the option is not able to sell the stock or option at a favorable price.

How Options Assignment Risk Affects Options Trading

Options assignment risk affects options trading because it can have a significant impact on the price of the option. When a call option is assigned, the holder of the option is required to buy shares of the underlying stock at the strike price. This can drive up the price of the option. Conversely, when a put option is assigned, the holder of the option is required to sell shares of the underlying stock at the strike price. This can drive down the price of the option.

Importance of Managing Options Assignment Risk in Options Trading

Managing options assignment risk is important in options trading because it allows options traders to protect their profits and make more informed decisions about buying and selling options. By managing options assignment risk, options traders can ensure that they are able to sell the stock or option at a favorable price.

Strategies for Managing Options Assignment Risk

There are several strategies that options traders can use to manage the risk associated with options assignment. These strategies include:

1. Choosing options with a high level of liquidity: By choosing options with a high level of liquidity, an options trader can reduce the risk of the option being assigned at an unfavorable price.
2. Using stop-loss orders: By using stop-loss orders, an options trader can limit their losses if the option is assigned at an unfavorable price.
3. Using options spreads: By using options spreads, an options trader can reduce the risk of the option being assigned at an unfavorable price.
4. Being aware of the expiration date of the option: By being aware of the expiration date of the option, an options trader can make sure to exercise or sell the option before it expires, to avoid any potential assignment at an unfavorable price.

5. Hedging positions: By hedging positions, an options trader can offset any potential losses from options assignment by holding a position in the underlying stock or another option with a different strike price.

Case Study

An options trader named Sarah is interested in trading the stock of ABC company. Sarah buys a call option on ABC company with an expiration date in three months. Sarah's analysis of the stock and the options market indicates that the stock is likely to decrease in value.

However, Sarah is concerned about the risk of options assignment. To manage this risk, Sarah chooses an option with a high level of liquidity and uses a stop-loss order to limit her losses if the option is assigned at an unfavorable price. Sarah also hedges her position by buying a put option on ABC company with a strike price lower than the call option.

Three months later, the stock price of ABC company has indeed decreased. However,

Sarah's call option is assigned and she is able to sell the stock at the strike price. The put option also increases in value, offsetting any potential losses from the assigned call option.

In this example, Sarah used strategies such as choosing options with a high level of liquidity, using stop-loss orders and hedging positions to manage the risk of options assignment. By understanding the importance of managing options assignment risk in options trading, Sarah was able to protect her profits and make more informed decisions.

In conclusion, options assignment risk is a key concept in options trading that can have a significant impact on the price of an option. It is important for options traders to understand how options assignment risk affects options trading and to have strategies in place to manage the risk associated with options assignment risk. By managing options assignment risk, options traders can ensure that they are able to sell the stock or option at a favorable price and protect their profits. However, as always, it's important to seek professional advice before making any trades and to keep in mind the expiration date of the option.

Chapter 22: Probability of Profit

Probability of profit (POP) is a key concept in options trading that refers to the likelihood that an options trade will be profitable. In this chapter, we will define probability of profit, explain how it affects options trading, discuss the importance of probability of profit in options trading, and provide strategies for maximizing probability of profit in options trading. We will also include a case study to illustrate the concepts discussed in this chapter.

Definition of Probability of Profit

Probability of profit is the likelihood that an options trade will be profitable. It is often expressed as a percentage and is determined by analyzing various factors such as the price of the option, the strike price, and the expiration date. A higher probability of profit means that the trade is more likely to be profitable, while a lower probability of profit means that the trade is less likely to be profitable.

How Probability of Profit Affects Options Trading

Probability of profit affects options trading because it is a key factor in determining the potential profitability of a trade. Traders who are able to identify options trades with a high probability of profit are more likely to make a profit, while traders who are unable to identify options trades with a high probability of profit are more likely to make a loss.

Importance of Probability of Profit in Options Trading

Probability of profit is important in options trading because it helps traders identify the most profitable trades. By analyzing the probability of profit, traders can make more informed decisions about buying and selling options and protect their profits.

Strategies for Maximizing Probability of Profit in Options Trading

There are several strategies that traders can use to maximize the probability of profit in options trading. These strategies include:

1. Analyzing historical data: By analyzing historical data, traders can identify patterns and trends that can help them predict the future price of an option.
2. Using technical analysis: By using technical analysis, traders can identify patterns and trends in the price of an option that can indicate a high probability of profit.
3. Using options spreads: By using options spreads, traders can reduce the risk of a trade and increase the probability of profit.
4. Using volatility as a metric: By using volatility as a metric, traders can identify options trades with a high probability of profit.

Case Study

An options trader named John is interested in trading the stock of XYZ company. John's analysis of the stock and the options market indicates that the stock is likely to increase in value.

To maximize the probability of profit, John analyzes historical data and uses technical analysis to identify patterns and trends in the price of the option. John also uses an options spread by buying a call option and selling a put option on XYZ company. He also uses volatility as a metric to identify options trades with a high probability of profit.

Three months later, the stock price of XYZ company has indeed increased. John's call option is profitable and the put option he sold expires worthless. By maximizing the probability of profit, John was able to protect his profits and make a profit on the trade.

In conclusion, probability of profit is a key concept in options trading that can have a significant impact on the potential profitability of a trade. It is important for options traders to understand how probability of profit affects options trading and to have strategies in place to maximize the probability of profit. By analyzing historical data, using technical analysis, implementing options spreads, and utilizing volatility as a metric, traders can increase the probability of making a profit on their options trades. In addition, it's also important to keep in mind that even with a high probability of profit, there are still risks involved in trading and traders should always have a risk management plan in place. Overall, by understanding the importance of probability of profit in options trading and utilizing the right strategies, traders can make more informed decisions and increase their chances of success in the market.

Chapter 23: Break-Even Price

Break-even price is a key concept in options trading that refers to the price at which an options trade will neither make a profit nor a loss. In this chapter, we will define break-even price, explain how it affects options trading, discuss the importance of break-even price in options trading, and provide strategies for using break-even price to make trades. We will also include a case study to illustrate the concepts discussed in this chapter.

Definition of Break-Even Price

Break-even price is the price at which an options trade will neither make a profit nor a loss. It is the point at which the cost of the trade is equal to the proceeds of the trade. For example, if an options trader buys a call option for $2 and sells it for $3, the break-even price would be $3.

How Break-Even Price Affects Options Trading

Break-even price affects options trading because it is a key factor in determining the potential profitability of a trade. Traders who are able to identify options trades with a low break-even price are more likely to make a profit, while traders who are unable to identify options trades with a low break-even price are more likely to make a loss.

Importance of Break-Even Price in Options Trading

Break-even price is important in options trading because it helps traders identify the most profitable trades. By analyzing the break-even price, traders can make more informed decisions about buying and selling options and protect their profits.

Strategies for Using Break-Even Price to Make Trades

There are several strategies that traders can use to use break-even price to make trades. These strategies include:

1. Analyzing historical data: By analyzing historical data, traders can identify patterns and trends that can help them predict the future price of an option.
2. Identifying options with a low break-even price: By identifying options with a low break-even price, traders can increase the probability of making a profit.
3. Using options spreads: By using options spreads, traders can reduce the risk of a trade and increase the probability of profit.
4. Using volatility as a metric: By using volatility as a metric, traders can identify options trades with a low break-even price.

Case Study

An options trader named John is interested in trading the stock of XYZ company. John's analysis of the stock and the options market indicates that the stock is likely to increase in value.

To use break-even price to make trades, John analyzes historical data and uses technical analysis to identify patterns and trends in the price of the option. He also identifies options with a low break-even price, uses an options spread by buying a call option and selling a put option on XYZ company, and uses volatility as a metric to identify options trades with a low break-even price.

Three months later, the stock price of XYZ company has indeed increased. John's call option is profitable and the put option he sold expires worthless. By identifying options with a low break-even price, John was able to protect his profits and make a profit on the trade.

In conclusion, break-even price is a key concept in options trading that can have a significant impact on the potential profitability of a trade. It is important for options traders to understand how break-even price affects options trading and to have strategies in place to use break-even price to make trades. By analyzing historical data, identifying options with a low break-even price, implementing options spreads, and utilizing volatility as a metric, traders can increase the probability of making a profit on their options trades. Additionally, by understanding the importance of break-even price in options trading, traders can make more informed decisions and protect their profits. In addition, traders should also keep in mind the other factors such as the volatility, current market conditions and the expiration date when determining their break-even price and making trades. Overall, by understanding break-even price and utilizing the right strategies, traders can increase their chances of success in the market.

Chapter 24: Return on Capital

Return on capital is a key metric in options trading that measures the profitability of a trade. In this chapter, we will define return on capital, explain how it affects options trading, discuss the importance of return on capital in options trading, and provide strategies for maximizing return on capital in options trading. We will also include a case study to illustrate the concepts discussed in this chapter.

Definition of Return on Capital

Return on capital is a measure of the profitability of a trade, calculated as the gain or loss on the trade divided by the amount of capital invested. This metric is used to evaluate the return on investment for a particular trade. It is typically expressed as a percentage.

How Return on Capital Affects Options Trading

Return on capital affects options trading by providing traders with a measure of the profitability of their trades. Traders who are able to generate a high return on capital are more likely to be successful, while traders who are unable to generate a high return on capital are more likely to struggle.

Importance of Return on Capital in Options Trading

Return on capital is important in options trading because it helps traders evaluate the profitability of their trades. By analyzing return on capital, traders can make more informed decisions about buying and selling options and protect their profits.

Strategies for Maximizing Return on Capital in Options Trading

There are several strategies that traders can use to maximize return on capital in options trading. These strategies include:

1. Identifying options trades with a high potential return on capital: By identifying options trades with a high potential return on capital, traders can

increase the probability of making a profit.
2. Using options spreads: By using options spreads, traders can reduce the risk of a trade and increase the return on capital.
3. Implementing risk management strategies: By implementing risk management strategies, traders can reduce the potential loss on a trade and increase the return on capital.
4. Diversifying the portfolio: By diversifying the portfolio, traders can reduce the risk of a trade and increase the return on capital.

Case Study

An options trader named Sarah is interested in trading the stock of ABC company. Sarah's analysis of the stock and the options market indicates that the stock is likely to increase in value.

To maximize return on capital, Sarah identifies options trades with a high potential return on capital, uses options spreads by buying a call option and selling a put option on ABC company, implements risk management strategies, and diversifies her portfolio by trading different options on different stocks.

Three months later, the stock price of ABC company has indeed increased, resulting in a profit for Sarah's options trades. By using the strategies discussed above, Sarah was able to maximize her return on capital, achieving a return of 20% on her initial investment.

In conclusion, return on capital is an important metric in options trading that provides traders with a measure of the profitability of their trades. By understanding the importance of return on capital, traders can make more informed decisions and protect their profits. By using strategies such as identifying options trades with a high potential return on capital, using options spreads, implementing risk management strategies, and diversifying the portfolio, traders can maximize their return on capital and achieve success in the options market.

Chapter 25: Implied Volatility: Historic vs Implied

In this chapter, we will explore the concept of implied volatility and how it differs from historic volatility. We will also discuss the importance of implied volatility in options trading and provide strategies for using implied volatility to make trades. Additionally, we will include a case study to illustrate the concepts discussed in this chapter.

Definition of Implied Volatility

Implied volatility refers to the expected volatility of a security's price, as implied by the current market price of options on that security. Implied volatility is calculated using a mathematical model such as the Black-Scholes model and is expressed as a percentage.

How Implied Volatility Differs from Historic Volatility

Historic volatility refers to the actual volatility of a security's price, as measured over a specific period of time. Implied volatility differs from historic volatility in that it is a forward-looking measure of volatility, while historic volatility is a backward-looking measure. Implied volatility is also affected by factors such as supply and demand for options, while historic volatility is only affected by the historical price movements of the underlying security.

Importance of Implied Volatility in Options Trading

Implied volatility is important in options trading because it can provide valuable information about the market's expectations for the future volatility of a security. Traders can use this information to make more informed decisions about buying and selling options, such as choosing options with higher implied volatility when expecting a volatile market, and options with lower implied volatility when expecting a stable market.

Strategies for Using Implied Volatility to Make Trades

1. Buying options with higher implied volatility: When expecting a volatile market, traders can buy options with higher implied volatility, which will increase the potential for profit.
2. Selling options with lower implied volatility: When expecting a stable market, traders can sell options with lower implied volatility, which will increase the potential for profit.
3. Using implied volatility to determine the best strike price for an options trade: Traders can use implied volatility to determine the best strike price for an options trade, as options with strike prices that are closer to the current stock price tend to have higher implied volatility.
4. Using implied volatility to determine the best expiration date for an options trade: Traders can use implied volatility to determine the best expiration date for an options trade, as options with expiration dates that are further in the future tend to have higher implied volatility.

Case Study

An options trader named John is interested in trading the stock of XYZ company. John's analysis of the stock and the options market indicates that the stock is likely to experience high volatility in the near future.

To take advantage of this expected volatility, John chooses to buy options with higher implied volatility on XYZ company. He also uses implied volatility to determine the best strike price and expiration date for his options trades. As a result, John is able to make profitable trades due to the higher implied volatility of the options he has chosen.

In conclusion, implied volatility is an important concept in options trading that can provide valuable information about the market's expectations for the future volatility of a security. By understanding the difference between implied volatility and historic volatility, traders can make more informed decisions about buying and selling options. Additionally, by using strategies such as buying options with higher implied volatility, selling options with lower implied volatility, and using implied volatility to determine the best strike price and expiration date for an options trade, traders can increase their potential for profit. It's important to note that implied volatility is not a guarantee of future volatility and traders should always conduct thorough research and analysis before making any trades. In this chapter, we have learned that Implied volatility is an important metric that can help traders make more informed decisions and increase their potential for profit in the options market.

Chapter 26: How Does Implied Volatility Impact Option Pricing

Options trading is a complex and dynamic field that requires a deep understanding of market conditions and factors that affect the value of options contracts. One of the most important concepts in options trading is implied volatility, which is the estimated volatility of a stock or other underlying asset over the life of an options contract. In this chapter, we will explore the definition of implied volatility impact on option pricing, how it affects options pricing, and the importance of implied volatility impact on option pricing in options trading. We will also examine strategies for using implied volatility impact on option pricing to make trades.

- Definition of Implied Volatility Impact on Option Pricing

- How Implied Volatility Affects Options Pricing
- Importance of Implied Volatility Impact on Option Pricing in Options Trading
- Strategies for Using Implied Volatility Impact on Option Pricing to Make Trades

Definition of Implied Volatility Impact on Option Pricing

Implied volatility is a measure of the expected volatility of an underlying asset over the life of an options contract. It is calculated using an options pricing model, such as the Black-Scholes model, which takes into account the current price of the underlying asset, the strike price of the options contract, the expiration date, the risk-free rate, and the dividend yield. Implied volatility is expressed as a percentage, and it reflects the market's expectation of how much the price of the underlying asset will fluctuate in the future.

How Implied Volatility Affects Options Pricing

Implied volatility has a direct impact on the price of options contracts. When implied volatility is high, options contracts are more expensive because there is a greater chance that the price of the underlying asset will fluctuate widely. Conversely, when implied volatility is low, options contracts are less expensive because there is a lower chance that the price of the underlying asset will fluctuate widely.

One of the most important factors that affects implied volatility is the expiration date of the options contract. Options contracts that expire in the near future have a lower implied volatility than options contracts that expire further out in time. This is because there is less time for the price of the underlying asset to fluctuate widely.

Importance of Implied Volatility Impact on Option Pricing in Options Trading

Understanding the impact of implied volatility on options pricing is crucial for making informed decisions in options trading. Implied volatility is one of the most important factors that affects the value of options contracts, and it can have a significant impact on the potential profit or loss of a trade.

Traders who are able to accurately predict changes in implied volatility can make profitable trades by buying options contracts when implied volatility is low and selling them when implied volatility is high. Additionally, traders can also use options contracts with different expiration dates to take advantage of changes in implied volatility.

Strategies for Using Implied Volatility Impact on Option Pricing to Make Trades

There are several strategies that traders can use to take advantage of changes in implied volatility. One popular strategy is to buy options contracts when implied volatility is low and sell them when implied volatility is high. This strategy is known as volatility trading, and it can be profitable if a trader is able to accurately predict changes in implied volatility.

Another strategy is to use options contracts with different expiration dates to take advantage of changes in implied volatility. For example, if a trader believes that implied volatility will increase in the near future, they can buy options contracts with expiration dates that are further out in time. If the trader's prediction is correct, the price of the options contracts will increase as implied volatility increases.

Case Study: Trading Options on Implied Volatility of Google Stock

In this case study, we will look at how a trader named Alex used implied volatility to make trades on Google stock. Alex believed that the implied volatility of Google stock would increase in the near future due to the release of new products and positive earnings reports. He decided to buy call options contracts with expiration dates that were further out and strike prices that were further out. As the implied volatility of Google stock increased, the price of the options contracts also increased, and Alex was able to make a large profit on his trade. Additionally, he also sold put options contracts with expiration dates that were closer to take advantage of the increase in implied volatility. Overall, Alex's strategy of using implied volatility to make trades on Google stock was a success and allowed him to profit from the market conditions.

In conclusion, implied volatility impact on option pricing is an important aspect of options trading that can be used to make profitable trades. By understanding how implied volatility affects options pricing and using strategies such as buying options contracts with different expiration dates, traders can take advantage of market conditions and potentially make large profits. It's important for traders to continuously monitor implied volatility and adjust their trading strategies accordingly. Additionally, it's also important to remember that implied volatility is just one of many factors that can affect options pricing and traders should always consider other market conditions as well.

Chapter 27: Implied Volatility Rank vs Implied Volatility Percentile

Options trading is a complex and dynamic field that requires a thorough understanding of various factors that affect the pricing of options. One such factor is implied volatility, which is the estimated volatility of a stock based on the market price of its options. In this chapter, we will delve into the concepts of implied volatility rank and implied volatility percentile and how they differ from each other. We will also discuss the importance of these concepts in options trading and strategies for using them to make trades.

Definition of implied volatility rank and implied volatility percentile:

Implied volatility rank (IV Rank) is a measure of how the implied volatility of a stock compares to the implied volatility of other stocks in the market. It is expressed as a percentage, with a higher percentage indicating a higher level of implied volatility compared to other stocks. For example, an IV Rank of 90% means that the stock's implied volatility is higher than 90% of other stocks in the market.

Implied volatility percentile (IV Percentile) is also a measure of how the implied volatility of a stock compares to the implied volatility of other stocks in the market. However, unlike IV Rank, it is expressed as a number between 0 and 100, with a higher number indicating a higher level of implied volatility compared to other stocks. For example, an IV Percentile of 75 means that the stock's implied volatility is higher than 75% of other stocks in the market.

How implied volatility rank and percentile differ:

The main difference between IV Rank and IV Percentile is the way they are expressed. IV Rank is expressed as a percentage, while IV Percentile is expressed as a number between 0 and 100. However, they both serve the same purpose of comparing the implied volatility of a stock to the implied volatility of other stocks in the market.

Importance of implied volatility rank and percentile in options trading:

Implied volatility rank and percentile are important concepts in options trading because they provide insight into the level of volatility of a stock compared to other stocks in the market. This information can be used to identify stocks that are more volatile than others, which can be useful for options traders looking to take advantage of high volatility.

For example, if Implied volatility rank and implied volatility percentile are two important concepts in options trading that can help traders make informed decisions. These concepts are closely related, but they measure different things and have different implications for options pricing. In this chapter, we will explore the definitions and differences between implied volatility rank and implied volatility percentile, and discuss the importance of these concepts in options trading. We will also provide strategies for using these concepts to make trades.

The first thing to understand is the difference between implied volatility rank and implied volatility percentile. Implied volatility rank (IVR) is a measure of how an option's implied volatility compares to the overall implied volatility of the underlying stock. For example, if an option's implied volatility is in the 90th percentile, it means that 90% of the options on that stock have a lower implied volatility. Implied volatility percentile (IVP) is a measure of how an option's implied volatility compares to the historical volatility of the underlying stock. For example, if an option's implied volatility is in the 80th percentile, it means that 80% of the historical volatility of that stock has been lower than the option's implied volatility.

It is important to note that IVR and IVP are not the same thing. IVR is a measure of relative volatility within the options market, while IVP is a measure of relative volatility within the stock market. IVR is useful for identifying options that are relatively overpriced or underpriced, while IVP is useful for identifying options that have a high probability of being profitable.

In terms of options trading, IVR and IVP can both be used to make trades. For example, if an option has a high IVR, it may be overpriced and a trader may want to sell that option. On the other hand, if an option has a high IVP, it may be underpriced and a trader may want to buy that option. It is important to note, however, that IVR and IVP should not be used in isolation. Traders should consider other factors such as the underlying stock's price, implied volatility, and time to expiration when making trades.

To illustrate the concepts of IVR and IVP, let's consider a case study of a stock XYZ. Currently, the stock is trading at $50 per share and has an implied volatility of 30%. The IVR for this stock is currently at the 50th percentile, meaning that 50% of stocks have a higher implied volatility than XYZ.

Now, let's say that the stock XYZ experiences a significant event, such as a positive earnings report, which causes the stock price to increase to $60 per share. Along with this increase in stock price, the implied volatility also increases to 40%. The IVR for this stock now jumps to the 75th percentile, meaning that only 25% of stocks have a higher implied volatility than XYZ.

The change in IVR can have a significant impact on options pricing and the profitability of options trades. A higher IVR usually means that options prices are higher, making it more expensive to purchase options contracts. However, a higher IVR also means that there is more potential for profit as the stock price can make larger moves.

In contrast, the IVP measures the implied volatility of a stock relative to its own historical volatility. Using our example above, if XYZ's implied volatility of 30% is at the 75th percentile of its own historical volatility, it means that 75% of the time in the past, the stock's implied volatility was lower than 30%.

Knowing the IVR and IVP can provide valuable insights into the potential volatility and profitability of a stock. For example, if a stock has a high IVR but a low IVP, it may indicate that the stock is currently experiencing unusually high volatility but has a history of being less volatile. In this case, it may be more profitable to sell options rather than buy them.

To utilize the IVR and IVP in options trading, traders can use a combination of technical analysis and fundamental analysis. Technical analysis can help identify potential trades based on chart patterns and indicators, while fundamental analysis can provide insights into the underlying factors driving the stock's volatility.

One strategy for using the IVR and IVP is to compare the current IVR or IVP of a stock to its historical IVR or IVP. If a stock's current IVR or IVP is significantly higher or lower than its historical average, it may indicate that the market is either overvaluing or undervaluing the stock's options. This information can then be used to make trades based on whether the stock is likely to move in the direction of its historical average IVR or IVP.

Another strategy is to use the IVR and IVP to identify stocks that are undervalued or overvalued in the options market. A stock with a high IVR or IVP may be considered overvalued, while a stock with a low IVR or IVP may be considered undervalued. By identifying these stocks, traders can make trades based on whether they believe the stock's options are undervalued or overvalued.

In addition, traders can use the IVR and IVP to identify stocks that are experiencing a change in volatility. For example, if a stock's IVR or IVP suddenly increases, it may indicate that the stock's volatility is increasing and that traders should be cautious. On the other hand, if a stock's IVR or IVP suddenly decreases, it may indicate that the stock's volatility is decreasing and that traders can take advantage of the opportunity to buy options at a lower price.

In conclusion, the IVR and IVP are important indicators for options traders to consider when making trades. By understanding the difference between the two and how they can impact options pricing, traders can use this information to make more informed decisions and potentially increase their probability of profit. It is always important to keep in mind that the market is constantly changing and that the IVR and IVP should be used as just one tool in a trader's toolbox to make informed trades.

Chapter 28: Standard Deviation

Standard deviation is a statistical measure that quantifies the volatility of a security's price. It is used to indicate the level of risk associated with a particular investment. In options trading, standard deviation plays an important role in determining the potential profitability of a trade and the level of risk involved. This chapter will provide an in-depth understanding of standard deviation, its impact on options trading, and strategies for using it to make trades.

Definition of standard deviation:

Standard deviation is a measure of how far the data points in a set of data are spread out from the mean or average. In other words, it measures the degree of variation of a set of data. In finance, standard deviation is used to measure the volatility of a security's price. The higher the standard deviation, the greater the volatility and the higher the risk associated with the security.

How standard deviation affects options trading:

Standard deviation plays an important role in options trading. It is used to measure the volatility of the underlying security's price, which in turn affects the price of the options. For example, if the standard deviation of a stock is high, the options will be more expensive than if the standard deviation is low. This is because options prices are affected by the volatility of the underlying security's price. The more volatile the underlying security's price, the more expensive the options will be.

Importance of standard deviation in options trading:

Standard deviation is an important measure of risk in options trading. It is used to determine the potential profitability of a trade and the level of risk involved. For example, if the standard deviation of a stock is high, the options will be more expensive, but they will also have a higher potential for profit. On the other hand, if the standard deviation is low, the options will be cheaper, but they will also have a lower potential for profit. Therefore, understanding standard deviation is crucial for making informed trading decisions.

Standard deviation is a statistical measurement that is used to indicate how much the individual data points in a given set deviate from the mean or average of that set. In other words, it is a measure of the dispersion or spread of data. In the context of options trading, standard deviation is used to measure the volatility of the underlying asset. The higher the standard deviation, the more volatile the asset is considered to be.

The importance of standard deviation in options trading cannot be overstated. It is a key metric that is used in the pricing of options, and it plays a crucial role in determining the probability of profit for a given trade. The standard deviation is used to calculate the implied volatility of an option, which is a key determinant of the option's price. The higher the implied volatility, the higher the price of the option.

There are several strategies for using standard deviation to make trades. One strategy is to use it to identify the most volatile options. This can be useful for traders who are looking to make high-risk, high-reward trades. Another strategy is to use standard deviation to identify options that are underpriced. This can be useful for traders who are looking to make more conservative trades.

Let's consider a case study to illustrate the concepts of standard deviation and its impact on options trading. Imagine that you are considering buying a call option on a stock that has a current price of $100. The option has a strike price of $110 and expires in one month. The current implied volatility of the option is 40%.

One strategy for using standard deviation in this scenario is to compare the current implied volatility of the option with the historical volatility of the underlying stock. If the current implied volatility is higher than the historical volatility, it may be a sign that the option is overpriced. In this case, the trader may choose to avoid the trade or to buy the option at a lower price.

On the other hand, if the current implied volatility is lower than the historical volatility, it may be a sign that the option is underpriced. In this case, the trader may choose to buy the option at a higher price.

Another strategy for using standard deviation in this scenario is to use it to identify options that have a high probability of profit. The standard deviation can be used to calculate the probability of the underlying stock price being above or below the strike price at expiration. If the probability of profit is high, the trader may choose to buy the option.

In conclusion, standard deviation is a key metric that is used in the pricing of options and plays a crucial role in determining the probability of profit for a given trade. Understanding standard deviation is crucial for making informed trading decisions and there are several strategies for using it to make trades. By studying the concepts of standard deviation and its impact on options trading, traders can gain a better understanding of how to use this metric to make more profitable trades.

Chapter 29: Implied Volatility & Standard Deviation

In options trading, implied volatility and standard deviation are two important concepts that are closely related. Implied volatility is a measure of the expected volatility of a stock's price, while standard deviation is a measure of the volatility of a stock's returns. Understanding the relationship between these two concepts is crucial for making informed trading decisions.

1. Definition of Implied Volatility and Standard Deviation:

Implied volatility (IV) is a measure of the expected volatility of a stock's price, calculated using the current price of options on the stock. It is a forward-looking measure, based on the market's expectation of future volatility. Standard deviation (SD) is a measure of the volatility of a stock's returns. It is a backward-looking measure, based on the historical volatility of the stock.

2. How Implied Volatility and Standard Deviation Interact:

The relationship between implied volatility and standard deviation is not always straightforward. Implied volatility is a measure of the market's expectation of future volatility, while standard deviation is a measure of historical volatility. However, the two concepts are often correlated, as higher levels of implied volatility tend to correspond to higher levels of standard deviation.

3. Importance of Understanding the Relationship Between Implied Volatility and Standard Deviation in Options Trading:

Understanding the relationship between implied volatility and standard deviation is crucial for making informed trading decisions. For example, if a stock has a high level of implied volatility, but a low level of standard deviation, it may indicate that the market is expecting a significant price movement in the near future. This can be useful information for options traders, as it may signal a potential opportunity to buy or sell options.

4. Strategies for Using Implied Volatility and Standard Deviation to Make Trades:

There are several strategies that options traders can use to take advantage of the relationship between implied volatility and standard deviation. For example, a trader may choose to buy options when implied volatility is high and standard deviation is low, as this may indicate a potential opportunity for a large price movement in the near future. On the other hand, a trader may choose to sell options when implied volatility is low and standard deviation is high, as this may indicate a potential opportunity for a small price movement in the near future.

Example of a Case Study:

Let's consider the example of a stock XYZ, which has an implied volatility of 20% and a standard deviation of 10%. The relationship between these two measures is not straightforward, as the implied volatility is higher than the standard deviation. This may indicate that the market is expecting a significant price movement in the near future, but it's not clear in which direction the movement will be.

One strategy for taking advantage of this information is to buy a call option on XYZ with a strike price that is slightly above the current stock price. This would allow the trader to benefit from a potential upward price movement in the stock. Additionally, the trader may also choose to buy a put option on XYZ with a strike price that is slightly below the current stock price. This would allow the trader to benefit from a potential downward price movement in the stock.

By combining these two strategies, the trader is able to benefit from both upward and downward price movements in the stock, while also taking into account the relationship between implied volatility and standard deviation. This can be a powerful way to make trades and potentially increase the chances of profitability.

In conclusion, understanding the relationship between implied volatility and standard deviation is crucial for making informed trading decisions in the options market. By understanding how these two concepts interact and how they impact option pricing, traders can make better decisions about when to enter and exit trades. Additionally, by utilizing strategies that take into account both implied volatility and standard deviation, traders can increase their chances of success in the options market. As always, it is important to remember to conduct thorough research and stay up-to-date on market conditions before making any trades. With a solid understanding of implied volatility and standard deviation, traders can make more informed decisions and increase their chances of success in the options market.

Chapter 30: Understanding Market Trends and Sentiment

Options trading is a highly dynamic field that requires traders to stay on top of market trends and sentiment at all times. The market is always changing and as a result, traders must adapt to new conditions and trends in order to be successful. In this chapter, we will delve into the topic of market trends and sentiment and how they impact options trading. We will explore the definition of market trends and sentiment, their importance in options trading, and strategies for using market trends and sentiment to make trades. Additionally, we will examine case studies and real-world examples of successful market trend and sentiment trading.

Definition of Market Trends and Sentiment

Market trends and sentiment refer to the general direction and mood of the market. Market trends can be seen in the price movement of a particular stock, index, or commodity.

Sentiment refers to the overall perception of the market and the emotions of market participants. These emotions can be driven by news, economic data, geopolitical events, and other factors. Market trends and sentiment play a crucial role in shaping the direction of the market and determining the price of assets.

How Market Trends and Sentiment Impact Options Trading

Market trends and sentiment play a significant role in options trading because they can impact the price of underlying assets. When the market is bullish, meaning that market participants are optimistic and the general sentiment is positive, prices tend to rise. Conversely, when the market is bearish, meaning that market participants are pessimistic and the general sentiment is negative, prices tend to fall. This, in turn, affects the price of options contracts. For example, if the market is bullish, call options are likely to become more expensive, while put options become cheaper.

Importance of Staying Up to Date on Market Trends and Sentiment in Options Trading

Staying up to date on market trends and sentiment is essential for options traders. It allows traders to make informed decisions about when to enter and exit trades, as well as which options contracts to trade. Traders who are able to accurately predict market trends and sentiment have a significant advantage over those who do not. They are able to make profitable trades and avoid losing trades, thus maximizing their profits.

Strategies for Using Market Trends and Sentiment to Make Trades

There are several strategies that traders can use to take advantage of market trends and sentiment in options trading. One strategy is to use technical analysis to identify market trends and sentiment. Technical analysis involves using charts and other tools to analyze market data and make predictions about future price movements. Another strategy is to stay informed about news and events that may impact the market. Traders can do this by monitoring financial news sources and paying attention to economic data releases, geopolitical events, and other news that may impact the market.

Case Studies and Real-World Examples of Successful Market Trend and Sentiment Trading

To gain a deeper understanding of the impact of market trends and sentiment on options trading, it is important to examine case studies and real-world examples of successful market trend and sentiment trading. One example is the 2008 financial crisis, when the stock market experienced a significant drop due to the collapse of the housing market and the subprime mortgage crisis. Many traders who were able to accurately predict the market trend and sentiment were able to make significant profits by trading put options. Another example is the bull market of the 1990s, when the stock market experienced a significant rally due to the growth of the internet and the dot-com boom. Traders who were able to accurately predict the market trend and sentiment were able to make significant profits by trading call options.

In conclusion, market trends and sentiment play a crucial role in options trading. Traders who are able to accurately predict market trends and sentiment have a distinct advantage over those who are not. Staying up to date on market trends and sentiment, using the right tools and techniques, and having a solid understanding of market conditions are key to successfully using market trends and sentiment to make profitable trades. Whether you are a beginner or an experienced trader, incorporating market trends and sentiment analysis into your options trading strategy can provide a significant edge and help you achieve your financial goals. Remember, it is important to always be vigilant, stay up to date, and continuously monitor market conditions to take advantage of the opportunities that arise from changes in market trends and sentiment.

Chapter 31: Volatility Skew

Volatility skew is a phenomenon that occurs when the implied volatility of options with different strike prices is not the same. In other words, it is the difference in implied volatility between options with the same expiration date but different strike prices. Understanding volatility skew is important for options traders because it can have a significant impact on options pricing and can be used to identify trading opportunities. In this chapter, we will explore the definition of volatility skew, how it affects options pricing, its importance in options trading, and strategies for using it to make trades.

Definition of Volatility Skew:

Volatility skew refers to the difference in implied volatility between options with the same expiration date but different strike prices. For example, if the implied volatility of a call option with a strike price of $50 is 30%, and the implied volatility of a call option with a strike price of $55 is 35%, then there is a volatility skew of 5% between the two options.

How Volatility Skew Affects Options Pricing:

Volatility skew can have a significant impact on options pricing because it affects the price of options with different strike prices differently. Options with a higher strike price generally have a higher implied volatility than options with a lower strike price. This is known as a positive volatility skew. On the other hand, options with a lower strike price generally have a lower implied volatility than options with a higher strike price, which is known as a negative volatility skew. The impact of volatility skew on options pricing can be seen in the Black-Scholes model, which is used to calculate the theoretical value of an option. The model takes into account factors such as the underlying asset's price, strike price, time to expiration, interest rate, and volatility. When volatility skew is present, the model will produce different results for options with different strike prices, even if all other factors are the same.

Importance of Volatility Skew in Options Trading:

Volatility skew can be used to identify trading opportunities in the options market. For example, if there is a positive volatility skew, it may be more profitable to sell options with a lower strike price and buy options with a higher strike price. This is because options with a lower strike price will have a lower implied volatility and will be cheaper to purchase, while options with a higher strike price will have a higher implied volatility and will be more expensive to purchase. On the other hand, if there is a negative volatility skew, it may be more profitable to buy options with a lower strike price and sell options with a higher strike price. This is because options with a lower strike price will have a higher implied volatility and will be more expensive to purchase, while options with a higher strike price will have a lower implied volatility and will be cheaper to purchase.

Strategies for Using Volatility Skew to Make Trades:

There are several strategies that options traders can use to take advantage of volatility skew. One strategy is to buy options with a lower strike price and sell options with a higher strike price when there is a positive volatility skew. Another strategy is to sell options with a lower strike price and buy options with a higher strike price when there is a negative volatility skew. Additionally, options traders can use volatility skew to identify overpriced options and underpriced options. If an option with a higher strike price has a lower implied volatility than an option with a lower strike price, it may be overpriced and a good candidate for selling. On the other hand, if an option with a lower strike price has a higher implied volatility than an option with a higher strike price, it may be underpriced and a good candidate for buying.

Example of a Case Study:

Let's consider a case study to illustrate the concept of volatility skew. XYZ Company is a tech giant with a strong track record of consistent growth. The stock has a current price of $200 and a strike price of $210 for a call option with a expiration date of one month from now. The implied volatility for the call option is 25%.

However, upon further analysis, it is found that the implied volatility for put options with the same strike price and expiration date is 30%. This is an example of volatility skew, where the implied volatility for put options is higher than the call options.

This skew can have a significant impact on options pricing and can affect the value of call and put options differently. In this scenario, the call option would be cheaper due to the lower implied volatility, while the put option would be more expensive due to the higher implied volatility.

One strategy for using volatility skew to make trades is to take advantage of the cheaper call options while also selling the more expensive put options. This can lead to a higher return on investment and can be a profitable strategy for those who can accurately predict and take advantage of volatility skew.

Another strategy is to use volatility skew to your advantage when creating a options trading portfolio. By having a diverse portfolio with options that are affected differently by volatility skew, you can mitigate risk and potentially increase profits.

It is important to note that volatility skew can change quickly and can be affected by various factors such as market conditions and company specific news. It is essential for options traders to constantly monitor volatility skew and make adjustments to their trading strategies accordingly.

In conclusion, understanding and utilizing volatility skew can greatly benefit options traders. It is important to understand how volatility skew affects options pricing and to have strategies in place to take advantage of it. By keeping a close eye on volatility skew and making informed trades, traders can potentially increase profits and mitigate risk.

Chapter 32: Contrarian Mindset

A contrarian mindset is the approach of going against the crowd and making decisions that are different from the majority. This mindset can be applied to many different areas, but in options trading, it is the practice of buying options when the market is bearish and selling options when the market is bullish. This approach can be beneficial for traders who are able to identify market trends and make informed decisions based on them.

Definition of Contrarian Mindset

A contrarian mindset is the practice of making decisions that go against the crowd. This can include buying stocks or options when the market is bearish, or selling options when the market is bullish. The idea behind this approach is that the market is often driven by emotions and that the majority of traders are often wrong. By going against the crowd, a trader can capitalize on these emotions and make profitable trades.

How a Contrarian Mindset Affects Options Trading

A contrarian mindset can have a significant impact on options trading. When the market is bearish, many traders will be selling options and closing their positions. A trader with a contrarian mindset will take advantage of this opportunity and buy options, betting that the market will eventually turn bullish. Similarly, when the market is bullish, many traders will be buying options and opening new positions. A trader with a contrarian mindset will take advantage of this opportunity and sell options, betting that the market will eventually turn bearish.

Importance of a Contrarian Mindset in Options Trading

A contrarian mindset is important in options trading because it allows traders to take advantage of market trends and emotions. The market is often driven by emotions and the majority of traders are often wrong. By going against the crowd, a trader can capitalize on these emotions and make profitable trades.

Additionally, a contrarian mindset allows traders to be more disciplined and patient, which are important characteristics for successful options trading.

Strategies for Using a Contrarian Mindset to Make Trades

There are several strategies that traders can use to take advantage of a contrarian mindset in options trading. One strategy is to use technical analysis to identify market trends and make informed decisions based on them. This can include using indicators such as moving averages and relative strength index (RSI) to identify trends and make trades. Another strategy is to use fundamental analysis to identify market trends and make informed decisions based on them. This can include using financial statements and news events to identify trends and make trades.

Case Study: Using a Contrarian Mindset to Trade Options on XYZ Stock

In this case study, we will look at how a trader named Michael used a contrarian mindset to trade options on XYZ stock. Michael believed that the market was bearish and that the price of XYZ stock would decrease. He bought call options with a strike price of $50 and an expiration date of 1 month. As the market continued to be bearish, the price of the options increased, and Michael was able to make a large profit on his trade.

In conclusion, a contrarian mindset is an important approach in options trading. By going against the crowd and making decisions that are different from the majority, traders can capitalize on market trends and emotions and make profitable trades. Traders should use technical and fundamental analysis to identify market trends and make informed decisions based on them. Additionally, traders should be disciplined, patient, and consistent in their approach to options trading. It's also important to always stay updated on the market trends and developments by regularly reading financial news and research.

Chapter 33: Implied Volatility Mean Reversion Explained

In options trading, understanding the concept of implied volatility mean reversion is crucial for making informed decisions. Implied volatility mean reversion is the tendency for implied volatility to return to its historical average after experiencing a significant deviation. In this chapter, we will discuss the definition of implied volatility mean reversion, how it affects options trading, its importance, and strategies for using it to make trades.

Definition of Implied Volatility Mean Reversion

Implied volatility mean reversion is the tendency for implied volatility to return to its historical average after experiencing a significant deviation. Implied volatility is a measure of the volatility of a security's price and is used to price options. Mean reversion is the idea that a stock's price will eventually return to its historical average after experiencing a significant deviation.

How Implied Volatility Mean Reversion Affects Options Trading

Implied volatility mean reversion can have a significant impact on options trading. When implied volatility is high, options prices will also be high. If implied volatility mean reversion is taking place, then options prices will eventually decrease as implied volatility returns to its historical average. Conversely, when implied volatility is low, options prices will also be low. If implied volatility mean reversion is taking place, then options prices will eventually increase as implied volatility returns to its historical average.

Importance of Implied Volatility Mean Reversion in Options Trading

Understanding implied volatility mean reversion is important for options traders because it can provide valuable information about the direction of options prices. If implied volatility is high and implied volatility mean reversion is taking place, then options prices will eventually decrease. This can provide an opportunity for options traders to sell options at a high price and buy them back at a lower price. Conversely, if implied volatility is low and implied volatility mean reversion is taking place, then options prices will eventually increase. This can provide an opportunity for options traders to buy options at a low price and sell them at a higher price.

Strategies for Using Implied Volatility Mean Reversion to Make Trades

One strategy for using implied volatility mean reversion to make trades is to buy options when implied volatility is low and sell options when implied volatility is high. This strategy is based on the idea that options prices will eventually increase when implied volatility is low and decrease when implied volatility is high.

Another strategy is to use volatility skew to make trades. Volatility skew is the difference in implied volatility between different strike prices. If there is a significant difference in implied volatility between different strike prices, then options traders can buy options at a low implied volatility strike price and sell options at a high implied volatility strike price.

Example of a Case Study

To illustrate the concepts of implied volatility mean reversion and volatility skew, let's consider a case study of XYZ Company. XYZ Company is a technology company that has a historical average implied volatility of 20%. One month ago, the implied volatility of XYZ Company was 30%. This deviation of 10% from the historical average implied volatility is significant.

According to the principle of implied volatility mean reversion, the implied volatility of XYZ Company will eventually return to its historical average of 20%. This means that the options prices of XYZ Company will decrease as implied volatility returns to its historical average.

Options traders can take advantage of this situation by selling options at a high price and buying them back at a lower price. For example, a call option with a strike price of $50 and expiration date of one month ago had a premium of $5. One month later, the premium of the same option decreased to $3 as implied volatility mean reversion.

In order to understand implied volatility mean reversion, we first need to define what we mean by implied volatility. Implied volatility is a measure of the expected volatility of a stock's price, as implied by the current market price of its options. It is calculated by taking the square root of the annualized implied variance, and is typically expressed as a percentage.

Mean reversion, on the other hand, is the tendency for a stock's price to move back towards its long-term average over time. This can be seen in a variety of different markets, including options markets.

When it comes to options trading, implied volatility mean reversion can have a significant impact on the pricing of options. This is because when implied volatility is high, options prices tend to be high as well. However, when implied volatility is low, options prices tend to be low.

One strategy for using implied volatility mean reversion to make trades is to buy options when implied volatility is high, and sell options when implied volatility is low. This can be a useful strategy for traders looking to take advantage of short-term fluctuations in implied volatility.

Another strategy for using implied volatility mean reversion to make trades is to buy options when implied volatility is low, and hold onto them until implied volatility rises. This can be a useful strategy for traders looking to take advantage of long-term trends in implied volatility.

In order to better understand the impact of implied volatility mean reversion on options trading, let's consider a case study. Let's say that we are looking at a stock with an implied volatility of 30%. Over the next several months, the implied volatility of this stock drops to 20%. Based on our understanding of implied volatility mean reversion, we might expect the implied volatility of this stock to rise back up to 30% over time.

In this scenario, a trader using the first strategy mentioned above would likely sell their options when implied volatility drops to 20%, and then buy back in when implied volatility rises back up to 30%. A trader using the second strategy would likely hold onto their options until implied volatility rises back up to 30%.

Overall, understanding implied volatility mean reversion can be a valuable tool for options traders looking to make informed trading decisions. By keeping an eye on changes in implied volatility, traders can better anticipate market movements and make trades that are more likely to be profitable.

Chapter 34: Market Awareness Explained: Understanding the Importance

Market awareness is the ability to stay informed and up-to-date on the latest market trends and events. It is essential for any trader, regardless of experience level, to have a deep understanding of the markets they are trading in. This knowledge can help traders make more informed decisions and increase their chances of success. In this chapter, we will explore the definition of market awareness, how it affects options trading, the importance of market awareness in options trading, and strategies for using market awareness to make trades.

Definition of Market Awareness

Market awareness refers to the ability to stay informed about the latest market trends and events. This includes understanding the economic and political factors that can impact the markets, as well as keeping track of the performance of individual stocks, indices, and other financial instruments. Market awareness also involves monitoring news and announcements that can impact the markets, such as earnings reports, mergers and acquisitions, and government policies.

How Market Awareness Affects Options Trading

Market awareness plays a critical role in options trading. It allows traders to stay informed about the latest market trends and events, which can impact the value of options contracts. For example, if a company is about to release its earnings report, the value of its options contracts may fluctuate depending on the results. If the earnings report is positive, the value of the options contracts may increase, while a negative report may cause the value to decrease. Market awareness also allows traders to anticipate market movements, which can help them make more informed decisions about when to buy or sell options contracts.

Importance of Market Awareness in Options Trading

Market awareness is crucial for options traders because it helps them make more informed decisions. When traders are aware of the latest market trends and events, they can anticipate market movements and make decisions that are more likely to be profitable. Market awareness also allows traders to identify opportunities that they may have otherwise missed. Additionally, market awareness can help traders avoid potential pitfalls, such as buying options contracts that are overvalued or selling options contracts that are undervalued.

Strategies for Using Market Awareness to Make Trades

1. Stay informed: The first step in using market awareness to make trades is to stay informed about the latest market trends and events. This can be done by reading financial news and announcements, monitoring stock and index performance, and keeping track of economic and political factors that can impact the markets.
2. Anticipate market movements: Once you have a good understanding of the latest market trends and events, you can start to anticipate market movements. This can be done by analyzing charts, using technical indicators, and studying historical data.
3. Identify opportunities: Market awareness can also help you identify opportunities that you may have otherwise missed. For

example, if you notice a stock that is underperforming, you may want to consider buying a put option on that stock.
4. Avoid pitfalls: Market awareness can also help you avoid potential pitfalls, such as buying options contracts that are overvalued or selling options contracts that are undervalued. This can be done by analyzing market conditions and studying historical data.

Example of a Case Study:

For example, let's say that a trader is considering buying call options on a stock that has recently released positive earnings. The trader has been monitoring the stock's performance and is aware of the positive earnings announcement. The trader also knows that the stock has been trending upward over the past few months and that the market is bullish. Based on this information, the trader can make an informed decision on whether or not to enter into a trade.

Definition of Market Awareness

Market awareness is the ability to understand and stay informed about the current market conditions and trends. This includes keeping track of economic indicators, news events, and other market data that may impact the price of a security. It also includes being aware of the broader market conditions, such as the overall trend of the market and any major events that may be impacting it.

How Market Awareness Affects Options Trading

Options trading is a highly dynamic and fast-paced activity that requires constant monitoring of market conditions. Being aware of the current market conditions and trends is essential for making informed trading decisions. For example, if the market is experiencing a period of volatility, it may be more risky to enter into a trade. On the other hand, if the market is stable and trending upward, it may be a good time to enter into a trade.

Importance of Market Awareness in Options Trading

Market awareness is crucial for making informed trading decisions. It allows traders to identify potential opportunities and risks in the market, and to make trades that align with their overall trading strategy. Additionally, market awareness helps traders to stay informed about any major events or changes that may impact their trades, such as changes in economic policy or major news events.

Strategies for Using Market Awareness to Make Trades

There are several strategies that traders can use to stay informed about market conditions and make trades that align with their overall trading strategy. One strategy is to regularly review market data and economic indicators, such as the stock market indices and key economic indicators like GDP and inflation. Additionally, traders can stay informed about market conditions by following news and analysis from reputable sources, such as financial news outlets and market research firms.

Another strategy is to use technical analysis tools, such as charts and indicators, to identify trends and patterns in the market. This can help traders to identify potential opportunities and risks, and to make trades that align with their overall trading strategy.

Case Study

Let's consider a trader who is interested in trading options on a specific stock. The trader has been following the stock for several months, and has been keeping track of the stock's performance and any major news events that may be impacting it.

The trader notices that the stock has been trending upward for several weeks, and that there has been a lot of positive news about the company's performance. Based on this information, the trader decides to enter into a long call option trade. The trader is able to successfully execute the trade, and is able to make a profit as the stock continues to trend upward.

In this example, the trader's market awareness helped them to identify an opportunity in the market and to make a profitable trade. The trader's understanding of the current market conditions and trends, as well as their ability to stay informed about any major events that may be impacting the stock, allowed them to make an informed decision and to successfully execute the trade.

Conclusion:

Market awareness is an essential skill for any trader, as it allows them to stay informed about current market conditions and trends and to make informed trading decisions. By understanding the importance of market awareness, traders can develop strategies for staying informed and for identifying opportunities and risks in the market. Additionally, by keeping track of market data and economic indicators, following news and analysis from reputable sources, and using technical analysis tools, traders can stay informed and make trades that align with their overall trading strategy.

Chapter 35: What is Options Delta & How to Trade it?

Options delta is a measure of the rate of change of an option's price with respect to a change in the underlying asset's price. It is often used as a way to gauge the risk of an option position and as a tool for making trading decisions. In this chapter, we will discuss the definition of options delta, how it affects options trading, and the importance of understanding options delta in order to make informed trades.

Definition of options delta

Options delta is a measure of the rate of change of an option's price with respect to a change in the underlying asset's price. It is often represented as a decimal between -1 and 1, with a positive delta indicating that the option's price will rise as the underlying asset's price rises, and a negative delta indicating that the option's price will fall as the underlying asset's price rises.

How options delta affects options trading

Options delta is an important concept to understand when trading options because it can help traders gauge the risk of an option position. A high delta option has a greater likelihood of ending in-the-money, and therefore has a higher risk than a low delta option. Additionally, options delta can also be used to determine the likelihood of an option expiring worthless.

Importance of options delta in options trading

Options delta is an important concept to understand when trading options because it can help traders make informed decisions about their trades. By understanding the delta of an option, traders can better gauge the risk of an option position and make decisions about when to enter or exit a trade. Additionally, options delta can also be used as a tool for hedging, where a trader can use options with opposite deltas to offset the risk of their portfolio.

Strategies for using options delta to make trades

One strategy for using options delta to make trades is to look for options with high delta when trading a bullish market, and options with low delta when trading a bearish market. Additionally, traders can also use options delta as a tool for hedging by using options with opposite deltas to offset the risk of their portfolio.

Example of a case study

Let's consider a case study where a trader has a portfolio of stock and wants to hedge against the risk of a market downturn. The trader decides to buy put options with a delta of -0.5, which means that the price of the option will increase by $0.50 for every $1 decrease in the underlying stock's price. If the stock's price does decrease, the trader can exercise the put option to sell the stock at a higher price, offsetting the loss in the stock.

In conclusion, options delta is an important concept to understand when trading options. It can be used as a tool to gauge the risk of an option position and make informed decisions about when to enter or exit a trade. Additionally, options delta can also be used as a tool for hedging, which can help traders offset the risk of their portfolio. By understanding and utilizing options delta, traders can make better trading decisions and potentially increase their chances of success in the options market.

Chapter 36: Delta & Directional Assumption Explained

Definition of delta and directional assumption:

Delta is a measure of the rate of change of an option's price with respect to the underlying stock's price. It is a Greek letter that is used to indicate the change in the price of an option relative to the underlying asset. It is represented as a decimal number between -1 and 1. A positive delta means that the option's price will increase as the underlying stock's price increases, and a negative delta means that the option's price will decrease as the underlying stock's price increases.

Directional assumption, on the other hand, refers to the expectation of the direction that the underlying stock's price will move. It is based on the analysis of various market indicators, such as charts, technical indicators, and market sentiment.

How delta and directional assumption interact:

Delta and directional assumption interact in the sense that the delta of an option can be used to determine the likelihood of the option expiring in the money. A call option with a delta of 0.5, for example, has a 50% chance of expiring in the money, while a put option with a delta of -0.5 has a 50% chance of expiring in the money.

The directional assumption, on the other hand, can be used to determine the likelihood of the underlying stock's price moving in a certain direction. A trader who believes that the stock's price will increase would be more likely to buy a call option with a positive delta, while a trader who believes that the stock's price will decrease would be more likely to buy a put option with a negative delta.

Importance of understanding delta and directional assumption in options trading:

Understanding delta and directional assumption is crucial for making informed trading decisions. The delta of an option can be used to determine the likelihood of the option expiring in the money, while the directional assumption can be used to determine the likelihood of the underlying stock's price moving in a certain direction.

By understanding these two concepts, traders can make more informed decisions about which options to buy and sell, and when to buy and sell them. They can also use these concepts to create more profitable trading strategies.

Strategies for using delta and directional assumption to make trades:

One strategy for using delta and directional assumption is to buy options with a high delta when the directional assumption is bullish and to buy options with a low delta when the directional assumption is bearish. This strategy is known as delta trading.

Another strategy is to use delta and directional assumption to create a delta neutral trading strategy. This strategy involves buying options with a high delta and selling options with a low delta. This can be used to create a portfolio that is not affected by the direction of the underlying stock's price.

Case Study:

Let's consider a trader who is interested in trading XYZ stock. The trader believes that the stock's price will increase in the next few months, and wants to buy a call option with a strike price of $100 and an expiration date of three months.

The trader looks at the option's delta and sees that it is 0.8. This means that the option's price will increase by 0.8 for every 1 point increase in the underlying stock's price. The trader also looks at the directional assumption and sees that it is bullish.

Based on this information, the trader decides to buy the call option. The stock's price does indeed increase, and the trader is able to make a profit on the option.

However, let's consider another scenario where the trader believes that the stock's price will decrease in the next few months.

In order to understand the concepts of delta and directional assumption, it is important to first define these terms. Delta is a measure of the rate of change of an option's price with respect to a change in the underlying asset's price. In simpler terms, it is the rate of change of an option's price in relation to the underlying stock or asset. Directional assumption is the assumption that the price of an underlying asset will move in a specific direction, either up or down.

The relationship between delta and directional assumption is important in options trading because it can help traders make informed decisions about which options to buy or sell. For example, if a trader believes that the price of a stock will go up, they may want to buy call options with a positive delta. This is because the call option will increase in value as the stock price goes up. Conversely, if a trader believes that the price of a stock will go down, they may want to buy put options with a negative delta. This is because the put option will increase in value as the stock price goes down.

The importance of understanding delta and directional assumption in options trading cannot be overstated. This is because delta and directional assumption are key factors in determining the value of an option and can greatly impact a trader's potential profits or losses. For example, if a trader buys a call option with a positive delta, they will make a profit if the stock price goes up, but will lose money if the stock price goes down. On the other hand, if a trader buys a put option with a negative delta, they will make a profit if the stock price goes down, but will lose money if the stock price goes up.

To illustrate the concepts of delta and directional assumption, let's consider a case study of a trader who believes that the price of XYZ stock will go up in the next few months. The trader buys a call option on XYZ stock with a strike price of $50 and a delta of 0.5. If the stock price goes up to $60, the trader will make a profit of $5 on the option ($60 - $50 = $10 x 0.5 = $5). This is because the option's delta is positive, which means that the option's price will increase as the stock price goes up.

One strategy for using delta and directional assumption to make trades is to look for options that have a high delta and a positive directional assumption. This is because these options will have the greatest potential for profit if the stock price goes up. Another strategy is to look for options that have a low delta and a negative directional assumption. This is because these options will have the greatest potential for profit if the stock price goes down.

In conclusion, understanding delta and directional assumption is crucial for making informed trading decisions. By understanding how these two factors interact, traders can make better decisions about which options to buy or sell and can increase their chances of making a profit. By using strategies such as looking for options with high delta and positive directional assumption, or options with low delta and negative directional assumption, traders can increase their chances of making a profit even further.

Chapter 37: Gamma Explained: What is it & How to Trade it

Gamma is an important concept in options trading that can have a significant impact on the price of an option. In this chapter, we will explore the definition of gamma, how it affects options trading, its importance in options trading, and strategies for using gamma to make trades.

Definition of Gamma

Gamma is a measure of the rate of change in an option's delta with respect to the underlying asset's price. In other words, it measures how much the delta of an option will change for a 1-point move in the underlying asset's price. Gamma is a Greek letter that is often used in finance to represent the rate of change of an option's delta.

Gamma is usually positive for call options and negative for put options. This is because as the underlying asset's price increases, the delta of a call option will also increase, while the delta of a put option will decrease.

How Gamma Affects Options Trading

Gamma is an important factor to consider when trading options because it affects the price of an option. As the underlying asset's price changes, the delta of an option will also change. This means that the price of an option will also change as the underlying asset's price changes.

Gamma is particularly important when trading options that are in-the-money or near-the-money. This is because the delta of these options will change more significantly as the underlying asset's price changes.

For example, let's say that an option trader has purchased a call option with a strike price of $50. The underlying asset's price is currently at $55, which means that the option is in-the-money. As the underlying asset's price increases, the delta of the option will also increase. This means that the price of the option will also increase as the underlying asset's price increases.

On the other hand, if the underlying asset's price decreases, the delta of the option will decrease, which means that the price of the option will also decrease. This is why it's important to consider gamma when trading options, as it can have a significant impact on the price of an option.

Importance of Gamma in Options Trading

Gamma is an important concept in options trading because it allows traders to better understand how the price of an option will change as the underlying asset's price changes. This can be useful for traders who are trying to predict how the underlying asset's price will move in the future.

Gamma is also important for traders who are trying to hedge their positions. For example, if a trader has a long call option position, they can use a short call option position to hedge their position. This is known as a gamma hedge.

Gamma is also important for traders who are trying to make a directional assumption. For example, if a trader believes that the underlying asset's price will increase in the next few months, they can purchase call options. This is because the delta of a call option will increase as the underlying asset's price increases.

Strategies for Using Gamma to Make Trades

There are several strategies that traders can use to make trades using gamma. These include:

1. Hedging: As mentioned earlier, traders can use a short call option position to hedge their long call option position. This is known as a gamma hedge.
2. Directional assumption: Traders can use gamma to make a directional assumption. For example, if a trader believes that the underlying asset's price will increase in the next few months, they can purchase call options.
3. Gamma scalping: Gamma scalping is a strategy that uses the gamma of options to make small, frequent trades in order to

take advantage of the volatility in the underlying asset. This strategy is often used by traders who are looking to make a quick profit in a short period of time.

Definition of gamma: Gamma is a measure of the rate of change of an option's delta with respect to the underlying asset's price. In other words, it measures how much the delta of an option will change as the price of the underlying asset changes. Gamma is often used in conjunction with delta to help traders understand the risk and reward of a trade.

How gamma affects options trading: Gamma can have a significant impact on the value of an option. A high gamma means that the delta of the option will change rapidly as the price of the underlying asset changes. This can make the option more valuable or less valuable depending on the direction of the price change. A low gamma means that the delta of the option will change more slowly, which can make the option less risky.

Importance of gamma in options trading: Gamma is an important measure for options traders because it helps them understand the risk and reward of a trade. By understanding gamma, traders can make more informed decisions about when to enter or exit a trade. Additionally, gamma can be used in conjunction with other measures, such as delta and theta, to help traders create more effective trading strategies.

Strategies for using gamma to make trades: There are several strategies that traders can use to take advantage of gamma. One strategy is to use gamma scalping, which involves making small, frequent trades in order to take advantage of the volatility in the underlying asset. Another strategy is to use gamma trading, which involves buying options with a high gamma and selling options with a low gamma. This can help traders profit from both the volatility in the underlying asset and the changes in the delta of the option.

Example of a case study:

A trader is looking to take advantage of the volatility in the price of XYZ stock. The trader believes that the price of XYZ stock will increase in the next few months, but is uncertain about the exact timing of the price increase. The trader decides to use a gamma trading strategy to profit from the volatility in the price of XYZ stock.

The trader buys a call option with a strike price of $100 and a gamma of 0.5. The trader also sells a call option with a strike price of $110 and a gamma of 0.3. The trader believes that the price of XYZ stock will increase, which will cause the delta of the first option to increase and the delta of the second option to decrease.

As the price of XYZ stock increases, the delta of the first option increases, making it more valuable. The delta of the second option decreases, making it less valuable. The trader is able to profit from the changes in the delta of the options, as well as the volatility in the price of XYZ stock.

Overall, the trader is able to take advantage of the volatility in the price of XYZ stock and make a profit by using the gamma trading strategy. This example highlights the importance of understanding gamma and how it can be used to make informed trading decisions.

As you can see, gamma is an important measure to understand in options trading, as it helps traders understand the risk and reward of a trade, and can be used in conjunction with other measures to create effective trading strategies. By understanding gamma and how to use it, traders can make more informed decisions and potentially increase their chances of success in the options market.

Chapter 38: Theta Explained: What is it & How to Trade it

Theta is a measure of the rate of decline in an option's value as time passes. It is one of the Greeks used in options trading and is often referred to as the "time decay" of an option. Theta is expressed as a negative number, as the value of an option decreases as time passes.

How theta affects options trading:

Theta is an important concept for options traders to understand, as it can have a significant impact on the value of an option. For example, a long call option will experience a decline in value as time passes, due to theta. This decline in value can be accelerated if the underlying stock's price remains stagnant or decreases. On the other hand, a short call option will benefit from theta, as the option's value will decline as time passes.

Importance of theta in options trading:

Theta is an important concept for options traders to understand, as it can have a significant impact on the value of an option. Traders need to be aware of theta when making decisions about when to enter or exit a trade. For example, if a trader is holding a long call option and theta is working against them, they may want to consider closing the position before the option's value declines too much.

Strategies for using theta to make trades:

There are several strategies that traders can use to take advantage of theta. One strategy is to sell options with high theta, as the option's value will decline rapidly as time passes. Another strategy is to buy options with low theta, as the option's value will decline at a slower rate. Traders can also use theta to their advantage by selling options that are close to expiration and buying options that have further expiration dates.

Example of a case study:

Let's consider a trader who is long a call option on XYZ stock with a strike price of $50 and an expiration date of one month. The option is currently trading at $2.50 and has a theta of -0.05. The trader is aware that theta is working against them and that the option's value will decline as time passes.

The trader decides to sell the option for $2.50, realizing a profit of $0.50. If the trader had held onto the option for another week, the option's value would have declined to $2.25 due to theta. By selling the option early, the trader was able to realize a profit before the option's value declined.

Research:

According to a study published in the Journal of Financial Economics, options traders can benefit from theta by selling options that have high theta and buying options that have low theta. The study found that options with high theta had a higher probability of expiring worthless, which made them more attractive to sell. On the other hand, options with low theta had a lower probability of expiring worthless, which made them more attractive to buy.

In conclusion, understanding theta and how it affects options trading is crucial for making informed decisions. Traders should be aware of theta when entering or exiting a trade, and can use theta to their advantage by selling options with high theta and buying options with low theta. By understanding theta, traders can make more profitable trades and increase their chances of success in the options market.

Chapter 39: Vega: What is it & How to Trade it

Vega, also known as the volatility factor, is an important measure in options trading that tells us how much an option's price is expected to change with a one percent change in implied volatility. In other words, it is a measure of an option's sensitivity to changes in volatility. Understanding vega and how it affects options pricing is crucial for any options trader. In this chapter, we will discuss the definition of vega, how it affects options trading, the importance of vega in options trading, and strategies for using vega to make trades.

Definition of Vega

Vega is a Greek letter that is used in options trading to measure the sensitivity of an option's price to changes in volatility. It is a measure of how much an option's price will change with a one percent change in implied volatility. Vega is expressed as a decimal, typically between 0 and

1, and is represented in the options chain as a percentage. A vega of 0.1, for example, means that an option's price will change by 0.1% for every 1% change in implied volatility.

How Vega Affects Options Trading

Vega is an important measure in options trading because it tells us how much an option's price is expected to change with a one percent change in implied volatility. Options prices are affected by changes in volatility because volatility is one of the key factors used to calculate the price of an option. When volatility is high, options prices are generally higher, and when volatility is low, options prices are generally lower.

Vega is also important because it tells us how much an option's price is expected to change with changes in volatility. When implied volatility is high, options prices are generally higher, and when implied volatility is low, options prices are generally lower. This means that options traders need to be aware of vega when making trades because changes in volatility can have a significant impact on the price of an option.

Importance of Vega in Options Trading

Vega is an important measure in options trading because it tells us how much an option's price is expected to change with changes in volatility. Understanding vega is crucial for any options trader because changes in volatility can have a significant impact on the price of an option. This means that options traders need to be aware of vega when making trades because changes in volatility can have a significant impact on the price of an option.

For example, if an options trader is bullish on a stock and buys a call option with a high vega, the option's price will increase if the implied volatility of the stock increases. On the other hand, if the options trader is bearish on a stock and buys a put option with a high vega, the option's price will decrease if the implied volatility of the stock decreases.

Strategies for Using Vega to Make Trades

Options traders use vega to make trades based on their expectations of how volatility will change in the future. For example, if an options trader expects volatility to increase in the future, they will buy options with a high vega. On the other hand, if an options trader expects volatility to decrease in the future, they will buy options with a low vega.

One strategy that options traders use to make trades based on vega is called volatility trading. Volatility trading is a strategy that involves buying options with a high vega when volatility is low and selling options with a high vega when volatility is high. This strategy is based on the assumption that volatility tends to revert to its mean over time.

Another strategy that options traders use to make trades using vega is known as "vega neutral" trading. This strategy involves adjusting an options position in order to neutralize the impact of vega on the trade. For example, a trader might sell an option with a high vega in order to offset the impact of a long option with a lower vega.

Another strategy that is commonly used when trading options is known as "vega trading." This involves taking advantage of changes in volatility in order to make profitable trades. For example, a trader might buy an option when volatility is low, and then sell it when volatility increases.

One of the most important things to keep in mind when trading options using vega is that the volatility of an underlying asset can change quickly and unpredictably. This means that it is important to be aware of the current volatility levels and to be prepared to adjust your options positions accordingly.

To conclude, vega is a very important concept in options trading. It is important to understand how vega affects options pricing and to use it as a tool to make profitable trades. Some of the strategies that can be used when trading options using vega include vega neutral trading, vega trading, and being aware of the current volatility levels. By understanding how vega works and how to trade it, you can greatly improve your chances of success when trading options.

Example of a case study and research:

In this case study, we will look at how a trader used vega to make a profitable trade. The trader in question was following the technology sector and noticed that the volatility of a particular stock, XYZ, was low. The trader believed that the volatility of XYZ would increase in the near future and decided to buy a call option with a high vega.

The trader was right, and the volatility of XYZ did increase. As a result, the value of the call option also increased, and the trader was able to sell it for a profit. In this case, the trader used vega to make a profitable trade by taking advantage of the expected increase in volatility.

Research shows that vega is a significant factor in options pricing, and it can be used to make profitable trades. Traders who are aware of the current volatility levels and are able to use vega to their advantage are more likely to be successful in the options market. By understanding how vega works and how to trade it, traders can greatly improve their chances of success when trading options.

In conclusion, understanding the concept of vega and how it affects options trading is crucial for any trader looking to make informed decisions. Vega is a measure of an option's sensitivity to changes in volatility and is an important factor to consider when evaluating options trades. By understanding the importance of vega, traders can develop strategies to take advantage of changes in volatility, whether it be through volatility trading or volatility hedging. The case study and research presented in this chapter provided valuable insights into how vega can be used in real-world trading scenarios and how it can impact the overall performance of a trade. By taking the time to understand vega and incorporating it into their trading strategy, traders can improve their chances of success in the options market.

Chapter 40: Vega's Impact On Longer-Dated Options

Options trading is a complex field that requires a deep understanding of the various factors that can affect the value of an option. One of the most important factors to consider is vega, which measures the sensitivity of an option's price to changes in implied volatility. In this chapter, we will explore how vega's impact on longer-dated options differs from shorter-dated options and how traders can use this information to make profitable trades.

Definition of vega's impact on longer-dated options

Vega is a Greek letter that is used to represent the sensitivity of an option's price to changes in implied volatility. Vega is measured in percentage points per percentage point of implied volatility. For example, if an option has a vega of 0.1, it means that for every 1%

increase in implied volatility, the option's price will increase by 0.1%.

When it comes to longer-dated options, vega's impact tends to be greater than it is for shorter-dated options. This is because longer-dated options have more time for implied volatility to change, which means that they are more sensitive to changes in implied volatility. Additionally, longer-dated options are more likely to be affected by events that can cause large changes in implied volatility, such as earnings reports or natural disasters.

How vega's impact on longer-dated options differs from shorter-dated options

The impact of vega on longer-dated options differs from shorter-dated options in a few key ways. Firstly, as mentioned earlier, longer-dated options tend to have a greater impact from changes in implied volatility than shorter-dated options. Additionally, longer-dated options are more likely to be affected by events that can cause large changes in implied volatility, such as earnings reports or natural disasters.

Furthermore, changes in implied volatility can have a greater impact on the value of longer-dated options than they do on shorter-dated options. This is because longer-dated options have more time for implied volatility to change, which means that they are more sensitive to changes in implied volatility.

Importance of understanding vega's impact on longer-dated options in options trading

Understanding vega's impact on longer-dated options is crucial for traders who are looking to make profitable trades. For example, if a trader is looking to buy a call option that is set to expire in six months, it is important for them to understand the impact of vega on that option. By knowing how sensitive the option is to changes in implied volatility, the trader can make a more informed decision about whether or not to buy the option.

Strategies for using vega's impact on longer-dated options to make trades

There are several strategies that traders can use to take advantage of vega's impact on longer-dated options. One strategy is to buy options that have a high vega, as these options are more likely to increase in value if implied volatility increases. Additionally, traders can use options with high vega to hedge against changes in implied volatility.

Another strategy is to sell options that have a low vega, as these options are less likely to increase in value if implied volatility increases. This strategy is commonly used by traders who are looking to generate income from their options trading.

Case Study:

One example of how vega's impact on longer-dated options can be used to make trades is a trader who is looking to buy a call option on a stock that is set to expire in six months. The trader is aware that the company is set to release its earnings report in three months and that this report can cause a large change in implied volatility.

In conclusion, understanding vega's impact on longer-dated options is crucial for any options trader looking to make informed trades. By understanding how vega differs for longer-dated options and how it can affect the value of an option, traders can use this information to make trades that are more likely to be profitable. Whether through utilizing different strategies or adjusting trade positions based on vega's impact, traders can increase their chances of success by understanding this important concept. In order to truly master options trading, it's essential to have a deep understanding of all the different factors that can affect an option's value, and vega's impact on longer-dated options is definitely one of them.

Chapter 41: Portfolio Management: Short Delta & Short Vega Explained

When it comes to options trading, portfolio management is an essential aspect to consider. One important aspect of portfolio management is understanding the concept of short delta and short vega. In this chapter, we will define short delta and short vega, explain how they affect options trading, and discuss the importance of using them in portfolio management. We will also provide strategies for using short delta and short vega to make trades, along with an example of a case study to illustrate these concepts in action.

Definition of short delta and short vega in portfolio management

Short delta refers to a strategy where an options trader sells options contracts, essentially betting that the underlying stock or index will not move as much as expected. This is the opposite of a long delta strategy, where an options trader buys options contracts, betting that the underlying stock or index will move in the desired direction.

Short vega, on the other hand, refers to a strategy where an options trader sells options contracts, betting that the volatility of the underlying stock or index will not increase as much as expected. This is the opposite of a long vega strategy, where an options trader buys options contracts, betting that the volatility of the underlying stock or index will increase.

How short delta and short vega affect options trading

Short delta and short vega strategies can be effective tools for portfolio management, as they allow traders to potentially profit from a lack of movement or volatility in the underlying stock or index. However, it is important to note that these strategies also come with risk. For example, if the underlying stock or index does move or experience an increase in volatility, the options trader will lose money.

Importance of using short delta and short vega in portfolio management

Short delta and short vega strategies can be useful for portfolio management as they provide a way for traders to potentially profit from a lack of movement or volatility in the underlying stock or index. Additionally, these strategies can also be used to hedge against potential losses in other positions in the portfolio.

Strategies for using short delta and short vega to make trades

One strategy for using short delta and short vega in options trading is to sell call options. This strategy can be profitable if the underlying stock or index does not move above the strike price of the call option. Another strategy is to sell put options, which can be profitable if the underlying stock or index does not move below the strike price of the put option.

Another strategy for using short delta and short vega is to sell options with a higher implied volatility than the historical volatility of the underlying stock or index. This strategy can be profitable if the implied volatility does not increase as much as expected.

Example of a case study

Consider a trader who is bearish on a particular stock and believes that the stock will not move much in the near future. The trader decides to sell a call option with a strike price of $50 and a expiration date of one month. The trader also sells a put option with a strike price of $45 and the same expiration date.

In this scenario, the trader is betting that the stock will not move above $50 or below $45 in the next month. If the stock does not move as expected, the trader will make a profit on the call and put options. However, if the stock does move above $50 or below $45, the trader will lose money on the call and put options.

In conclusion, short delta and short vega are important concepts to understand in options trading, as they provide a way for traders to potentially profit from a lack of movement or volatility in the underlying

In conclusion, understanding short delta and short vega in portfolio management is crucial for options traders looking to make informed and profitable trades. By utilizing the right strategies, such as delta and vega neutral hedging, traders can manage their portfolio risk and maximize their returns. However, it is important to remember that these strategies should be used in conjunction with other market analysis and research to make the most informed decisions. Ultimately, a comprehensive understanding of short delta and short vega can greatly enhance a trader's ability to navigate the ever-changing market landscape and make successful trades.

Chapter 42: Day Trading Using SPY Explained

Day trading using SPY refers to the practice of buying and selling options contracts based on the S&P 500 ETF (SPY) within the same trading day. The SPY ETF is a popular choice for day traders due to its high liquidity and correlation with the broader market.

How day trading using SPY affects options trading

Day trading using SPY can be a highly profitable strategy, but it also comes with a high level of risk. Because options contracts have a limited lifespan, day traders must be able to accurately predict market movements in a short period of time. This requires a high level of market knowledge and the ability to quickly react to changes in the market.

Importance of day trading using SPY in options trading

Day trading using SPY is a popular strategy among options traders because it allows them to take advantage of short-term market movements. By buying and selling options contracts based on the SPY ETF, traders can profit from both bullish and bearish market conditions. Additionally, day trading using SPY can be a useful tool for managing risk in a portfolio.

Strategies for using SPY to make day trades

There are a variety of strategies that traders can use when day trading using SPY. Some popular strategies include:

1. Bullish strategies: These strategies involve buying call options on the SPY ETF in anticipation of a bullish market. This can include buying call options at-the-money or in-the-money, as well as using options spreads such as a bull call spread.
2. Bearish strategies: These strategies involve buying put options on the SPY ETF in anticipation of a bearish market.

This can include buying put options at-the-money or in-the-money, as well as using options spreads such as a bear put spread.
3. Volatility strategies: These strategies involve buying options contracts based on the volatility of the SPY ETF. This can include buying options that are sensitive to changes in volatility, such as long straddles or strangles.

Example of a case study

To illustrate the potential of day trading using SPY, let's look at a hypothetical example.

Imagine that a trader believes that the market is going to decline in the short-term. In this case, the trader could buy put options on the SPY ETF with a strike price of $290 and an expiration date of the same day. The trader could then sell these options later in the day if the market does decline, thereby profiting from the decline in the market.

In this example, the trader was able to profit from a bearish market movement without having to actually sell the underlying SPY ETF. This is one of the key advantages of day trading using SPY – it allows traders to profit from market movements without having to take on the risk of actually buying and selling the underlying asset.

Conclusion

Day trading using SPY can be a highly profitable strategy for options traders, but it also comes with a high level of risk. By understanding the basics of day trading using SPY, including the importance of market knowledge and the ability to quickly react to changes in the market, traders can increase their chances of success. Additionally, by using a variety of strategies such as bullish, bearish, and volatility strategies, traders can take advantage of different market conditions to make profitable trades.

Chapter 43: Stock Correlation Explained

Stock correlation is a statistical measure of how two stocks move in relation to each other. It is a number between -1 and 1, where 1 indicates perfect positive correlation (meaning the two stocks move in the same direction), -1 indicates perfect negative correlation (meaning the two stocks move in opposite directions), and 0 indicates no correlation (meaning the two stocks are completely independent of each other).

Understanding stock correlation is important in options trading because it can help traders identify potential trade opportunities and risk management strategies. For example, if two stocks have a high positive correlation, a trader may consider creating a long call spread strategy using options on both stocks. On the other hand, if two stocks have a high negative correlation, a trader may consider creating a long call spread strategy using options on one stock and a short call spread strategy using options on the other stock.

One strategy for using stock correlation in options trading is to look for pairs of stocks that have a high positive correlation and then create a long call spread strategy using options on both stocks. This strategy is known as a "pair trade" and can be a way to profit from a market move without having to predict which stock will perform better. Another strategy is to look for pairs of stocks that have a high negative correlation and then create a long call spread strategy using options on one stock and a short call spread strategy using options on the other stock. This strategy is known as a "market neutral" strategy and can be a way to profit from market moves without having to predict which direction the market will go.

An example of a case study where stock correlation was used in options trading is the following:

A trader noticed that the stock prices of Company A and Company B were highly correlated. The trader decided to create a long call spread strategy using options on both stocks, with the expectation that if the market moved in a positive direction, both stocks would increase in value and the options would expire in the money. The trader also decided to set a stop loss order at a certain price level to limit potential losses.

In this case, the trader was able to profit from the market move without having to predict which stock would perform better. The trader was also able to limit potential losses by using a stop loss order.

It is important to note that while stock correlation can be a useful tool in options trading, it should not be the only factor considered when making trades. Traders should also consider other factors such as the overall market conditions, the individual stock's fundamentals, and any relevant news or events that may affect the stock's price.

In conclusion, stock correlation is a statistical measure of how two stocks move in relation to each other. Understanding stock correlation can help traders identify potential trade opportunities and risk management strategies in options trading. Some strategies for using stock correlation include pair trading and market neutral strategies. However, it is important to consider other factors in addition to stock correlation when making trades.

Chapter 44: Beta Explained: What is it & How to Trade it

In the world of options trading, understanding the various factors that affect the value of an option is crucial to making informed trades. One such factor is beta, which is a measure of a stock's volatility in relation to the overall market. In this chapter, we will delve into the definition and importance of beta, as well as strategies for using it to make trades.

Definition of beta:

Beta is a measure of a stock's volatility in relation to the overall market. It is calculated by comparing the stock's returns to the returns of a benchmark index, such as the S&P 500. A beta of 1 means that the stock's returns move in line with the market, while a beta greater than 1 indicates that the stock is more volatile than the market, and a beta less than 1 indicates that the stock is less volatile than the market.

How beta affects options trading:

The value of an option is affected by a number of factors, including the underlying stock's price, strike price, and expiration date. Beta is also an important factor, as it is used to estimate the volatility of the underlying stock. A high beta stock is considered more volatile than a low beta stock, which can have an impact on the value of the option. For example, a call option on a high beta stock may be more expensive than a call option on a low beta stock.

Importance of beta in options trading:

Beta is an important factor to consider when trading options, as it can help traders identify stocks that are likely to experience more volatility. This can be useful when making trades, as options on volatile stocks can have higher premiums. Additionally, beta can be used to determine the level of risk associated with a particular option trade. A high beta stock is generally considered to be more risky than a low beta stock, which can be useful information when determining the level of risk that a trader is willing to take on.

Strategies for using beta to make trades:

1. Trading options on high beta stocks: One strategy for using beta to make trades is to focus on options on high beta stocks. These stocks are generally considered to be more volatile than low beta stocks, which can result in higher premiums for options.
2. Hedging with options on low beta stocks: Another strategy for using beta to make trades is to use options on low beta stocks to hedge against the risk of high beta stocks. This can be done by purchasing options on low beta stocks and selling options on high beta stocks, which can help to offset the risk of the high beta stocks.
3. Using beta to identify potential trades: Beta can also be used to identify potential trades. For example, a trader may use beta to identify stocks that are likely to experience more volatility in the future, and then use this information to make trades.

Example of a case Study:

A trader is interested in trading options on a stock that has a beta of 1.5, meaning that it is 50% more volatile than the overall market. The trader decides to use a delta neutral strategy, where the delta of their options positions is equal to zero. This means that the trader is not exposed to any directional risk and is only affected by changes in volatility.

The trader buys a call option with a strike price of $50 and a theta of -0.05. This means that the option will decrease in value by $0.05 for every day that passes. The trader also buys a put option with a strike price of $50 and a gamma of 0.02. This means that the option's delta will increase by 2% for every 1% move in the underlying stock's price.

The trader's goal is to profit from changes in volatility while minimizing their exposure to directional risk. In this case, the trader is expecting the stock's volatility to increase. If the stock's volatility increases, the call option's value will increase as well, due to its positive vega. The put option's value will also increase, due to its positive gamma. The trader will profit from both options, as they are both positively impacted by an increase in volatility.

However, if the stock's volatility decreases, the call option's value will decrease, due to its negative vega. The put option's value will also decrease, due to its negative gamma. The trader will lose money on both options, as they are both negatively impacted by a decrease in volatility.

Overall, the trader's strategy is to profit from changes in volatility while minimizing their exposure to directional risk. The trader is able to do this by using a delta neutral strategy and buying options with positive vega and positive gamma. This strategy can be used by other traders who are interested in profiting from changes in volatility while minimizing their exposure to directional risk.

Conclusion:

In this chapter, we discussed the four factors for measuring risk in options trading: delta, gamma, theta, and vega. Each of these factors can be used to make trades and manage risk in different ways. We also discussed a case study of a trader who used a delta neutral strategy and bought options with positive vega and positive gamma to profit from changes in volatility while minimizing their exposure to directional risk. Understanding and utilizing these factors can be crucial for any options trader looking to make profitable trades and manage their risk effectively.

Chapter 45: Four Factors for Measuring Risk: Delta, Gamma, Theta, and Vega

When it comes to options trading, understanding and managing risk is crucial for success. One way to do this is by understanding and utilizing four key factors that can help measure and manage risk: delta, gamma, theta, and vega. In this chapter, we will define each of these factors, explain how they affect options trading, and explore strategies for using them to make trades and manage risk.

Definition of delta, gamma, theta, and vega as factors for measuring risk

Delta is a measure of how much the price of an option changes in relation to the price of the underlying asset. It is often referred to as the "hedge ratio" because it tells us how much of the underlying asset we need to purchase or sell in order to hedge our option position.

Gamma is a measure of how much delta changes as the price of the underlying asset changes. It is often referred to as the "delta accelerator" because it tells us how much delta will change as the underlying price moves.

Theta is a measure of how much the price of an option changes over time. It is often referred to as the "time decay" because it tells us how much the option will lose value over time.

Vega is a measure of how much the price of an option changes in relation to changes in volatility. It is often referred to as the "volatility sensitivity" because it tells us how much the option will gain or lose value as volatility changes.

How each of these factors affects options trading

Delta, gamma, theta, and vega are all important factors to consider when trading options. Delta tells us how much of the underlying asset we need to purchase or sell in order to hedge our option position, while gamma tells us how much delta will change as the underlying price moves. Theta tells us how much the option will lose value over time, while vega tells us how much the option will gain or lose value as volatility changes.

Importance of understanding these four factors in options trading

By understanding delta, gamma, theta, and vega, we can make more informed decisions about when to enter and exit trades, how much to risk, and how to manage our positions. For example, if we know that an option has a high theta, we may want to exit the trade before expiration in order to avoid losing too much value due to time decay. If we know that an option has a high vega, we may want to consider hedging our position in order to protect against changes in volatility.

Strategies for using these four factors to measure and manage risk

One strategy for using delta, gamma, theta, and vega is to use them to calculate the "Greeks" of an option. The Greeks are a set of measures that can help us understand the risk and reward of an option. By calculating the delta, gamma, theta, and vega of an option, we can get a better sense of how the option will perform under different market conditions.

Another strategy for using these four factors is to use them to make trades. For example, if we know that an option has a high delta, we may want to enter a long call option in order to benefit from upward movements in the underlying asset. If we know that an option has a high vega, we may want to enter a long call option in order to benefit from increased volatility.

Example of a case study

In this case study, we will look at how an options trader might use delta, gamma, theta, and vega to measure and manage risk in their portfolio. Let's say that the trader has a portfolio of options that is heavily skewed towards long positions. In order to measure the risk of this portfolio, the trader would first look at the delta of each option. Delta measures the change in the value of the option for every one-point change in the underlying asset. In this case, the trader would want to have a low delta, as this would indicate that the portfolio is not highly sensitive to changes in the underlying asset.

Next, the trader would look at the gamma of each option. Gamma measures the rate of change in delta. In other words, it measures how quickly the delta of an option changes as the underlying asset moves. A high gamma would indicate that the portfolio is highly sensitive to changes in the underlying asset, and that it is at a high risk of losing value quickly. In this case, the trader would want to have a low gamma, as this would indicate that the portfolio is less sensitive to changes in the underlying asset.

The trader would then look at the theta of each option. Theta measures the rate of change in the value of the option as time passes. In other words, it measures how quickly the option is losing value as time passes. A high theta would indicate that the portfolio is at a high risk of losing value as time passes, and that it is not well-suited for long-term investments. In this case, the trader would want to have a low theta, as this would indicate that the portfolio is well-suited for long-term investments.

Finally, the trader would look at the vega of each option. Vega measures the rate of change in the value of the option as volatility changes. In other words, it measures how quickly the option is losing value as volatility changes. A high vega would indicate that the portfolio is at a high risk of losing value as volatility changes, and that it is not well-suited for volatile markets. In this case, the trader would want to have a low vega, as this would indicate that the portfolio is well-suited for volatile markets.

By using these four factors, the trader is able to get a comprehensive view of the risk in their portfolio. They can see which areas of the portfolio are most at risk, and can take steps to reduce that risk. For example, if the trader sees that the portfolio has a high delta, they might reduce their position in that option. If they see that the portfolio has a high gamma, they might take steps to reduce the rate of change in the delta of that option. By using these four factors, the trader is able to make informed decisions about how to manage the risk in their portfolio.

In conclusion, delta, gamma, theta, and vega are four important factors that can be used to measure and manage risk in options trading. By understanding how each of these factors affects the value of an option, traders can make informed decisions about how to manage the risk in their portfolio. By using these four factors in combination, traders can get a comprehensive view of the risk in their portfolio and can take steps to reduce that risk. As always, it is important to remember that risk management is an ongoing process and that traders should regularly review their portfolio and make adjustments as needed.

Chapter 46: Rolling an options trade explained

Rolling an options trade is a strategy that is used by options traders to adjust or extend the life of an existing options position. This technique is often used to manage risk or to take advantage of changes in market conditions. In this chapter, we will define what rolling an options trade is, explain how it affects options trading, and discuss the importance of this strategy in options trading. We will also provide some strategies for rolling options trades and include a case study to illustrate how this technique can be used in practice.

1. Definition of rolling an options trade

Rolling an options trade refers to the process of closing an existing options position and simultaneously opening a new options position with a different strike price or expiration date. This strategy is often used to manage risk or to take advantage of changes in market conditions. For example, if an options trader is holding a long call option and the underlying stock price has increased, they might roll their position to a higher strike price to lock in profits. Alternatively, if an options trader is holding a long put option and the underlying stock price has decreased, they might roll their position to a lower strike price to reduce their risk.

2. How rolling an options trade affects options trading

Rolling an options trade can affect options trading in a number of ways. For one, it can be used to manage risk by adjusting the strike price or expiration date of an existing options position. Additionally, it can be used to take advantage of changes in market conditions by adjusting the strike price or expiration date of an existing options position. For example, if an options trader is holding a long call option and the underlying stock price has increased, they might roll their position to a higher strike price to lock in profits. Alternatively, if an options trader is holding a long put option and the underlying stock price has decreased, they might roll their position to a lower strike price to reduce their risk.

3. Importance of rolling an options trade in options trading

Rolling an options trade is an important strategy in options trading because it allows traders to manage risk and take advantage of changes in market conditions. By adjusting the strike price or expiration date of an existing options position, traders can lock in profits, reduce risk, or extend the life of an existing position. Additionally, rolling an options trade can be used to generate additional income through the collection of option premiums.

4. Strategies for rolling options trades

There are several strategies for rolling options trades that traders can use. One strategy is to roll an options position to a higher strike price when the underlying stock price has increased. This can be used to lock in profits and reduce risk. Another strategy is to roll an options position to a lower strike price when the underlying stock price has decreased. This can also be used to reduce risk. Additionally, traders can roll an options position to a later expiration date in order to extend the life of the position.

Example of a case study

In this case study, we will look at how an options trader might use rolling an options trade to manage risk and take advantage of changes in market conditions. The trader is holding a long call option on XYZ stock with a strike price of $50 and an expiration date of June. The underlying stock price has increased to $55, and the trader decides to roll their position to a higher strike price of $60. By doing this, the trader has locked in a profit of $5 per share ($55 - $50) and reduced their risk. Additionally, the trader has also collected additional option premiums by rolling the position to a higher strike price.

In conclusion, rolling an options trade is a powerful strategy that can be used to manage risk and capitalize on market movements. By understanding the definition and mechanics of rolling an options trade, as well as its impact on options trading, traders can effectively use this strategy to their advantage. Additionally, by being aware of the importance of rolling an options trade and utilizing different strategies, traders can make informed decisions and potentially increase their chances of success in the options market. As always, it is important to continually educate oneself and stay up-to-date on the latest market trends and strategies in order to make the most profitable trades.

Chapter 47: Keeping Track of Rolled Options Explained

Definition of keeping track of rolled options

When an options trader rolls an options trade, it means that they are closing out an existing options position and opening a new one with a different expiration date or strike price. Keeping track of rolled options refers to the process of monitoring and managing these rolled trades. This includes keeping track of the strike prices, expiration dates, and positions size of each trade, as well as keeping track of any profit or loss.

How keeping track of rolled options affects options trading

Keeping track of rolled options is an important part of managing risk in options trading. By monitoring these trades, traders can ensure that they are not over-exposing themselves to risk and that they are making trades that align with their overall trading strategy. Additionally, keeping track of rolled options allows traders to easily adjust their positions as market conditions change, which can help them to minimize losses and maximize profits.

Importance of keeping track of rolled options in options trading

Keeping track of rolled options is essential for any options trader who wants to be successful. It allows traders to understand their risk and exposure, and to adjust their positions as needed. Without keeping track of rolled options, traders may find themselves in a position where they are over-exposed to risk and unable to adjust their positions in time to avoid losses.

Strategies for keeping track of rolled options

There are several strategies that traders can use to keep track of rolled options. One approach is to use a spreadsheet or a trading journal to record all of the details of each trade, including the strike price, expiration date, and position size. This allows traders to quickly and easily track their rolled options and make adjustments as needed. Another approach is to use a trading software or app that automatically tracks and records all of the details of each trade. This can be a convenient and efficient way to keep track of rolled options, but it may also be more expensive.

Example of a case study:

To illustrate the importance of keeping track of rolled options, let's consider the example of a trader named John. John is a new options trader and is not familiar with the concept of rolling options. He starts trading with a single call option contract on a stock that he believes is undervalued. After a few weeks, the stock starts to rise and John wants to lock in his profits. However, instead of rolling the option, he closes the position and takes the profits. A few days later, the stock continues to rise and John wishes he had kept the option open to capture more profits.

John quickly realizes the importance of rolling options and starts to keep track of his rolled options using a spreadsheet. He records the strike price, expiration date, and position size of each trade. He also makes a note of the reason for rolling the trade and any adjustments that he makes. He also starts to use a trading software that keeps track of his rolled options and alerts him when it is time to adjust his positions.

John's trading improves significantly and he starts to see consistent profits. He is able to adjust his positions quickly and effectively, which helps him to capture more profits and minimize losses. He also starts to see how rolling options can help him to manage risk and adjust his positions as market conditions change.

In conclusion, keeping track of rolled options is an important part of options trading. It allows traders to understand their risk and exposure, and to adjust their positions as needed. By keeping track of rolled options, traders can make better trading decisions, capture more profits, and minimize losses. Traders should consider using a spreadsheet or trading software to keep track of their rolled options and make adjustments as needed.

Chapter 48: Locking in Profit by Purchasing Options

As an options trader, one of the most important skills to master is the ability to lock in profit. This means taking advantage of favorable market conditions to secure a profit, rather than holding onto a position and hoping for the best. One way to do this is by purchasing options. In this chapter, we will explore the definition, effects, importance, and strategies for locking in profit by purchasing options.

Definition of Locking in Profit by Purchasing Options

Purchasing options is a strategy that allows traders to secure a profit by buying an option contract at a specific price. This price is known as the strike price. When an option is purchased, the trader has the right, but not the obligation, to buy or sell the underlying asset at the strike price. This allows the trader to lock in a profit if the market moves in their favor.

How Locking in Profit by Purchasing Options Affects Options Trading

Locking in profit by purchasing options can have a significant impact on options trading. One of the key benefits of this strategy is that it allows traders to secure a profit without having to hold onto a position for an extended period of time. This can be particularly useful in volatile markets, where prices can change rapidly. Additionally, purchasing options can help traders manage risk by allowing them to limit their potential losses.

Importance of Locking in Profit by Purchasing Options in Options Trading

Understanding the importance of locking in profit by purchasing options is crucial for any options trader. This strategy can help traders to minimize risk, maximize returns, and make more informed trading decisions. Additionally, it can help traders to manage their positions more effectively, which can be especially useful in volatile markets.

Strategies for Locking in Profit by Purchasing Options

There are several strategies that traders can use when locking in profit by purchasing options. One of the most popular is the covered call strategy. This involves purchasing a stock and simultaneously selling a call option on the same stock. This can help traders to lock in a profit if the stock price rises, while also limiting potential losses if the stock price falls. Another strategy is the protective put strategy. This involves purchasing a stock and simultaneously buying a put option on the same stock. This can help traders to lock in a profit if the stock price falls, while also limiting potential losses if the stock price rises.

Example of a Case Study

In this case study, we will look at how an options trader might use the covered call strategy to lock in a profit. The trader is bullish on XYZ stock and decides to purchase 100 shares at $50 per share. The trader also sells a call option at a strike price of $55 with a expiration date of one month. This option gives the buyer the right, but not the obligation, to purchase the stock at $55.

The stock price rises to $60 within the month and the trader exercises their right to sell the stock at $55. The trader makes a profit of $500 ($55 x 100 shares) minus the premium received from selling the call option. In this scenario, the trader was able to lock in a profit and limit potential losses by utilizing the covered call strategy.

In conclusion, locking in profit by purchasing options is a powerful strategy that can be used to manage risk and maximize returns in options trading. By understanding the definition, effects, importance, and strategies for this technique, traders can make more informed trading decisions and achieve greater success in the market. It is essential to research and understand the different strategies available and to have a clear plan in place when implementing them.

Chapter 49: Option Spread Differences

Options trading is a complex and dynamic field that requires a deep understanding of various strategies and concepts. One such concept is option spread differences, which can greatly impact the outcome of a trade. In this chapter, we will explore the definition of option spread differences, how they affect options trading, the importance of understanding option spread differences, and strategies for using them to make trades.

Option spread differences refer to the difference in price between two different options contracts, such as a call option and a put option. These differences can be caused by a variety of factors, such as the underlying stock price, the strike price, and the expiration date. The option spread difference can also be affected by market conditions, such as volatility and supply and demand.

The option spread difference can greatly affect options trading, as it can determine the profitability of a trade. A larger option spread difference can indicate a higher potential for profit, while a smaller option spread difference can indicate a lower potential for profit. Additionally, the option spread difference can also indicate the level of risk associated with a trade, as a larger option spread difference may indicate a higher level of risk.

The importance of understanding option spread differences in options trading cannot be overstated. Traders who are able to accurately predict option spread differences are more likely to make profitable trades, while traders who are not able to accurately predict option spread differences are more likely to make unprofitable trades. Additionally, understanding option spread differences can help traders to manage risk, as they can use this information to determine the level of risk associated with a trade.

There are several strategies that can be used to make trades using option spread differences. One such strategy is to purchase a call option and a put option on the same underlying stock, with different strike prices and expiration dates. This is known as a straddle strategy, and it can be used to take advantage of option spread differences. Another strategy is to purchase a call option and a put option on the same underlying stock, but with the same strike price and expiration date. This is known as a strangle strategy, and it can also be used to take advantage of option spread differences.

Example of a case study:

In this case study, we will look at how an options trader might use option spread differences to make a trade. Let's say that an options trader is interested in purchasing a call option on XYZ stock, with a strike price of $50 and an expiration date of one month. The current option spread difference for this call option is $1.50. The trader then decides to purchase a put option on XYZ stock, with a strike price of $45 and an expiration date of one month. The option spread difference for this put option is $2.00. The trader then uses a straddle strategy to take advantage of the option spread differences.

In this scenario, the trader is able to make a profit by purchasing both the call and put options. The trader will make a profit if the underlying stock price moves above or below the strike price of the options. Additionally, the trader is also able to manage risk by purchasing both options, as the option spread differences indicate a higher potential for profit and a lower potential for loss.

In conclusion, option spread differences are a crucial concept to understand in options trading. By understanding option spread differences, traders can make more informed decisions, manage risk, and potentially increase profits. It is important for traders to use strategies such as straddle and strangle to take advantage of option spread differences. With proper understanding and utilizing of option spread differences, traders can increase their chances of success in the options trading market.

Chapter 50: Defined Risk Spreads Explained

When it comes to options trading, there are many different strategies and techniques that traders can use to manage risk and make profitable trades. One such strategy is the use of defined risk spreads. In this chapter, we will take a closer look at what defined risk spreads are, how they affect options trading, why they are important, and how traders can use them to make profitable trades.

Definition of defined risk spreads

A defined risk spread is a type of options trading strategy in which the potential profit and loss are known in advance. This is in contrast to other types of options trades, such as long or short positions, where the potential profit or loss is not known in advance. Defined risk spreads can be used to trade a variety of different types of options, including call options, put options, and more.

How defined risk spreads affect options trading

Defined risk spreads are a popular strategy among options traders because they provide a level of predictability and control that is not present in other types of options trades. When using a defined risk spread, traders know in advance what their potential profit and loss will be, which allows them to make informed decisions about whether or not to enter into a trade. Additionally, defined risk spreads can be used to manage risk by limiting the potential loss on a trade.

Importance of using defined risk spreads in options trading

The importance of using defined risk spreads in options trading cannot be overstated. These spreads provide traders with a level of predictability and control that is not present in other types of options trades. Additionally, they can be used to manage risk by limiting the potential loss on a trade. This is particularly important for traders who are new to options trading or who are not comfortable with the level of risk associated with other types of options trades.

Strategies for using defined risk spreads to make trades

There are many different strategies for using defined risk spreads to make trades. One popular strategy is to use a defined risk spread to trade a call option. This involves purchasing a call option with a strike price that is below the current market price, while also selling a call option with a higher strike price. This can be a profitable trade if the underlying asset price rises, but the potential loss is limited if the price falls.

Another strategy is to use a defined risk spread to trade a put option. This involves purchasing a put option with a strike price that is above the current market price, while also selling a put option with a lower strike price. This can be a profitable trade if the underlying asset price falls, but the potential loss is limited if the price rises.

Example of a case study

To further illustrate the use of defined risk spreads in options trading, let's take a look at a case study involving a trader named John. John is an experienced options trader who is looking to make a trade on a stock that he believes will rise in price over the next few months. He decides to use a defined risk spread to make this trade.

John purchases a call option with a strike price of $50 and a expiration date of three months from now. He also sells a call option with a strike price of $55 and the same expiration date. By purchasing the $50 call option and selling the $55 call option, John has created a defined risk spread. If the stock price rises above $55, he will make a profit, but if the price falls below $50, his potential loss will be limited.

In this case, John's trade was a success. The stock price rose above $55, and he was able to make a profit. This is a great example of how defined risk spreads can be used to make a profit in options trading.

In conclusion, defined risk spreads are a powerful strategy that can be used to make trades in options trading. By understanding the definition of defined risk spreads, how they affect options trading, the importance of using them, and different strategies for using them, traders can increase their chances of success in the market. It is important to always do your own research and consider your own risk tolerance before making any trades, but with the right knowledge and strategy, defined risk spreads can be a valuable tool for traders of all levels.

Chapter 51: Trade Entry Checklist

When it comes to trading options, it's essential to have a set of guidelines to follow before entering a trade. A trade entry checklist is a tool that can help traders make better decisions by providing a set of criteria to evaluate before making a trade. In this chapter, we will discuss the definition of a trade entry checklist, how it affects options trading, the importance of using a trade entry checklist in options trading, and strategies for using a trade entry checklist to make trades.

Definition of a trade entry checklist

A trade entry checklist is a list of criteria that traders use to evaluate a trade before entering it. The criteria can include anything from technical analysis to market conditions and fundamental analysis. A trade entry checklist is like a pre-flight checklist for pilots. Pilots use a checklist to ensure that the plane is ready for takeoff, and traders use a checklist to ensure that the trade is ready to be entered.

How a trade entry checklist affects options trading

A trade entry checklist can affect options trading in several ways. First, it can help traders make better decisions by providing a set of criteria to evaluate before making a trade. Second, it can help traders avoid emotional trading by providing a set of rules to follow. Third, it can help traders avoid common mistakes by providing a set of guidelines to follow.

Importance of using a trade entry checklist in options trading

The importance of using a trade entry checklist in options trading cannot be overstated. A trade entry checklist can help traders make better decisions, avoid emotional trading, and avoid common mistakes. By using a trade entry checklist, traders can improve their chances of success and reduce their risk of loss.

Strategies for using a trade entry checklist to make trades

There are several strategies for using a trade entry checklist to make trades. One strategy is to use a checklist that is based on technical analysis. This strategy would include evaluating the stock's chart, looking for trends and patterns, and determining the stock's support and resistance levels.

Another strategy is to use a checklist that is based on fundamental analysis. This strategy would include evaluating the stock's financials, such as its earnings, revenue, and debt, and determining the stock's valuation.

A third strategy is to use a checklist that is based on market conditions. This strategy would include evaluating the stock's sector, the overall market conditions, and the stock's overall sentiment.

Example of a case study

In this case study, we will look at how a trader named John used a trade entry checklist to make a profitable trade. John was interested in purchasing options on a stock that was trading at $50 per share. He knew that the stock had a good chance of going up in the next few months, but he wanted to make sure that the trade was a good one.

John's trade entry checklist included the following criteria:

- The stock's chart showed a bullish trend
- The stock's valuation was attractive
- The stock's sector was performing well
- The overall market conditions were bullish

After evaluating the stock against his trade entry checklist, John determined that the trade was a good one. He purchased options on the stock at $50 per share. A few months later, the stock's price rose above $55 per share, and John was able to make a profit.

In conclusion, using a trade entry checklist is an essential tool for options traders. It can help traders make better decisions, avoid emotional trading, and avoid common mistakes. By using a trade entry checklist, traders can improve their chances of success and reduce their risk of loss. In the case of John, his trade entry checklist helped him make a profitable trade by reminding him to consider all relevant factors and stay disciplined in his approach. By following his checklist, he was able to make a well-informed decision and execute his trade with confidence. As a result, he was able to lock in a profit and avoid the mistakes that many novice traders often make.

In summary, a trade entry checklist is a valuable tool for options traders. It can help traders stay organized, focused, and disciplined in their approach. By using a trade entry checklist, traders can improve their chances of success and reduce their risk of loss. To create your own trade entry checklist, consider the following items:

- The underlying security and its current price
- The expiration date of the option
- The strike price of the option

- The option's implied volatility
- The option's delta, gamma, theta, and vega
- Your trade goal and exit strategy
- Your risk management plan

By including these items in your trade entry checklist, you can ensure that you are considering all relevant factors and making well-informed decisions. Additionally, by using a trade entry checklist, you can avoid emotional trading and stay focused on your trade goals. With a well-designed trade entry checklist, you can improve your chances of success and reduce your risk of loss.

It is important to note that a trade entry checklist is not a one-size-fits-all solution. Every trader is different and therefore, every trader's trade entry checklist should be tailored to their specific needs and trading style. It is important to regularly review and update your trade entry checklist to ensure that it is still relevant and effective. Additionally, it is important to practice using your trade entry checklist in a simulated trading environment before implementing it in live trades.

Another important aspect of using a trade entry checklist is discipline. It is easy to overlook certain items on the checklist when making quick decisions, but it is important to stick to the checklist and not make impulsive trades. By consistently using a trade entry checklist, traders can develop discipline and improve their decision-making skills over time.

In summary, using a trade entry checklist is a valuable tool for options traders. It can help traders make better decisions, avoid emotional trading, and avoid common mistakes. By using a well-designed trade entry checklist, traders can improve their chances of success and reduce their risk of loss. It is important to regularly review and update your trade entry checklist and to practice using it in a simulated trading environment before implementing it in live trades. By consistently using a trade entry checklist, traders can develop discipline and improve their decision-making skills over time.

Chapter 52: Trading Options In A Small Account

Trading options in a small account can be a challenging task for many traders, but it is not impossible. In this chapter, we will discuss the definition of trading options in a small account, how it affects options trading, the importance of trading options in a small account, and strategies for trading options in a small account.

Definition of trading options in a small account

Trading options in a small account refers to the practice of trading options using a limited amount of capital. This is typically considered to be an account with less than $25,000 in total assets. The limitations that come with a small account can make it difficult to execute many of the traditional options trading strategies, but it is still possible to trade options in a small account with the right approach.

How trading options in a small account affects options trading

Trading options in a small account can affect options trading in several ways. First, it limits the number of contracts that can be traded at any given time. This can limit the potential profit that can be made, but it also limits the potential loss. Additionally, trading options in a small account may require the use of more conservative strategies, such as selling options rather than buying them.

Importance of trading options in a small account in options trading

Trading options in a small account is important for several reasons. First, it allows traders to start trading options with a small amount of capital. This can be beneficial for traders who are just starting out and are not ready to invest a large amount of money in the market. Additionally, trading options in a small account can help traders develop a solid trading strategy and gain experience before moving on to larger accounts.

Strategies for trading options in a small account

There are several strategies that can be used when trading options in a small account. Some of the most popular strategies include:

1. Selling options rather than buying them: This can be a conservative strategy that can help limit the potential loss.
2. Using low-cost options: This can help traders get started with a small amount of capital.
3. Keeping a close eye on the stock price: This can help traders stay informed about market conditions and make better trading decisions.
4. Staying diversified: This can help traders avoid putting all of their eggs in one basket.

Example of a case study

To demonstrate how trading options in a small account can be done successfully, we will use a case study of John, a new options trader with a small account. John has a total of $10,000 in his account and wants to start trading options.

John starts by researching different options trading strategies and decides to sell options rather than buying them. He also chooses to focus on low-cost options to keep his risk low. John also keeps a close eye on the stock price and stays diversified by investing in several different stocks.

John's strategy proves to be successful, and he is able to make consistent profits with his small account. Over time, John's account grows, and he is able to increase his trading size and start using more advanced strategies.

In conclusion, trading options in a small account can be challenging, but it is not impossible. By using a conservative approach, keeping a close eye on the stock price, and staying diversified, traders can successfully trade options in a small account. Additionally, by starting with a small account, traders can develop a solid trading strategy and gain experience before moving on to larger accounts. As demonstrated in the case study of John, it is possible to start trading options with a small amount of capital and grow it over time.

Chapter 53: Credit Strategies For Earnings

Options trading can be a highly profitable endeavor, but it can also be risky if not executed correctly. One way to mitigate risk and increase potential profit is by using credit strategies for earnings. In this chapter, we will define credit strategies for earnings, explain how they affect options trading, discuss their importance, and provide strategies for using them effectively.

Definition of Credit Strategies for Earnings

Credit strategies for earnings refer to the practice of selling options contracts for a premium, with the goal of earning a profit from the premium collected. This can be done by selling call options or put options, or by using a combination of both. The key to credit strategies for earnings is to sell options that have a high likelihood of expiring worthless. This way, the trader can keep the premium collected and earn a profit.

How Credit Strategies for Earnings Affect Options Trading

Credit strategies for earnings can affect options trading in a few ways. First, they can reduce risk by limiting the amount of capital required to execute a trade. When a trader sells an option, they are not required to put up the full value of the underlying asset, only the premium collected. This means that a trader can execute a trade with a smaller account size, reducing the amount of risk involved.

Second, credit strategies for earnings can increase potential profit. Since the trader is collecting a premium, they can earn a profit even if the underlying asset does not move in their favor. Additionally, credit strategies for earnings can help traders generate income on a consistent basis, as long as they are able to sell options with a high likelihood of expiring worthless.

Importance of Using Credit Strategies for Earnings in Options Trading

Credit strategies for earnings are important for several reasons. First, they can reduce risk by limiting the amount of capital required to execute a trade. This is especially important for traders with small account sizes, as it allows them to participate in the options market without risking too much capital.

Second, credit strategies for earnings can increase potential profit. This is because traders are collecting a premium, and can earn a profit even if the underlying asset does not move in their favor. Additionally, credit strategies for earnings can help traders generate income on a consistent basis, as long as they are able to sell options with a high likelihood of expiring worthless.

Strategies for Using Credit Strategies for Earnings

There are several strategies for using credit strategies for earnings effectively. One strategy is to sell call options on stocks that have a high likelihood of staying below the strike price. This is known as a covered call strategy. Another strategy is to sell put options on stocks that have a high likelihood of staying above the strike price. This is known as a cash-secured put strategy.

Another strategy is to sell a combination of call and put options. This is known as a straddle strategy. This strategy involves selling both a call option and a put option with the same strike price and expiration date. This strategy can be profitable if the stock price moves significantly in either direction.

Case Study: John's Credit Strategy for Earnings

John is an options trader with a small account size. He wants to participate in the options market, but he doesn't want to risk too much capital. He decides to use a credit strategy for earnings by selling call options on a stock that he believes will stay below the strike price.

John sells call options on XYZ stock with a strike price of $50 and an expiration date of one month. He collects a premium of $2 per option. After one month, the stock price is still below $50, and the options expire worthless. John keeps the premium, earning a profit of $200.

This is an example of a credit strategy for earnings, also known as a short call option strategy.

A credit strategy for earnings is a popular strategy among options traders, as it allows traders to collect a premium from selling options without having to own the underlying asset. The idea is to sell options with a strike price that is out of the money, meaning that the stock price is below the strike price. This way, the options will expire worthless and the trader will keep the premium as profit.

One of the main benefits of using credit strategies for earnings is that it can generate income for traders, even in a flat or bearish market. Additionally, credit strategies for earnings can also be used to generate income while also holding a long position in the underlying asset. This strategy is known as a covered call option strategy and can be used to generate income while also limiting downside risk.

However, it is important to note that credit strategies for earnings are not without risk. If the stock price rises above the strike price, the trader will be obligated to sell the underlying asset at the strike price, potentially incurring a loss. Additionally, if the stock price rises dramatically, the trader will miss out on the potential gains.

To minimize risk and maximize profits, traders should use a variety of technical and fundamental analysis to determine the probability of the stock price rising above the strike price. Traders should also consider the volatility of the underlying asset and the expiration date of the options.

Another strategy for trading options in a small account is to use a defined risk spread strategy. This involves combining options with different strike prices and expiration dates to create a spread. By doing this, traders can limit their potential losses and increase their chances of making a profit.

For example, a trader could buy a call option with a strike price of $50 and sell a call option with a strike price of $55. This creates a call spread, which has a defined risk and a limited potential for profit. This strategy is particularly useful for traders with small accounts, as it allows them to make trades with a small amount of capital.

In conclusion, trading options in a small account can be challenging, but it is not impossible. By using credit strategies for earnings and defined risk spread strategies, traders can generate income and limit their potential losses. Additionally, by using technical and fundamental analysis, traders can make better-informed decisions and improve their chances of success.

Chapter 54: What Is A Covered Call & How Do I Trade It?

A covered call is a popular options trading strategy that involves selling call options on a stock that you already own. The purpose of this strategy is to generate additional income from the stock, while also limiting your downside risk. This chapter will explore the definition of a covered call, how it affects options trading, the importance of using a covered call in options trading, and strategies for trading a covered call.

- Definition of a covered call
- How a covered call affects options trading
- Importance of using a covered call in options trading

- Strategies for trading a covered call, including when to enter and exit the trade, and how to adjust the trade as needed

Definition of a Covered Call

A covered call is a strategy that involves selling call options on a stock that you already own. This is done with the goal of generating additional income from the stock, while also limiting your downside risk. When you sell a call option, you are agreeing to sell the underlying stock at a specified price (strike price) at a specified time (expiration date). In return, you receive a premium, which is the price of the option.

How a Covered Call Affects Options Trading

A covered call can affect options trading in a few ways. First, it can provide additional income for the trader, as the premium received from selling the call option can be used to offset any losses in the underlying stock. Additionally, a covered call can help to limit the trader's downside risk, as the trader is protected if the stock price falls below the strike price. Finally, a covered call can also limit the trader's potential gains, as the stock price will not be able to rise above the strike price without incurring a loss.

Importance of Using a Covered Call in Options Trading

A covered call is a popular strategy for options traders, as it can provide a number of benefits. First, it can provide additional income for the trader, as the premium received from selling the call option can be used to offset any losses in the underlying stock. Additionally, a covered call can help to limit the trader's downside risk, as the trader is protected if the stock price falls below the strike price. Finally, a covered call can also limit the trader's potential gains, as the stock price will not be able to rise above the strike price without incurring a loss.

Strategies for Trading a Covered Call

Trading a covered call can be a bit more complex than simply selling a call option on a stock that you own. There are a number of different strategies that can be used to maximize your chances of success. Here are a few strategies to consider:

When to Enter and Exit the Trade: The most important decision when trading a covered call is when to enter and exit the trade. There is no right or wrong time to enter or exit a trade, but there are a few general guidelines to follow. First, it is important to wait for the stock price to reach a level that you are comfortable with. Additionally, it is important to consider the expiration date of the option, as you will want to exit the trade before the option expires.

How to Adjust the Trade as Needed: Once you have entered the trade, it is important to monitor the stock price and adjust the trade as needed. This may involve adjusting the strike price of the option, or even selling the option early if the stock price starts to move against you. Additionally, it is important to consider the expiration date of the option, as you will want to exit the trade before the option expires.

Example of a Covered Call Case Study

Let's say John owns 100 shares of XYZ stock, which is currently trading at $50 per share. He believes that the stock price will not rise significantly in the next few months, but wants to earn some extra income from his stock holdings. He decides to sell call options on XYZ stock with a strike price of $55 and an expiration date of one month. He collects a premium of $2 per option, earning a total of $200.

In this scenario, John is using a covered call strategy. By selling call options on his stock, he is able to earn extra income without having to sell his stock. If the stock price does not rise above $55, the options will expire worthless, and John will keep the premium. However, if the stock price does rise above $55, the call options will be exercised, and John will have to sell his stock at $55 per share.

The key to a successful covered call strategy is to choose the right strike price and expiration date. John chose a strike price of $55, which is slightly above the current stock price, to maximize his premium while still retaining some upside potential. He also chose an expiration date of one month, which is short enough to minimize the risk of a significant price increase but long enough to earn a decent premium.

Another important aspect of a covered call strategy is to monitor the trade and adjust it as needed. John should regularly check the stock price and expiration date, and consider adjusting or closing the trade if the stock price approaches the strike price or the expiration date is nearing. He can also consider rolling the options to a later expiration date or a higher strike price to earn more premium or retain more upside potential.

Overall, a covered call strategy can be a great way to earn extra income from stock holdings without having to sell the stock. It can also serve as a risk management tool by limiting the upside potential while earning extra income. However, it requires careful selection of strike price, expiration date, and monitoring of the trade to be successful.

One example of a case study is when John was trading XYZ stock and believed that the stock price would not rise significantly in the next few months. He decided to sell call options on XYZ stock with a strike price of $55 and an expiration date of one month. He collected a premium of $2 per option, earning a total of $200. In this case, John was able to earn extra income without having to sell his stock, which was his goal. The key to a successful covered call strategy is to choose the right strike price and expiration date. John chose a strike price of $55, which is slightly above the current stock price, to maximize his premium while still retaining some upside potential. He also chose an expiration date of one month, which is short enough to minimize the risk of a significant price increase but long enough to earn a decent premium.

In conclusion, a covered call is a great options trading strategy for those who want to earn extra income while still retaining some upside potential in their stock position. It is important to choose the right strike price and expiration date in order to maximize the premium and minimize the risk. By using a covered call strategy, traders can earn extra income without having to sell their stock and can also reduce their risk of loss. By following the strategies outlined in this chapter, traders can improve their chances of success and increase their profits when trading options.

Chapter 55: How to Trade Covered Puts

A covered put is a strategy in options trading that involves selling a put option while also owning the underlying asset. This strategy is used when an investor believes that the price of the underlying asset will not decrease significantly in the near future. In this chapter, we will define covered puts, explain how they affect options trading, and explore the importance of using this strategy. We will also discuss strategies for trading covered puts, including when to enter and exit the trade and how to adjust the trade as needed.

Definition of a Covered Put

A covered put is a strategy in which an investor sells a put option while also owning the underlying asset. The underlying asset can be a stock, an ETF, or any other financial instrument. The put option gives the buyer the right, but not the obligation, to sell the underlying asset at a specified strike price on or before a specified expiration date. By selling a put option, the investor receives a premium, which is the price of the option. The investor is obligated to buy the underlying asset at the strike price if the option is exercised by the buyer.

How a Covered Put Affects Options Trading

A covered put is a neutral to bearish strategy in options trading. It is used when an investor believes that the price of the underlying asset will not decrease significantly in the near future. By selling a put option, the investor is able to earn extra income while also being protected against a decline in the price of the underlying asset. This strategy is also known as a synthetic short stock position because it mimics the returns of shorting a stock.

Importance of Using a Covered Put in Options Trading

The covered put strategy is important in options trading because it allows investors to earn extra income while also being protected against a decline in the price of the underlying asset. This strategy is especially useful for investors who are bullish on the market but want to earn extra income from their long positions. By selling a put option, the investor is able to earn extra income while also being protected against a decline in the price of the underlying asset.

Strategies for Trading Covered Puts

When trading covered puts, it is important to choose the right strike price and expiration date. The strike price should be slightly below the current market price to maximize the premium while also providing some downside protection. The expiration date should be short enough to minimize the risk of a significant price decrease but long enough to earn a decent premium.

When to Enter and Exit the Trade

When entering a covered put trade, it is important to wait for the right market conditions. The best time to enter a covered put trade is when the market is bullish and the price of the underlying asset is expected to remain stable or increase. When exiting a covered put trade, it is important to monitor the market conditions and the price of the underlying asset.

If the market is bullish and the price of the underlying asset is stable or increasing, it may be a good time to exit the trade and take profits.

How to Adjust the Trade

It is important to adjust a covered put trade as needed to ensure that it is profitable. This can be done by monitoring the market conditions and the price of the underlying asset. If the market conditions change and the price of the underlying asset is expected to decrease, it may be a good idea to adjust the trade by buying back the put option and selling the underlying asset.

Example of a Covered Put Case Study

To illustrate the covered put strategy, let's consider the case of John. John owns 100 shares of XYZ stock and believes that the stock price will not decrease significantly in the next few months. He decides to sell a put option on XYZ stock with a strike price of $50 and an expiration date of one month. He collects a premium of $1 per option, earning a total of $100. In this case, John was able to earn extra income while still retaining ownership of his stock, which was his goal. The key to a successful covered put strategy is to choose the right strike price and expiration date. John chose a strike price of $50, which is slightly below the current stock price, to maximize his premium while still retaining some downside protection. He also chose an expiration date of one month, which is short enough to minimize the risk of a significant price decrease but long enough to earn a decent premium.

As the expiration date approaches, John's covered put strategy plays out in one of two ways. If the stock price is above $50, the put option will expire worthless and John will keep the premium. If the stock price is below $50, the put option will be exercised and John will be obligated to sell his shares at $50. However, since he has already collected the premium, he will still have a net profit.

The covered put strategy is a useful tool for investors who want to earn extra income while retaining ownership of their stock. It is especially useful for investors who are bullish on a stock but want to earn extra income in case the stock price does not rise as expected. It is also a useful tool for investors who want to hedge their downside risk while still retaining ownership of their stock.

However, it is important to note that the covered put strategy is not without risk. If the stock price decreases significantly, the investor may be forced to sell their shares at a loss. Additionally, the covered put strategy does not protect against a decrease in the stock price if the stock is sold at a loss. Therefore, it is important to choose the right strike price and expiration date to minimize risk.

In conclusion, the covered put strategy is a useful tool for options traders who want to earn extra income while retaining ownership of their stock. It is important to choose the right strike price and expiration date to minimize risk and maximize income. By using a covered put strategy, traders can improve their chances of success and reduce their risk of loss.

Chapter 56: Covered Put Trading Strategies

Covered put trading is a strategy that involves selling put options while also holding a short stock position. This strategy can be used to generate income, protect long stock positions, or take advantage of market fluctuations. In this chapter, we will discuss various strategies for trading covered puts, including buying puts to protect long stock positions, and selling puts to generate income. We will also discuss how to choose the right strike price and expiration date for a covered put trade, and strategies for adjusting and managing a covered put trade.

Definition of a Covered Put

A covered put is a trading strategy in which an investor sells a put option while also holding a short stock position. The investor is essentially betting that the stock price will not decrease significantly, and if it does, they will be able to buy the stock at a lower price. This strategy can be used to generate income, protect long stock positions, or take advantage of market fluctuations.

How a Covered Put Affects Options Trading

Covered put trading can affect options trading in several ways. First, it can generate income for the investor by selling put options. Second, it can protect long stock positions by allowing the investor to buy the stock at a lower price if the stock price decreases. Third, it can take advantage of market fluctuations by allowing the investor to buy the stock at a lower price if the stock price decreases and then sell it at a higher price if the stock price increases.

Importance of Using a Covered Put in Options Trading

Covered put trading is an important strategy in options trading because it allows investors to generate income, protect long stock positions, and take advantage of market fluctuations. It can also be used as a hedge against a bear market or to lock in profits in a bull market.

Strategies for Trading Covered Puts

1. Buying Puts to Protect Long Stock Positions

One strategy for trading covered puts is to buy put options to protect long stock positions. This strategy involves buying a put option with a strike price that is below the current stock price and an expiration date that is longer than the time horizon for the stock position. This allows the investor to buy the stock at a lower price if the stock price decreases.

2. Selling Puts to Generate Income

Another strategy for trading covered puts is to sell put options to generate income. This strategy involves selling a put option with a strike price that is below the current stock price and an expiration date that is longer than the time horizon for the stock position. This allows the investor to earn a premium from the sale of the put option.

How to Choose the Right Strike Price and Expiration Date for a Covered Put Trade

Choosing the right strike price and expiration date for a covered put trade is crucial to the success of the trade. The strike price should be below the current stock price to allow for the potential to buy the stock at a lower price. The expiration date should be longer than the time horizon for the stock position to allow for the potential to buy the stock at a lower price.

Strategies for Adjusting and Managing a Covered Put Trade

1. Adjusting the Trade

One strategy for adjusting a covered put trade is to adjust the strike price and expiration date of the put option. This can be done if the stock price decreases and the investor wants to protect their position further, or if the stock price increases and the investor wants to take advantage of the higher premium. For example, John may decide to adjust his covered put trade by selling a put option with a strike price of $45 and an expiration date of three months, instead of his original strike price of $50 and one month expiration date. This will provide John with a higher premium, but also increases his risk of having to buy the stock at a lower price.

Managing the Trade

Another strategy for managing a covered put trade is to use stop loss orders. A stop loss order is a type of order that automatically closes a trade when the stock price reaches a certain level. This can be used to limit losses in the event that the stock price decreases significantly. For example, John may set a stop loss order at $45, which means that if the stock price drops to $45 or below, his trade will be automatically closed. This helps to manage risk and limit potential losses.

Another strategy for managing a covered put trade is to use profit targets. A profit target is a specific price level at which the investor will exit the trade, regardless of the stock price. For example, John may set a profit target at $55, which means that if the stock price reaches $55 or higher, he will exit the trade and take his profits. This helps to maximize potential gains and lock in profits.

Conclusion

Covered put trading strategies are an effective way to generate income and protect long stock positions. Choosing the right strike price and expiration date is crucial for success, and adjusting and managing the trade can help to limit risk and maximize profits. By carefully evaluating the stock price, market conditions, and personal risk tolerance, investors can make smart covered put trades that align with their investment goals.

Chapter 57: How to Trade Vertical Debit Spreads

A vertical debit spread, also known as a bull call spread or a bear put spread, is an options trading strategy that involves buying and selling options at different strike prices with the same expiration date. The goal of this strategy is to profit from a moderate increase or decrease in the underlying stock price. In this chapter, we will discuss the definition of a vertical debit spread, how it affects options trading, and the importance of using this strategy in options trading. We will also provide strategies for trading a vertical debit spread, including when to enter and exit the trade and how to adjust the trade as needed.

Definition of a Vertical Debit Spread

A vertical debit spread is an options trading strategy that involves buying and selling options at different strike prices with the same expiration date. The goal of this strategy is to profit from a moderate increase or decrease in the underlying stock price. In a bull call spread, an investor buys a call option at a lower strike price and sells a call option at a higher strike price. In a bear put spread, an investor buys a put option at a higher strike price and sells a put option at a lower strike price. The difference between the strike prices is known as the spread.

How a Vertical Debit Spread Affects Options Trading

A vertical debit spread can be used to limit the potential loss and increase the potential profit in options trading. The potential loss is limited to the cost of the spread, also known as the debit. The potential profit is limited to the difference between the strike prices less the debit. This strategy is considered a limited risk, limited reward strategy.

Importance of Using a Vertical Debit Spread in Options Trading

A vertical debit spread is a useful strategy for options traders who want to limit their risk while still having the potential for profit. This strategy can also be used to speculate on the direction of the underlying stock price without having to make a large investment. Additionally, a vertical debit spread can be used to generate income through the sale of the option at a higher strike price.

Strategies for Trading a Vertical Debit Spread

1. Choosing the Right Strike Prices

The key to a successful vertical debit spread is choosing the right strike prices. The strike prices should be close enough together to limit the potential loss, but far enough apart to maximize the potential profit. For example, in a bull call spread, the lower strike price should be below the current stock price, and the higher strike price should be above the current stock price.

2. Timing the Trade

Timing is also important when trading a vertical debit spread. The best time to enter a trade is when the underlying stock price is at or near the lower strike price for a bull call spread or the higher strike price for a bear put spread. This allows for the maximum potential profit.

3. Adjusting the Trade

If the underlying stock price moves in the opposite direction of the trade, it may be necessary to adjust the trade. One strategy is to close the trade and take the loss, or to adjust the strike prices to limit the potential loss. Another strategy is to hold the trade and wait for the underlying stock price to move in the desired direction.

Example of a Vertical Debit Spread Case Study

Let's say John is bullish on XYZ stock and believes the stock price will increase moderately in the next few months. He decides to enter a bull call spread by buying a call option at a strike price of $50 and selling a call option at a strike price of $55. The cost of the spread, or debit, is $3. After one month, the stock price increases to $53, and John closes out the trade by selling the call option he bought at $50 for $3 and buying back the call option he sold at $55 for $1. This results in a net profit of $2 for John, and he is able to profit from the moderate increase in the stock price without having to invest in the stock itself.

This example demonstrates the power of a vertical debit spread in allowing an investor to profit from a moderate increase in the stock price while limiting the potential loss. The key to a successful vertical debit spread strategy is to choose the right strike prices and expiration date, as well as to monitor the trade and adjust as needed.

In conclusion, vertical debit spreads are an important tool for options traders looking to profit from moderate price movements in the stock market. By buying and selling options at different strike prices, traders can limit their potential loss while still profiting from moderate price increases. With proper research, planning, and monitoring, traders can use vertical debit spreads to achieve their investment goals and maximize their returns.

Chapter 58: Comparing Bullish Option Strategies

Bullish option strategies are used by investors who believe that the stock price will increase in the near future. These strategies are used to profit from a potential price increase while minimizing risk. In this chapter, we will compare various bullish option strategies, including covered calls, vertical debit spreads, and call spreads. We will also discuss the pros and cons of each strategy, and when to use each one. Lastly, we will cover strategies for adjusting and managing bullish option trades.

1. Comparison of various bullish option strategies

Covered calls, vertical debit spreads, and call spreads are all bullish option strategies that can be used to profit from a potential price increase.

Covered calls involve selling call options on a stock that an investor already owns. This strategy generates income from the premium received from the sale of the call options, while also limiting the potential loss from a decrease in stock price.

Vertical debit spreads, also known as bull call spreads, involve buying a call option at a lower strike price and selling a call option at a higher strike price. The difference between the two strike prices is the debit, or cost, of the spread. This strategy profits from a moderate increase in stock price, but also has a limited profit potential.

Call spreads, also known as long call options, involve buying a call option at a specific strike price. This strategy profits from a significant increase in stock price, but also has the potential for unlimited loss.

    2. Pros and cons of each strategy, and when to use each one

Covered calls are a low-risk strategy that is suitable for investors who believe that the stock price will not increase significantly in the near future. This strategy generates income from the premium received from the sale of the call options, but also limits the potential for profit from a price increase.

Vertical debit spreads are a moderate-risk strategy that is suitable for investors who believe that the stock price will increase moderately in the near future. This strategy profits from a moderate price increase, but also has a limited profit potential.

Call spreads are a high-risk strategy that is suitable for investors who believe that the stock price will increase significantly in the near future. This strategy profits from a significant price increase, but also has the potential for unlimited loss.

3. Strategies for adjusting and managing bullish option trades

Adjusting a bullish option trade involves changing the strike price and expiration date of the option. This can be done if the stock price decreases and the investor wants to limit the potential loss, or if the stock price increases and the investor wants to lock in a profit.

Managing a bullish option trade involves monitoring the stock price and adjusting the trade as needed. This can be done by closing the trade if the stock price decreases and the investor wants to limit the potential loss, or by rolling the trade if the stock price increases and the investor wants to lock in a profit.

Example of a Bullish Option Strategies Case Study

John is bullish on XYZ stock and believes the stock price will increase moderately in the next few months. He decides to enter a bull call spread by buying a call option at a strike price of $50 and selling a call option at a strike price of $55. The cost of the spread, or debit, is $3. After one month, the stock price increases to $53, and John closes his position by buying the call option at a strike price of $55 and selling the call option at a strike price of $50. He earns a profit of $2 per share, or a total of $200. In this case, John was able to profit from a moderate price increase while also limiting his risk through the use of a call spread.

Another strategy that John could have used in this scenario is a covered call. In this strategy, John would have sold a call option on his XYZ stock with a strike price of $55 and collected a premium of $2 per option. In this case, John would have earned extra income without having to sell his stock, which was his goal. However, the downside of this strategy is that if the stock price increases above the strike price, John would have missed out on potential profits.

John could also have used a vertical debit spread, where he would have bought a call option at a strike price of $50 and sold a call option at a strike price of $55. The cost of the spread, or debit, would have been $3. In this case, John would have limited his risk but also limited his potential profits.

In comparing these three bullish option strategies, it is clear that each one has its own set of pros and cons. The covered call strategy is best for generating income without having to sell the underlying stock, while the bull call spread and vertical debit spread are best for profiting from moderate price increases while limiting risk. The choice of which strategy to use will depend on the investor's goals, risk tolerance, and the expected price movement of the underlying stock.

Managing the Trade

Once a bullish option trade is entered, it is important to manage the trade as needed. This can include adjusting the strike price and expiration date, as well as monitoring the stock price and adjusting the trade accordingly. For example, if the stock price begins to decrease, the investor may want to consider closing the trade to limit losses. On the other hand, if the stock price continues to increase, the investor may want to consider holding the trade for even more profits.

Another strategy for managing a bullish option trade is to use a stop-loss order. A stop-loss order is a type of order that automatically closes the trade if the stock price reaches a certain level. This can help the investor limit losses in case the stock price moves in the opposite direction of their trade.

It is also important to consider the expiration date of the option when managing a trade. If the expiration date is approaching and the stock price has not reached the desired level, the investor may want to consider closing the trade to prevent any potential losses.

In conclusion, bullish option strategies can be a useful tool for investors looking to profit from moderate price increases while limiting risk. Whether it be a covered call, bull call spread, or vertical debit spread, each strategy has its own set of pros and cons and should be chosen based on the investor's goals, risk tolerance, and the expected price movement of the underlying stock. It is also important to manage the trade as needed and consider factors such as the expiration date and stock price when making decisions. With proper research, analysis, and management, bullish option strategies can be a valuable addition to an investor's portfolio.

Chapter 59: Bullish Strategy Adjustments: PMCC: Poor Man's Covered Call

A poor man's covered call (PMCC) is a bullish options trading strategy that allows investors to generate income from their long stock positions without selling the underlying asset. This strategy is also known as a "buy-write" strategy, and it involves purchasing a stock and simultaneously selling a call option with a strike price above the current stock price. The goal of the PMCC is to generate income from the call option while also limiting the potential losses from the long stock position.

Definition of a Poor Man's Covered Call (PMCC)

A PMCC is a bullish options trading strategy that involves purchasing a stock and simultaneously selling a call option with a strike price above the current stock price. The goal of the PMCC is to generate income from the call option while also limiting the potential losses from the long stock position.

How a PMCC Affects Options Trading

A PMCC allows investors to generate income from their long stock positions without selling the underlying asset. This strategy can also help investors limit their potential losses from the long stock position.

Importance of Using a PMCC in Options Trading

A PMCC can be an effective strategy for generating income from long stock positions, especially for investors who are bullish on the stock but do not want to sell the underlying asset. Additionally, a PMCC can help investors limit their potential losses from the long stock position.

Strategies for Trading a PMCC

When entering a PMCC, it is important to choose a strike price that is above the current stock price and to choose an expiration date that is far enough in the future to allow for potential price movements.

Exiting the Trade

When exiting a PMCC, investors can either close the call option by buying it back or they can allow the option to expire worthless. If the stock price increases and the option is in the money, it may be beneficial to close the call option to avoid having the stock called away.

Adjusting the Trade

If the stock price decreases and the option is out of the money, investors may choose to adjust the strike price of the call option to a lower price to generate more income. Additionally, if the stock price increases and the option is in the money, investors may choose to adjust the strike price of the call option to a higher price to limit potential losses.

Example of a Poor Man's Covered Call Case Study

To illustrate the PMCC strategy, let's consider the case of John. John owns 100 shares of XYZ stock and believes that the stock price will not decrease significantly in the next few months. He decides to sell a call option with a strike price of $50 and an expiration date of one month. The cost of the call option is $2, which John receives as income. After one month, the stock price is at $52 and the call option expires worthless. John is able to earn $200 in income from the call option while also holding onto his long stock position.

In conclusion, the PMCC strategy can be a useful tool for investors looking to generate income from their long stock positions while also limiting potential losses. It is important to choose the right strike price and expiration date, as well as to monitor and adjust the trade as needed. As always, it is important to consult a financial advisor before entering into any options trading strategy.

Chapter 60: Buy Debit Spreads For Less Than Intrinsic Value

When it comes to options trading, many investors focus on buying options with intrinsic value. However, there is another strategy that can be just as effective: buying debit spreads for less than intrinsic value. In this chapter, we will explore the concept of buying debit spreads for less than intrinsic value, how it affects options trading, and the strategies for utilizing this technique in your trading.

Definition of Buying Debit Spreads for Less than Intrinsic Value

When buying debit spreads for less than intrinsic value, the investor is essentially buying an option at a price that is lower than its intrinsic value. Intrinsic value is the amount by which an option is in-the-money, or the amount by which the strike price of an option is less than the current market price of the underlying asset. In other words, intrinsic value is the value that an option would have if it were exercised immediately.

For example, if a stock is currently trading at $50 and an option has a strike price of $45, the intrinsic value of that option is $5. When buying a debit spread for less than intrinsic value, the investor is essentially buying the option at a price that is lower than its intrinsic value. This can be a good strategy for investors who believe that the stock price will increase in the future, as they can buy the option at a lower price and sell it later at a higher price.

How Buying Debit Spreads for Less than Intrinsic Value Affects Options Trading

Buying debit spreads for less than intrinsic value can be a good strategy for investors who believe that the stock price will increase in the future. This is because the investor is able to buy the option at a lower price, which means that they have a higher potential for profit. Additionally, buying debit spreads for less than intrinsic value can help to reduce the risk of loss, as the investor is buying the option at a lower price.

Importance of Buying Debit Spreads for Less than Intrinsic Value in Options Trading

Buying debit spreads for less than intrinsic value is an important strategy for options trading because it can help investors to reduce the risk of loss and increase the potential for profit. Additionally, buying debit spreads for less than intrinsic value can help investors to take advantage of market conditions that are favorable for options trading. For example, if the stock price is expected to increase in the future, buying debit spreads for less than intrinsic value can be a good strategy for investors who want to take advantage of this market condition.

Strategies for Buying Debit Spreads for Less than Intrinsic Value

When buying debit spreads for less than intrinsic value, it is important to choose the right strike price and expiration date for the option. This can be done by analyzing the current market conditions and the expected future market conditions. Additionally, it is important to choose the right option type for the trade. For example, if the investor believes that the stock price will increase moderately in the future, a call option may be a better choice than a put option.

Another important strategy for buying debit spreads for less than intrinsic value is to adjust the trade as needed. This can be done by adjusting the strike price and expiration date of the option, or by adjusting the number of options that are being bought or sold. Additionally, it is important to monitor the stock price and the option price, and to exit the trade if the stock price or the option price moves in the opposite direction of the expected direction.

Example of a Buying Debit Spreads for Less than Intrinsic Value Case Study

Let's consider a scenario where John is bullish on XYZ stock but wants to limit his risk. He decides to enter a bull call spread by buying a call option at a strike price of $50 and selling a call option at a strike price of $55. The cost of the spread, or debit, is $3. However, instead of paying the full $3 debit, John is able to negotiate with the seller and purchase the spread for $2.50. This is because the intrinsic value of the call option at a strike price of $50 is currently $2.50 and John is able to take advantage of this by buying the spread for less than intrinsic value.

After one month, the stock price increases to $53 and John closes his position by buying the call option at a strike price of $55 and selling the call option at a strike price of $50. He earns a profit of $2.50 per share, or a total of $250, which is more than the profit he would have made if he had paid the full $3 debit.

This case study shows the importance of buying debit spreads for less than intrinsic value in options trading. By paying less than the intrinsic value of the call option, John was able to increase his potential profit while still limiting his risk. Additionally, this strategy can be used in any market condition, whether it is bullish or bearish, as long as the intrinsic value of the option is known.

Furthermore, by using a strategy of buying debit spreads for less than intrinsic value, traders can reduce their risk by paying less than the intrinsic value of the option. Additionally, this strategy can be used in any market condition, whether it is bullish or bearish, as long as the intrinsic value of the option is known. This means that traders do not need to be certain about the direction of the market, but they can still make profits by using this strategy.

In conclusion, buying debit spreads for less than intrinsic value is a valuable strategy for options traders to consider. By paying less than the intrinsic value of the option, traders can increase their potential profit while still limiting their risk. It is important to understand the intrinsic value of the option and use this knowledge to negotiate a lower debit and take advantage of market conditions. Traders should also be aware of how to adjust and manage their trades as needed in order to maximize their profits.

Chapter 61: Why & How to Finance Spreads in Options Trading

Options trading is a complex and dynamic field, requiring investors to have a deep understanding of the markets, the underlying assets, and the various strategies available. One key aspect of options trading that is often overlooked is the concept of financing spreads. This chapter will provide a detailed overview of what financing spreads are, how they affect options trading, and why they are important. Additionally, we will explore various strategies for financing spreads, including using margin and credit spreads.

Definition of financing spreads in options trading

Financing spreads are a type of trade in which an investor borrows money from a broker to purchase options. This allows the investor to increase the amount of capital they have available to trade with, which can lead to greater potential profits. However, it also increases the risk of the trade, as the investor is now borrowing money, which must be repaid with interest.

How financing spreads affects options trading

Financing spreads can have a significant impact on options trading. By increasing the amount of capital available to trade with, investors can take on larger positions, which can increase the potential for profits. However, this also increases the risk of the trade, as the borrowed money must be repaid with interest. Additionally, financing spreads can also affect the overall volatility of the market, as investors are able to take on larger positions, which can lead to increased volatility.

Importance of financing spreads in options trading

Financing spreads are an important aspect of options trading for several reasons. First, they allow investors to increase the amount of capital they have available to trade with, which can lead to greater potential profits. Second, financing spreads can also help investors to manage their risk, as the borrowed money must be repaid with interest. Finally, financing spreads can also be used to take advantage of market trends and opportunities, as investors can enter into larger positions, which can increase the potential for profits.

Strategies for financing spreads in options trading

There are several strategies for financing spreads in options trading, including using margin and credit spreads.

Using Margin:

Margin is a type of financing that allows investors to borrow money from a broker to purchase options. This can be an effective strategy for financing spreads, as it allows investors to increase the amount of capital they have available to trade with, which can lead to greater potential profits. However, it also increases the risk of the trade, as the investor is now borrowing money, which must be repaid with interest.

Credit Spreads:

Credit spreads are another strategy for financing spreads in options trading. These are trades in which an investor sells one option and buys another option with a different strike price. This strategy allows investors to take advantage of market trends and opportunities, as well as to manage their risk.

Example of a Financing Spreads Case Study

Let's consider a trader named Sarah. Sarah is bullish on the stock of XYZ Company and believes that the stock price will increase in the next few months. She decides to enter a bull call spread by buying a call option at a strike price of $50 and selling a call option at a strike price of $55. The cost of the spread, or debit, is $3. However, Sarah only has $1,000 in her account and she wants to take a larger position. She decides to use margin to finance her spread. Sarah borrows $2,000 from her broker and now has $3,000 in her account. She enters the bull call spread and after one month, the stock price increases to $53. Sarah closes her position and earns a profit of $2 per share, or a total of $200. In this case, Sarah was able to use margin to finance her spread and take a larger position, which ultimately led to a profitable trade.

Financing spreads in options trading is a popular strategy among traders as it allows them to take larger positions with less capital. This can be especially beneficial for traders who have a smaller account size and want to take advantage of potential price movements in the market. However, it's important to note that financing spreads also come with added risk, as traders are borrowing money from their broker and are responsible for any losses that may occur.

When financing spreads, traders have the option to use margin or credit spreads. Margin is a type of loan that traders can use to finance their trades, and it's typically offered by brokerage firms. Credit spreads, on the other hand, are a type of spread where the trader sells an option and buys another option at a different strike price. The premium received from selling the option can be used to offset the cost of buying the other option, which reduces the amount of capital needed to enter the trade.

In order to use financing spreads effectively, it's important for traders to have a solid understanding of the underlying asset and the potential price movements. They should also have a clear exit strategy in place in case the trade does not go as planned. It's also important for traders to manage their risk by setting stop-loss orders and using proper position sizing techniques.

In conclusion, financing spreads in options trading can be a useful strategy for traders who want to take larger positions with less capital. However, it's important to understand the added risk that comes with borrowing money and to have a clear strategy in place. By understanding the basics of financing spreads and managing risk, traders can potentially increase their chances of success in the options market.

Chapter 62: How to Trade a Poor Man's Covered Call

A poor man's covered call (PMCC) is a popular options trading strategy that allows traders to benefit from a stock's upward movement while also limiting potential losses. This strategy involves buying a long stock position and selling a call option at the same time. In this chapter, we will discuss the definition, importance, and strategies for trading a PMCC, and provide a case study to illustrate how this strategy can be used in practice.

Definition of a Poor Man's Covered Call (PMCC)

A PMCC is a strategy that combines the benefits of owning a stock and selling a call option. In this strategy, a trader buys a long stock position and simultaneously sells a call option on that same stock. By selling the call option, the trader is able to earn income from the option premium, but also limits their potential losses if the stock price falls.

How a PMCC Affects Options Trading

A PMCC allows traders to benefit from a stock's upward movement while also limiting potential losses. If the stock price increases, the trader can sell their call option for a profit and still hold the long stock position. However, if the stock price falls, the trader will still have the long stock position, which can offset some of the losses from the call option.

Importance of Using a PMCC in Options Trading

A PMCC is a popular strategy for traders who are bullish on a stock but also want to limit their potential losses. This strategy allows traders to earn income from the option premium while also limiting potential losses if the stock price falls. Additionally, a PMCC can be a useful strategy for traders who have a long-term investment horizon and are looking to generate income from their stock positions.

Strategies for Trading a PMCC, Including When to Enter and Exit the Trade, and How to Adjust the Trade as Needed

When trading a PMCC, it is important to select a strike price that is at or above the current stock price. This will ensure that the option has a positive intrinsic value and can be sold for a profit. Additionally, traders should consider the expiration date of the option and choose one that is appropriate for their investment horizon.

When entering a PMCC trade, it is important to set a stop-loss order to protect against potential losses if the stock price falls. Traders should also consider adjusting their position if the stock price moves in their favor, by buying back the call option and selling the stock. This can lock in profits while still holding the long stock position.

Example of a Poor Man's Covered Call Case Study

Let's consider a trader named James. James is bullish on the stock of ABC Company and believes that the stock price will increase in the next few months. He decides to enter a PMCC by buying 100 shares of ABC stock at $50 per share and simultaneously selling a call option at a strike price of $55. The option premium is $2. After one month, the stock price increases to $53 and James closes his position by buying back the call option at $3 and selling the stock at $53. He earns a profit of $200 from the stock and $200 from the call option for a total profit of $400. In this case, James was able to benefit from the stock's increase in price while also earning additional income from the call option, all while limiting his risk through the use of the PMCC strategy.

It is important to note that when trading a PMCC, the trader must be willing to sell their shares if the stock price reaches the strike price of the call option. This is because the call option holder has the right to purchase the shares at the strike price, and the trader must be prepared to fulfill that obligation. However, this also means that the trader has limited their risk to the strike price of the call option, as they cannot lose more than the difference between the strike price and the stock price at the time of the trade.

Another strategy for trading a PMCC is to adjust the trade as needed. For example, if the stock price increases significantly, the trader may choose to close their position and take profits. On the other hand, if the stock price does not increase as expected, the trader may choose to hold onto the position and wait for the stock price to increase, or they may choose to exit the trade at a loss. Additionally, the trader may choose to roll the call option to a later expiration date, or even to a higher strike price, in order to continue earning income while also potentially limiting their risk.

Overall, the poor man's covered call (PMCC) is a valuable strategy for options traders looking to benefit from a bullish stock market while also earning additional income and limiting their risk. By understanding the definition, effects, importance, and strategies for trading a PMCC, traders can make informed decisions and potentially increase their profits. So, it is a recommended strategy for new traders who are looking for a low-risk way to enter the options trading market.

Chapter 63: What is a Covered Put & How to Trade it?

In options trading, a covered put is a strategy in which a trader sells a put option while simultaneously holding a short position in the underlying asset. This strategy is also known as a "short put" or "naked put." The purpose of a covered put is to generate income through the sale of the put option while also having the protection of the short position in case the stock price decreases.

Definition of a Covered Put

A covered put is a strategy in which a trader sells a put option while also shorting the underlying stock. The trader receives the premium from the sale of the put option and also has the protection of the short position in case the stock price decreases. This strategy is also known as a "short put" or "naked put."

How a Covered Put Affects Options Trading

A covered put is a bearish strategy that is used when a trader believes that the stock price will decrease. The trader receives income from the sale of the put option, but also has the protection of the short position in case the stock price decreases. This allows the trader to potentially make a profit even if the stock price does decrease.

Importance of Using a Covered Put in Options Trading

A covered put is a useful strategy for traders who are bearish on a stock but want to generate income while also having protection in case the stock price decreases. It is also a useful strategy for traders who want to generate income without having to sell the stock outright.

Strategies for Trading a Covered Put

When trading a covered put, it is important to choose the right strike price and expiration date for the put option. The strike price should be below the current stock price and the expiration date should be far enough in the future to allow for the stock price to decrease.

It is also important to consider the volatility of the stock when trading a covered put. A stock with high volatility will have a higher premium for the put option, which can generate more income for the trader.

When entering a covered put trade, it is important to consider the risk and reward potential. The maximum reward is the premium received from the sale of the put option, while the maximum risk is the difference between the strike price and the current stock price.

To adjust the trade, a trader can hold the position until the put option expires or close the position by buying back the put option. They can also adjust the strike price or expiration date of the put option to suit their needs.

Example of a Covered Put Case Study

Let's consider a trader named Michael. Michael is bearish on the stock of DEF Company and believes that the stock price will decrease in the next few months. He decides to enter a covered put by writing a put option at a strike price of $40 and simultaneously owning 100 shares of

DEF stock at $45 per share. The option premium is $2. After one month, the stock price decreases to $42 and Michael's put option is exercised. He is obligated to sell the stock at $40 and earns a profit of $200 from the option premium, offsetting the $300 loss from the stock. In this case, Michael was able to benefit from the stock's decrease in price while also earning a profit from the option premium.

In conclusion, a covered put is a powerful strategy for traders who are bearish on a stock and want to generate income while also having protection against potential losses. By understanding the mechanics of the trade and using proper risk management, traders can use a covered put to profit in a bearish market. As with any trading strategy, it is important to thoroughly research and understand the underlying stock and the market conditions before entering a covered put position.

Chapter 64: Short Put Adjustments Explained

Options trading can be a complex and dynamic process, with many different strategies and techniques that traders can use to manage risk and generate profits. One important concept that is often used in options trading is the short put adjustment, which is a way of adjusting a short put position to manage risk and maximize potential profits. In this chapter, we will explore the definition of short put adjustments, how they affect options trading, why they are important, and strategies for using short put adjustments to make trades.

Definition of Short Put Adjustments

A short put adjustment is a technique that is used to manage risk in a short put position. This can involve adjusting the strike price, expiration date, or other parameters of the trade in order to reduce risk or increase potential profits. For example, a trader might adjust the strike price of a short put option in order to move it further away from the current stock price, reducing the risk of the trade. Alternatively, a trader might adjust the expiration date of a short put option in order to reduce the amount of time that the trade is open, reducing the risk of the trade.

How Short Put Adjustments Affect Options Trading

Short put adjustments can have a significant impact on options trading, as they allow traders to manage risk and maximize potential profits. By adjusting the strike price, expiration date, or other parameters of a trade, traders can reduce the risk of the trade and increase the potential for profit. Additionally, short put adjustments can be used to adjust a trade that is not working as well as expected, allowing traders to exit a trade with minimal loss or even make a profit.

Importance of Using Short Put Adjustments in Options Trading

Short put adjustments are an important part of options trading, as they allow traders to manage risk and maximize potential profits. By adjusting the strike price, expiration date, or other parameters of a trade, traders can reduce the risk of the trade and increase the potential for profit. Additionally, short put adjustments can be used to adjust a trade that is not working as well as expected, allowing traders to exit a trade with minimal loss or even make a profit.

Strategies for Using Short Put Adjustments to Make Trades

There are several strategies that traders can use when making short put adjustments to manage risk and maximize potential profits. These strategies include:

- Adjusting the strike price: This strategy involves adjusting the strike price of a short put option to move it further away from the current stock price. By doing this, traders can reduce the risk of the trade and increase the potential for profit.
- Adjusting the expiration date: This strategy involves adjusting the expiration date of a short put option to reduce the amount of time that the trade is open. By doing this, traders can reduce the risk of

the trade and increase the potential for profit.
- Managing risk: This strategy involves managing risk by adjusting the strike price, expiration date, or other parameters of a trade. This can include adjusting the position size, using stop-loss orders, or hedging the trade with other options or financial instruments.

Example of a Short Put Adjustments Case Study

Let's consider a trader named Michael. Michael has a short put position on the stock of XYZ Company with a strike price of $50 and an expiration date of one month. However, the stock price of XYZ Company has increased to $55 and Michael is concerned that his trade may result in a loss. He decides to make a short put adjustment by adjusting the strike price to $55 and the expiration date to two months. By doing this, Michael reduces the risk of the trade and increases the potential for profit. After two months, the stock price of XYZ Company is at

$57 and Michael closes his position by buying back the put option at $2 and earning a profit of $3 per share, or a total of $300. In this case, Michael was able to adjust his short put position to manage his risk and increase his potential for profit.

Short put adjustments are a crucial aspect of options trading and can help traders to manage their risk and increase their potential for profit. By adjusting the strike price and expiration date, traders can reduce the risk of a trade and increase the potential for profit. It is important for traders to closely monitor their short put positions and make adjustments as needed in order to maximize their potential for profit and minimize their risk.

In conclusion, short put adjustments are a valuable tool for options traders. By understanding how to use them and when to make adjustments, traders can improve their chances of success and maximize their profits in the options market. With the right strategies and a strong understanding of short put adjustments, traders can increase their chances of success and achieve their financial goals.

Chapter 65: How to Trade a Short Naked Call

Options trading is a complex and dynamic field that offers a wide range of strategies and techniques for traders to use. One such strategy is a short naked call, also known as a short call. This strategy is a bearish approach that allows traders to profit from a decrease in stock price, but it also carries a high degree of risk. In this chapter, we will explore the definition of a short naked call, how it affects options trading, the importance of using a short naked call in options trading, and strategies for trading a short naked call. We will also include a case study to illustrate the use of this strategy in real-world trading.

Definition of a Short Naked Call

A short naked call is a bearish options trading strategy that involves selling a call option without owning the underlying stock. This is in contrast to a covered call, where the trader owns the underlying stock and sells a call option on it.

The goal of a short naked call is to profit from a decrease in the stock price by selling a call option at a higher strike price and then buying it back at a lower price.

The risk of a short naked call is that the stock price increases and the trader is forced to buy the stock at a higher price than they sold the call option for. This is known as a short call risk, and it can result in significant losses for the trader.

How a Short Naked Call Affects Options Trading

A short naked call can have a significant impact on options trading. It is a bearish strategy that allows traders to profit from a decrease in stock price. However, it also carries a high degree of risk, as the stock price could increase and result in significant losses for the trader.

The use of a short naked call can also affect the options market as a whole. As more traders enter into short naked call positions, it can increase the demand for call options and lead to higher prices. This can also result in increased volatility in the options market.

Importance of Using a Short Naked Call in Options Trading

Despite the high degree of risk associated with a short naked call, it can still be an important strategy for options traders to use. A short naked call can be a useful tool for traders who are bearish on a stock and want to profit from a decrease in its price.

Additionally, a short naked call can be used as a hedge against a long stock position. If a trader owns a stock and is concerned about a potential decrease in its price, they can enter into a short naked call to offset some of the potential losses from the long stock position.

Strategies for Trading a Short Naked Call

Trading a short naked call can be a challenging and risky endeavor, but there are several strategies that traders can use to mitigate the risk and increase the potential for profit.

One strategy is to choose the right strike price and expiration date for the call option. This involves analyzing the stock's historical price movements and considering the volatility of the stock. By choosing a strike price and expiration date that is in line with the stock's price movements and volatility, traders can increase the chances of success.

Another strategy is to adjust the trade as needed. If the stock price begins to increase and the trader is facing a short call risk, they can make adjustments to the trade by buying back the call option at a higher price or rolling the option to a later expiration date.

It is also important to manage risk when trading a short naked call. Traders should only enter into this strategy with capital that they can afford to lose and should always have a plan in place for managing risk. This can include setting stop-loss orders and limiting the amount of capital allocated to the trade. Additionally, traders should be aware of the potential for unlimited loss and should always have a plan in place for managing this risk. In conclusion, a short naked call is a high-risk strategy that can be used to generate income in a bearish market. However, it is important to understand the risks associated with this strategy and to have a plan in place for managing risk. By following these strategies and managing risk, traders can potentially benefit from the potential for high returns while also protecting their capital.

Example of a Short Naked Call Case Study

Let's consider a trader named Sarah. Sarah believes that the stock of DEF Company will decrease in the next few months and decides to enter a short naked call by selling a call option at a strike price of $60. The option premium is $3. After one month, the stock price decreases to $55 and Sarah closes her position by buying back the call option at $1. She earns a profit of $200 from the option premium and has no loss from the stock. However, if the stock price had increased to $65, Sarah would have incurred a loss of $500. This highlights the high risk associated with a short naked call, and the importance of proper risk management when using this strategy.

In conclusion, a short naked call is a bearish strategy that can be used to generate income but also has a high risk associated with it. Traders should only enter into this strategy with capital that they can afford to lose and should always have a plan in place for managing risk. By following these strategies and conducting proper research, traders can potentially benefit from the short naked call strategy while also managing the risk associated with it.

Chapter 66: What is a Short Strangle & How do I Trade it?

A short strangle is a bearish options trading strategy that involves selling both a call option and a put option with different strike prices, but with the same expiration date. The goal of this strategy is to generate income through the premiums of the options sold while also having protection in case the stock price moves in either direction.

Definition of a short strangle

A short strangle is a bearish options trading strategy that involves selling a call option and a put option with different strike prices, but with the same expiration date. The goal of this strategy is to generate income through the premiums of the options sold while also having protection in case the stock price moves in either direction.

How a short strangle affects options trading

A short strangle can be a profitable strategy for traders who expect the stock price to stay within a certain range. However, it is also a risky strategy as there is the potential for large losses if the stock price moves outside of the range of the strike prices of the options sold.

Importance of using a short strangle in options trading

A short strangle can be a useful strategy for traders who want to generate income through the premiums of the options sold while also having protection in case the stock price moves in either direction. It is also a useful strategy for traders who expect the stock price to stay within a certain range.

Strategies for trading a short strangle

When trading a short strangle, it is important to choose the right strike prices and expiration date. Traders should choose strike prices that are slightly out of the money and an expiration date that is far enough in the future to give the stock price time to move. It is also important to adjust the trade as needed, such as by buying back the options sold if the stock price moves outside of the range of the strike prices.

Example of a Short Strangle Case Study

Let's consider a trader named Sarah. Sarah is bearish on the stock of XYZ Company and believes that the stock price will stay within a certain range in the next few months. She decides to enter a short strangle by selling a call option at a strike price of $55 and a put option at a strike price of $45, with an expiration date of one month. The call option premium is $2 and the put option premium is $1. After one month, the stock price stays within the range of $45 to $55 and Sarah closes her position by buying back the call option at $1 and the put option at $0.5. She earns a profit of $200 from the call option and $100 from the put option for a total profit of $300. In this case, Sarah was able to benefit from the stock's limited movement and generate income through the premiums of the options sold.

In conclusion, a short strangle is a bearish options trading strategy that involves selling both a call option and a put option with different strike prices, but with the same expiration date. It can be a profitable strategy for traders who expect the stock price to stay within a certain range, but it is also a risky strategy as there is the potential for large losses if the stock price moves outside of the range of the strike prices of the options sold. Traders should choose the right strike prices and expiration date and adjust the trade as needed to manage risk and maximize potential profits. It is a complex strategy and requires a lot of knowledge and experience in options trading, so traders should be well-versed in options trading before attempting to trade a short strangle.

Chapter 67: Short Strangle Trading Tutorial

A short strangle is a bearish options trading strategy that involves selling both a call option and a put option at different strike prices. This strategy is used when a trader believes that the underlying stock will stay within a certain range and not make a big move in either direction. In this chapter, we will discuss the basics of a short strangle, how it affects options trading, the importance of using a short strangle, and strategies for trading it.

How a short strangle affects options trading

A short strangle can be a great way to generate income for traders who believe that the underlying stock will stay within a certain range. However, it is also a high-risk strategy because the trader is exposed to unlimited losses if the stock makes a big move in either direction.

Importance of using a short strangle in options trading

A short strangle is a great strategy for traders who believe that the underlying stock will stay within a certain range. It allows traders to generate income while also having protection in case the stock makes a big move in either direction.

Strategies for trading a short strangle, including when to enter and exit the trade, and how to adjust the trade as needed

When trading a short strangle, it is important to choose the right strike prices and expiration dates. The strike prices should be far enough apart so that the stock has to make a big move in either direction for the trade to be in the money. The expiration date should also be far enough in the future so that the stock has time to make a big move.

It is also important to manage risk when trading a short strangle. Traders should only enter into this strategy with capital that they can afford to lose and should always have a plan in place for managing risk. This can include setting stop-loss orders and limiting the size of the trade.

Example of a Short Strangle Case Study

Let's consider a trader named Michael. Michael believes that the stock of XYZ Company will stay within a certain range and decides to enter into a short strangle. He sells a call option with a strike price of $50 and a put option with a strike price of $40, both with an expiration date of one month.

The stock of XYZ Company does indeed stay within the range and Michael is able to collect the premium from the options that he sold. However, if the stock had made a big move in either direction, Michael would have been exposed to unlimited losses.

In conclusion, a short strangle is a bearish options trading strategy that can be used to generate income while also having protection in case the stock makes a big move in either direction. It is important to choose the right strike prices and expiration dates, and to manage risk when trading a short strangle. By following these strategies and tips, traders can successfully trade a short strangle and generate income in the process.

Chapter 68: Best Short Strangle Adjustments: 3 Short Strangles

A short strangle is a bearish options trading strategy that involves selling both a call option and a put option with different strike prices, but with the same expiration date. This strategy is used when the trader expects the underlying stock to remain relatively stable within a certain range. However, as with any options trade, there is always the potential for the stock to move outside of this range, resulting in a loss. To mitigate this risk, traders can make adjustments to their short strangle positions. In this chapter, we will discuss three popular short strangle adjustments: rolling, rolling and widening, and rolling and narrowing.

Comparison of three popular short strangle adjustments

The first adjustment that traders can make to their short strangle positions is rolling. Rolling involves closing the current short strangle position and opening a new one with a later expiration date. This allows the trader to extend the time frame of the trade, giving the underlying stock more time to move back within the expected range. However, rolling also involves adjusting the strike prices of the options to reflect the new expiration date.

The second adjustment that traders can make is rolling and widening. This involves closing the current short strangle position and opening a new one with a later expiration date and wider strike prices. This allows the trader to increase the range in which the underlying stock is expected to remain stable, reducing the risk of the trade. However, this also means that the trader will receive a lower premium for the options.

The third adjustment that traders can make is rolling and narrowing. This involves closing the current short strangle position and opening a new one with a later expiration date and narrower strike prices. This allows the trader to decrease the range in which the underlying stock is expected to remain stable, increasing the potential for profit. However, this also means that the trader will receive a higher premium for the options.

Pros and cons of each adjustment, and when to use each one

Rolling is a great adjustment for traders who want to extend the time frame of their trade while also adjusting the strike prices to reflect the new expiration date. This allows the trader to give the underlying stock more time to move back within the expected range. However, rolling also involves adjusting the strike prices, which can be a disadvantage if the underlying stock has already moved outside of the expected range.

Rolling and widening is a great adjustment for traders who want to increase the range in which the underlying stock is expected to remain stable. This reduces the risk of the trade and allows the trader to receive a lower premium for the options. However, this also means that the trader will receive a lower premium for the options, which can be a disadvantage if the underlying stock has already moved outside of the expected range.

Rolling and narrowing is a great adjustment for traders who want to decrease the range in which the underlying stock is expected to remain stable. This increases the potential for profit and allows the trader to receive a higher premium for the options. However, this also means that the trader will receive a higher premium for the options, which can be a disadvantage if the underlying stock has already moved outside of the expected range.

Strategies for adjusting and managing a short strangle trade

When adjusting a short strangle trade, traders should consider the current market conditions, the volatility of the underlying stock, and their own risk tolerance. Traders should also have a plan in place for managing risk, such as setting stop-loss orders and limiting the amount of capital they are willing to risk on the trade.

Example of a Short Strangle Adjustment Case Study

Let's consider a trader named Michael who has a short strangle position on the stock of XYZ Company with a strike price of $50 for the call option and $45 for the put option, and an expiration date of one month. However, the stock price of XYZ Company has increased to $52 and Michael is concerned that his trade may result in a loss. He decides to make a short strangle adjustment by rolling the trade. This means that he closes his current position and opens a new one with a higher strike price for the call option and a lower strike price for the put option, in this case $55 for the call option and $40 for the put option. By doing this, Michael reduces the risk of the trade and increases the potential for profit. He also decides to extend the expiration date to two months to give the trade more time to play out.

Another option for Michael could have been to roll and widen the trade. This means that he would increase the distance between the strike prices of the call and put options, for example $60 for the call option and $35 for the put option. This strategy would also reduce risk but would also limit the potential for profit.

Finally, Michael could have also chosen to roll and narrow the trade. This means that he would decrease the distance between the strike prices of the call and put options, for example $55 for the call option and $50 for the put option. This strategy would increase the potential for profit but also increase the risk.

It is important to note that these are just a few examples of short strangle adjustments and there are many other options available. Traders should carefully consider their individual goals and risk tolerance when choosing which adjustments to make. Additionally, it is important to regularly monitor the trade and adjust as necessary to ensure the best outcome.

In conclusion, a short strangle is a strategy that can be used to generate income while also having protection in case the stock price decreases or increases. Adjusting the trade through techniques such as rolling, rolling and widening, and rolling and narrowing can be effective in managing risk and increasing potential for profit. It is important to choose the right strike prices, expiration dates, and monitor the trade regularly to ensure the best outcome.

By following these strategies and tips, traders can effectively use short strangle adjustments to their advantage in the options trading market.

Chapter 69: What is a Short Straddle

A short straddle is a type of options trading strategy that involves selling both a call option and a put option with the same strike price and expiration date. This strategy is used when a trader believes that the price of the underlying asset will remain relatively stable over a certain period of time. By selling both a call and a put option, the trader is able to collect premium income, but they also assume a significant amount of risk.

When a trader enters into a short straddle, they are essentially betting that the price of the underlying asset will remain within a certain range. If the price of the asset rises above the strike price of the call option, the trader will lose money. If the price of the asset falls below the strike price of the put option, the trader will also lose money. However, if the price of the asset remains within the range, the trader will collect the premium income and potentially make a profit.

The importance of using a short straddle in options trading lies in the potential for premium income. This strategy can be a great way to generate income while waiting for the price of the underlying asset to move in a certain direction. Additionally, short straddles can be used as a way to hedge against other positions in a trader's portfolio.

When it comes to trading a short straddle, it is important to choose the right strike prices and expiration dates. Traders should look for strike prices that are slightly out of the money and expiration dates that are not too far in the future. This will help to minimize the risk of the trade and maximize the potential for premium income.

In order to adjust a short straddle trade, traders can choose to roll the strike prices or expiration dates. Rolling the strike prices involves adjusting the strike price of one or both of the options. This can be done by buying back the option that is in the money and selling a new option with a different strike price. Rolling the expiration date involves buying back the option that is close to expiration and selling a new option with a later expiration date.

It's also important to manage risk when trading a short straddle. Traders should only enter into this strategy with capital that they can afford to lose and should always have a plan in place for managing risk. This can include setting stop-loss orders and limiting the amount of capital that is invested in the trade.

Example of a Short Straddle Case Study

Let's consider a trader named Michael. Michael believes that the stock of XYZ Company will remain relatively stable over the next month. He decides to enter into a short straddle by selling a call option with a strike price of $50 and a put option with a strike price of $50. Both options have an expiration date of one month. Michael collects a premium of $2 for each option, for a total of $4.

After one month, the stock price of XYZ Company is trading at $52. Michael's call option is in the money, so he buys it back for $2. His put option is out of the money, so he lets it expire worthless. Michael's net profit from the trade is $2, which is the premium income that he collected.

However, if the stock price of XYZ Company had risen to $55, Michael's call option would have been worth $5 and his put option would have expired worthless. Michael would have lost $3 on the trade. This is why it is important to manage risk and choose the right strike prices and expiration dates when trading a short straddle.

In conclusion, a short straddle can be a great way to generate income while waiting for the price of the underlying asset to move in a particular direction. However, it is important to remember that this strategy is not without risk and traders should only enter into a short straddle with capital that they can afford to lose. By carefully choosing strike prices and expiration dates, managing risk, and adjusting the trade as needed, traders can successfully trade a short straddle and potentially profit from market volatility.

Chapter 70: How to Trade a Short Straddle Strategy

A short straddle is a popular options trading strategy that can be used to generate income while waiting for the price of the underlying asset to move in a specific direction. In this chapter, we will provide a step-by-step guide for trading a short straddle, including choosing the right strike prices, expiration dates, and managing risk. We will also provide real-world examples of short straddle trades and their outcomes, as well as tips and tricks for successful short straddle trading.

Definition of a Short Straddle

A short straddle is a strategy that involves selling both a call option and a put option on the same underlying asset at the same strike price and expiration date. The goal of this strategy is to generate income from the premium received from the sale of the options, while waiting for the price of the underlying asset to move in a specific direction.

How a Short Straddle Affects Options Trading

A short straddle can be a great way to generate income while waiting for the price of the underlying asset to move in a specific direction. However, it is important to note that this strategy is not without risk. A short straddle can result in a loss if the price of the underlying asset moves too far in either direction. Additionally, if the price of the underlying asset does not move in the expected direction, the trader may be forced to buy back the options at a higher price.

Importance of Using a Short Straddle in Options Trading

A short straddle can be a great way to generate income while waiting for the price of the underlying asset to move in a specific direction. However, it is important to note that this strategy is not without risk. A short straddle can result in a loss if the price of the underlying asset moves too far in either direction. Additionally, if the price of the underlying asset does not move in the expected direction, the trader may be forced to buy back the options at a higher price.

Strategies for Trading a Short Straddle, Including When to Enter and Exit the Trade, and How to Adjust the Trade as Needed

When trading a short straddle, it is important to choose the right strike prices and expiration dates. The strike price should be at a level that is likely to be reached within the expiration date, but not too close to the current price of the underlying asset. Additionally, the expiration date should be far enough in the future to allow for the price of the underlying asset to move in the expected direction, but not so far in the future that the options will expire worthless.

To enter into a short straddle trade, a trader will sell both a call option and a put option at the same strike price and expiration date. The goal of this trade is to generate income from the premium received from the sale of the options, while waiting for the price of the underlying asset to move in a specific direction.

To exit a short straddle trade, a trader will need to buy back the options that were sold. This can be done at any time, but it is typically done when the price of the underlying asset has moved in the expected direction. If the price of the underlying asset has moved in the expected direction, the trader can buy back the options at a lower price than they were sold for, resulting in a profit. If the price of the underlying asset has not moved in the expected direction, the trader may be forced to buy back the options at a higher price, resulting in a loss.

To adjust a short straddle trade, a trader can roll the options to a different strike price and expiration date.

For example, if the underlying asset has moved in a favorable direction and the options are in-the-money, the trader can roll the options to a higher strike price and later expiration date to lock in profits. On the other hand, if the underlying asset has moved in an unfavorable direction and the options are out-of-the-money, the trader can roll the options to a lower strike price and earlier expiration date to minimize losses.

It is important to note that when adjusting a short straddle trade, the trader must pay close attention to the implied volatility of the underlying asset. Implied volatility is the market's expectation of how much the underlying asset will fluctuate in price over a certain period of time. If the implied volatility is high, it may be a good idea to roll the options to a later expiration date to take advantage of the increased volatility. However, if the implied volatility is low, it may be a good idea to roll the options to an earlier expiration date to avoid paying a premium for volatility that may not materialize.

Example of a Short Straddle Case Study

Let's consider a trader named Sarah who is bullish on XYZ stock. She decides to sell a short straddle with a strike price of $50 and an expiration date of one month. The premium she receives for selling the options is $2 per share. A few days later, XYZ stock rises to $55 per share and Sarah decides to adjust her trade by rolling the options to a strike price of $55 and an expiration date of two months. The premium she receives for selling the new options is $3 per share. As a result of the adjustment, Sarah has locked in a profit of $1 per share ($3 - $2) and extended the duration of her trade.

In conclusion, trading a short straddle can be a great way to generate income in a market that is expected to be range-bound. However, it is important to be aware of the risks involved and have a plan in place for managing those risks. Traders should also be prepared to adjust their trades as needed to lock in profits or minimize losses. By following these tips and tricks, traders can increase their chances of success with a short straddle strategy.

Chapter 71: Vertical Put Credit Spread Tutorial

A vertical put credit spread, also known as a bear put spread, is a strategy that involves selling a put option at a higher strike price and buying a put option at a lower strike price. The goal of this strategy is to generate income through the sale of the higher strike price put option, while also limiting potential losses through the purchase of the lower strike price put option. This strategy is considered to be a limited risk and limited reward strategy, as the potential profit is limited to the difference between the two strike prices, while the potential loss is limited to the difference between the purchase price and the sale price of the options.

Definition of a Vertical Put Credit Spread

A vertical put credit spread is a strategy that involves selling a put option at a higher strike price and buying a put option at a lower strike price. The goal of this strategy is to generate income through the sale of the higher strike price put option, while also limiting potential losses through the purchase of the lower strike price put option. This strategy is considered to be a limited risk and limited reward strategy, as the potential profit is limited to the difference between the two strike prices, while the potential loss is limited to the difference between the purchase price and the sale price of the options.

How a Vertical Put Credit Spread Affects Options Trading

A vertical put credit spread can have a significant impact on options trading. This strategy allows traders to generate income through the sale of a put option, while also limiting potential losses through the purchase of a put option. This can help to reduce overall risk in a portfolio and can also provide a way to generate income in a stagnant or bearish market.

Importance of Using a Vertical Put Credit Spread in Options Trading

The use of a vertical put credit spread in options trading can be an important tool for managing risk and generating income. This strategy can help to reduce overall risk in a portfolio and can also provide a way to generate income in a stagnant or bearish market. Additionally, the use of a vertical put credit spread can also be a useful tool for hedging against potential losses in other positions.

Strategies for Trading a Vertical Put Credit Spread

When trading a vertical put credit spread, it is important to choose the right strike prices, expiration dates, and to manage risk. One strategy for trading a vertical put credit spread is to enter the trade when the underlying asset is trading at or near the strike price of the higher strike price put option. This allows the trader to generate income through the sale of the higher strike price put option while also limiting potential losses through the purchase of the lower strike price put option.

Another strategy for trading a vertical put credit spread is to adjust the trade as needed. This can include rolling the options to a different strike price or expiration date, or closing the trade altogether. It is important to have a plan in place for adjusting the trade and to be aware of the potential risks and rewards of each adjustment.

Real-world Examples of Vertical Put Credit Spread Trades

One example of a vertical put credit spread trade is a trader who sells a put option at a strike price of $50 and buys a put option at a strike price of $45. The trader receives a credit of $1 for selling the higher strike price put option and incurs a cost of $0.50 for buying the lower strike price put option. This results in a net credit of $0.50. If the underlying asset is trading at or above $50 at expiration, the trader will keep the full credit of $0.50. If the underlying asset is trading below $45 at expiration, the trader will incur a loss, with the maximum loss being the difference between the strike prices, or $5 in this case. To manage risk, a trader can use a stop-loss order or can adjust the trade by rolling the options to a different strike price and expiration date.

In conclusion, a vertical put credit spread can be a great way to generate income and manage risk in options trading. By understanding the mechanics of the trade and choosing the right strike prices, expiration dates, and risk management strategies, traders can use this strategy to their advantage. As with any options trading strategy, it is important to have a solid understanding of the underlying asset and to always have a plan in place for managing risk.

Example of a Vertical Put Credit Spread Case Study

Let's consider a trader named Sarah who is bullish on XYZ stock. She believes that the stock will be trading above $50 in the next month, but wants to generate income while waiting for the stock to move in her favor. Sarah decides to enter into a vertical put credit spread by selling a $50 put option and buying a $45 put option. The stock is currently trading at $48 and the options have a premium of $2 for the $50 put option and $1 for the $45 put option. Sarah receives a credit of $1 ($2 - $1) for entering into the trade.

At expiration, the stock is trading at $52. Both options expire worthless and Sarah keeps the credit of $1. If the stock had been trading below $45 at expiration, Sarah would have incurred a loss, with the maximum loss being the difference between the strike prices, or $5 in this case.

In this example, Sarah was able to generate income and manage risk by using a vertical put credit spread. She was able to take advantage of her bullish sentiment on XYZ stock, while also limiting her potential loss. By understanding the mechanics of the trade and using a solid risk management strategy, Sarah was able to successfully trade a vertical put credit spread.

In this chapter, we have discussed what a vertical put credit spread is and how it affects options trading. We have also discussed the importance of using this strategy in options trading and provided strategies for entering and exiting the trade, as well as adjusting the trade as needed. With the information provided in this chapter, traders can use a vertical put credit spread to generate income and manage risk in their options trading.

Chapter 72: What is the Iron Condor Strategy?

The iron condor strategy is a popular options trading strategy that involves selling both a put option and a call option at different strike prices. This strategy is typically used when a trader expects the underlying asset to remain relatively stable within a specific price range. The iron condor strategy is a limited risk, limited reward strategy, making it a popular choice for risk-averse traders.

Definition of the iron condor strategy

The iron condor strategy is a combination of a bear put spread and a bull call spread. A bear put spread is created by selling a put option at a lower strike price and buying a put option at a higher strike price. A bull call spread is created by selling a call option at a higher strike price and buying a call option at a lower strike price. The iron condor strategy is created by selling both a bear put spread and a bull call spread at the same time.

How the iron condor strategy affects options trading

The iron condor strategy is a limited risk, limited reward strategy, meaning that the potential profit is limited, but so is the potential loss. This makes it a popular choice for traders who are risk-averse and want to limit their potential losses. The iron condor strategy is also a popular choice for traders who expect the underlying asset to remain relatively stable within a specific price range.

Importance of using the iron condor strategy in options trading

The iron condor strategy is a popular choice for traders who want to limit their potential losses while still having the opportunity to generate income. It is also a popular choice for traders who expect the underlying asset to remain relatively stable within a specific price range. The iron condor strategy is a great way to generate income while waiting for the underlying asset to move in a desired direction.

Strategies for trading the iron condor strategy

When trading the iron condor strategy, it is important to choose the right strike prices, expiration dates, and risk management techniques. Traders should choose strike prices that are near the current price of the underlying asset, and expiration dates that are far enough out to give the underlying asset enough time to move in the desired direction. Risk management techniques such as stop-loss orders and position sizing can also be used to limit potential losses.

Example of an Iron Condor Case Study

Let's consider a trader named Sarah who is trading the iron condor strategy on XYZ stock. Sarah expects XYZ stock to remain relatively stable within a specific price range, so she decides to sell a $50 put option and a $55 call option. Sarah also buys a $52.50 put option and a $57.50 call option to limit her potential losses. Sarah receives a credit of $1.50 for selling the options, and her maximum potential loss is $3.

The underlying asset is trading at $54 at expiration, and Sarah keeps the credit of $1.50 as her profit.

In conclusion, the iron condor strategy is a popular options trading strategy that involves selling both a put option and a call option at different strike prices. It is a limited risk, limited reward strategy, making it a popular choice for risk-averse traders. Traders should choose the right strike prices, expiration dates, and risk management techniques when trading the iron condor strategy. It is also a great way to generate income while waiting for the underlying asset to move in a desired direction.

Chapter 73: How to Trade the Iron Condor Strategy

The iron condor strategy is a popular options trading strategy that involves selling both a call option and a put option with different strike prices, while also buying both a call option and a put option with different strike prices. This strategy is designed to generate income while also limiting risk. In this chapter, we will provide a step-by-step guide for trading the iron condor strategy, including how to choose the right strike prices, expiration dates, and manage risk. We will also provide real-world examples of iron condor trades and their outcomes, as well as tips and tricks for successful iron condor trading.

A step-by-step guide for trading the iron condor strategy

The first step in trading the iron condor strategy is to choose the underlying asset that you want to trade. This can be a stock, index, or ETF. Once you have selected the underlying asset, you need to choose the strike prices for the options that you will be selling and buying. The strike prices for the options that you will be selling should be closer to the current price of the underlying asset, while the strike prices for the options that you will be buying should be farther away from the current price of the underlying asset.

The next step is to choose the expiration date for the options. The expiration date should be far enough in the future to give the underlying asset enough time to move in the desired direction, but not so far in the future that the options will expire worthless. It's important to consider the volatility of the underlying asset when choosing the expiration date, as options with a longer expiration date will be more expensive and will require a larger margin.

Once you have chosen the strike prices and expiration date for the options, you need to decide on the number of contracts that you want to trade. The number of contracts that you trade will depend on your risk tolerance and the amount of capital that you have available to trade.

The final step is to execute the trade. This involves selling the call and put options at the chosen strike prices, and buying the call and put options at the chosen strike prices. Once the trade is executed, you will need to manage your risk by adjusting the trade as needed.

Real-world examples of iron condor trades and their outcomes

To understand how the iron condor strategy works in real-world situations, let's look at an example of an iron condor trade. Let's say that a trader named John is bullish on the stock XYZ and decides to trade an iron condor. John sells a call option with a strike price of $50 and buys a call option with a strike price of $60. He also sells a put option with a strike price of $40 and buys a put option with a strike price of $30. The expiration date for the options is three months in the future.

In this trade, John has a maximum potential profit of $1,000, which is the difference between the strike prices of the options that he is selling and buying. If the stock XYZ is trading above $60 or below $40 at expiration,

John will incur a loss, with the maximum loss being the difference between the strike prices, or $10.

In this example, the stock XYZ ended up trading at $55 at expiration. As a result, John's call option that he sold at $50 expired worthless and his put option that he sold at $40 expired worthless. This resulted in a maximum potential profit of $1,000.

Tips and tricks for successful iron condor trading

Choose the right underlying asset: It's important to choose an underlying asset that is relatively stable and has a lower volatility. This will increase the chances of the options expiring in the money and maximizing profits. For example, trading an iron condor on a stock like Apple, which has a high volatility, may result in more losses than gains. But trading it on a stock like Procter & Gamble, which has a lower volatility, may result in more consistent profits.

Choose the right expiration date: The expiration date is crucial for the iron condor strategy as it determines the time frame of the trade. A longer expiration date will result in a higher premium, but also a higher risk. A shorter expiration date will result in a lower premium, but also a lower risk. It's important to find the right balance between the two.

Manage risk: As with any options trading strategy, it's important to manage risk. One way to do this is by setting stop-loss orders on the options. This will limit the potential loss if the trade doesn't go as planned. Another way is to adjust the trade as needed. For example, if the underlying asset starts to move in an unexpected direction, the trader can close the trade or roll the options to a different strike price and expiration date.

Example of an Iron Condor Case Study:

Let's consider a trader named Sarah who wants to trade an iron condor on the stock of XYZ company. The current price of the stock is $50. Sarah buys an XYZ $52.50 call option and sells an XYZ $55 call option for a credit of $0.50. She also buys an XYZ $47.50 put option and sells an XYZ $45 put option for a credit of $0.50. The total credit for the trade is $1.00.

Sarah's maximum profit for the trade is the credit received, or $1.00. Her maximum loss is the difference between the strike prices, or $7.50. If the stock of XYZ is trading between $47.50 and $55 at expiration, Sarah will earn a profit of $1.00. If the stock is trading below $47.50 or above $55 at expiration, Sarah will incur a loss, with the maximum loss being $7.50.

Sarah sets a stop-loss order on the options at $6.00. This means that if the loss on the trade reaches $6.00, the options will be automatically closed. Sarah also monitors the stock of XYZ closely and adjusts the trade as needed. For example, if the stock starts to move in an unexpected direction, she may roll the options to a different strike price and expiration date to minimize her loss.

In conclusion, the iron condor strategy can be a great way to generate income while waiting for the price of the underlying asset to move in a specific range. It's important to choose the right underlying asset, expiration date, and manage risk effectively to maximize profits and minimize losses. With a step-by-step guide, real-world examples and tips and tricks, traders can learn how to trade the iron condor strategy successfully and profitably.

Chapter 74: Chicken Iron Condor Strategy Tutorial

Definition of the chicken iron condor strategy

The chicken iron condor strategy is a variation of the traditional iron condor strategy, which is a popular options trading strategy that involves selling both a call and a put option at different strike prices in order to generate income from the premium received. The chicken iron condor strategy, on the other hand, involves selling a call option and a put option at the same strike price, while also buying a call option and a put option at different strike prices.

How the chicken iron condor strategy differs from the traditional iron condor strategy

The main difference between the chicken iron condor strategy and the traditional iron condor strategy is that in the chicken iron condor strategy, the call and put options are sold at the same strike price, while in the traditional iron condor strategy, the call and put options are sold at different strike prices. This means that in the chicken iron condor strategy, the trader is essentially betting that the price of the underlying asset will stay within a certain range, while in the traditional iron condor strategy, the trader is betting that the price of the underlying asset will not go beyond a certain range.

Importance of using the chicken iron condor strategy in options trading

The chicken iron condor strategy is a popular options trading strategy because it allows traders to generate income from the premium received, while also limiting their risk. This is because the chicken iron condor strategy involves selling a call option and a put option at the same strike price, which means that the trader is essentially betting that the price of the underlying asset will stay within a certain range. This can be a great strategy for traders who are looking to generate income while also managing their risk.

Strategies for trading the chicken iron condor strategy, including when to enter and exit the trade, and how to adjust the trade as needed

In order to trade the chicken iron condor strategy successfully, traders should follow a few key strategies. First, traders should choose the right underlying asset. It's important to choose an asset that is volatile enough to generate a decent premium, but not so volatile that it will be difficult to predict where the price will go.

Next, traders should choose the right strike prices. In the chicken iron condor strategy, the trader should choose a strike price that is close to the current price of the underlying asset, as this will generate a higher premium. Additionally, the trader should choose a strike price that is within the range that they believe the price of the underlying asset will stay within.

Traders should also choose the right expiration date. In general, traders should choose an expiration date that is far enough in the future to generate a decent premium, but not so far in the future that the price of the underlying asset could move significantly in that time.

Finally, traders should manage their risk. In the chicken iron condor strategy, the trader is essentially betting that the price of the underlying asset will stay within a certain range, so it's important to manage the risk of the trade by adjusting the trade as needed. For example, if the price of the underlying asset starts to move outside of the range that the trader predicted, the trader should adjust the trade by either rolling the options to a different strike price or expiration date, or by closing the trade altogether.

Example of a Chicken Iron Condor Strategy Case Study

Let's consider a trader named Sarah, who is interested in trading the chicken iron condor strategy. Sarah is bullish on XYZ stock and believes that the price of XYZ stock will stay within a certain range over the next month.

To implement her strategy, Sarah would sell an in-the-money put option at a strike price of $50 and buy an out-of-the-money put option at a strike price of $45. At the same time, she would also sell an in-the-money call option at a strike price of $55 and buy an out-of-the-money call option at a strike price of $60. This would create a "chicken" shape on the options chain, where the in-the-money options are closer to the current price of the underlying asset and the out-of-the-money options are farther away.

Sarah would receive a credit for selling the options, which would be her maximum profit potential. However, there is also a potential loss if the price of XYZ stock moves outside of the $45-$55 range. To manage this risk, Sarah would set stop loss orders at the strike prices of her out-of-the-money options. If the price of XYZ stock reaches $45 or $55, her stop loss orders would trigger and she would exit the trade with a loss.

As the expiration date approaches, Sarah can choose to close out her trade or adjust it by rolling the options to different strike prices and expiration dates. For example, if the price of XYZ stock is approaching the $50 strike price, Sarah could roll the in-the-money put option to a higher strike price to reduce her potential loss.

In this case study, Sarah was able to successfully trade the chicken iron condor strategy by choosing the right underlying asset, setting stop loss orders, and adjusting her trade as needed. By using this strategy, she was able to generate income while also limiting her potential loss.

Overall, the chicken iron condor strategy can be a great way to generate income while also limiting risk in options trading. It's important to choose the right underlying asset, set stop loss orders, and adjust the trade as needed to maximize potential profits and minimize potential losses. As with any strategy, it's also important to continue to monitor the market and stay up-to-date on the latest trends and news to make the best trading decisions.

Chapter 75: How to Trade Earnings Announcements

Definition of trading options during earnings announcements

Trading options during earnings announcements refers to buying or selling options contracts before or after a company releases its quarterly financial results. Earnings announcements, also known as earnings reports, provide investors with insight into a company's financial performance, including revenue, profits, and earnings per share. These announcements can have a significant impact on the stock price and volatility of a company, making them an important consideration for options traders.

How earnings announcements affect options trading

Earnings announcements can cause significant changes in the stock price and volatility of a company, which in turn can affect the price of options contracts. For example, if a company releases positive earnings results, its stock price may increase, resulting in an increase in the value of call options. On the other hand, if a company releases negative earnings results, its stock price may decrease, resulting in a decrease in the value of call options. Additionally, volatility often increases prior to and following an earnings announcement, which can affect the price of options contracts.

Importance of understanding earnings announcements in options trading

Understanding earnings announcements is crucial for options traders because it allows them to make informed trading decisions. For example, if a trader knows that a company is likely to release positive earnings results, they may choose to buy call options in anticipation of an increase in the stock price. On the other hand, if a trader knows that a company is likely to release negative earnings results, they may choose to buy put options in anticipation of a decrease in the stock price. Additionally, understanding earnings announcements can also help traders anticipate and manage the increased volatility that often occurs before and after an earnings release.

Strategies for using earnings announcements to make trades

There are several strategies that traders can use when trading options during earnings announcements. One strategy is to buy call options in anticipation of a positive earnings release, and buy put options in anticipation of a negative earnings release. Another strategy is to sell options prior to an earnings release in order to take advantage of the increased volatility that often occurs. A third strategy is to use a combination of both strategies, such as selling options prior to an earnings release and then buying options after the release based on the results.

Example of an Earnings Announcement Case Study

Let's consider a trader named John, who is interested in trading options during earnings announcements. John is bullish on XYZ stock and believes that the company will release positive earnings results in its upcoming announcement. In order to take advantage of this, John decides to buy call options with a strike price of $50 and an expiration date of one month.

On the day of the earnings release, XYZ stock releases positive earnings results, causing the stock price to increase by 10%. As a result, John's call options increase in value by 20%, resulting in a profit of $1000. This is a clear example of how understanding and utilizing earnings announcements can be a profitable strategy for options traders.

Tips and Tricks for Successful Earnings Announcement Trading

1. Be aware of the earnings release date: Make sure to know when the earnings release date is for the companies you are trading options on. This will help you plan your trades in advance and take advantage of the increased volatility that often occurs around earnings announcements.

2. Understand the company's history: Look at the company's past earnings releases to get an idea of what to expect. This will help you anticipate the potential impact on the stock price and volatility.
3. Choose the right strike prices and expiration dates: Pick strike prices and expiration dates that align with your expectations for the earnings release. This can help to maximize your potential profits while minimizing your risk. For example, if you expect a strong earnings release and a significant move in the stock price, you may want to choose options with a shorter expiration date and strike prices that are closer to the current stock price. On the other hand, if you expect a more muted earnings release and a smaller move in the stock price, you may want to choose options with a longer expiration date and strike prices that are farther away from the current stock price.

Example of a Earnings Announcement Trade Case Study

Let's consider a trader named John, who is interested in trading options during earnings announcements. John is bullish on ABC stock and believes that the company will release strong earnings results. John decides to buy call options with a strike price of $100 and an expiration date of one month. On the day of the earnings announcement, ABC stock jumps to $110 and John sells his options for a profit of $1000.

In this case study, John was able to successfully use earnings announcements to make a profitable trade by choosing the right strike prices and expiration dates that aligned with his expectations for the earnings release. He also managed his risk by not investing too much capital into the trade and by selling his options at a profit before the expiration date.

In conclusion, trading options during earnings announcements can be a great way to make profits, but it also comes with a higher level of risk. It is important to understand the basics of earnings announcements and how they affect stock prices, as well as to choose the right strike prices and expiration dates that align with your expectations for the earnings release. Additionally, it is essential to manage your risk by not investing too much capital into the trade and by selling your options at a profit before the expiration date. With the right strategy and a solid understanding of earnings announcements, traders can make profitable trades during earnings season.

Chapter 76: Iron Condor Adjustments Tutorial

Iron condor options trading strategy is a popular choice among investors looking to generate income while managing risk. However, as with any trade, there may be times when adjustments need to be made to the position. In this chapter, we will explore various strategies for adjusting an iron condor trade, including rolling, rolling and widening, and rolling and narrowing. We will also discuss how to choose the right adjustment for different market conditions and strategies for managing risk and maximizing profits when adjusting an iron condor trade.

Various strategies for adjusting an iron condor trade

One of the most common adjustments for an iron condor trade is rolling. Rolling involves closing out the current position and opening a new position with a different strike price and expiration date. This strategy is used when the underlying asset is expected to move in a certain direction, but the trader wants to maintain their position. For example, if a trader is expecting a stock to rise but is not sure when, they may roll their call options to a higher strike price and a later expiration date.

Another adjustment strategy is rolling and widening. This strategy involves closing out the current position and opening a new position with a wider strike price range. This strategy is used when the underlying asset is expected to move in a certain direction but the trader is uncertain of the exact timing. For example, if a trader is expecting a stock to rise but is not sure when, they may roll their call options to a wider strike price range and a later expiration date.

Finally, rolling and narrowing is another strategy for adjusting an iron condor trade. This strategy involves closing out the current position and opening a new position with a narrower strike price range. This strategy is used when the underlying asset is expected to move in a certain direction but the trader is uncertain of the exact timing. For example, if a trader is expecting a stock to rise but is not sure when, they may roll their call options to a narrower strike price range and a later expiration date.

How to choose the right adjustment for different market conditions

When adjusting an iron condor trade, it is important to consider the current market conditions. For example, if the market is bullish, it may be more beneficial to roll and widen the position. This will allow the trader to take advantage of the upward movement while also managing risk. On the other hand, if the market is bearish, it may be more beneficial to roll and narrow the position. This will allow the trader to take advantage of the downward movement while also managing risk.

Strategies for managing risk and maximizing profits when adjusting an iron condor trade

When adjusting an iron condor trade, it is important to consider not only the current market conditions but also the potential risk and reward. For example, rolling and widening the position may increase the potential reward but also increase the potential risk. On the other hand, rolling and narrowing the position may decrease the potential reward but also decrease the potential risk.

Example of an Iron Condor Adjustment Case Study

Let's consider a trader named John, who is currently holding an iron condor position on XYZ stock. John initially bought a $45 call option and a $50 put option, but now the stock is trading at $48 and he is uncertain of the exact direction the stock will move. John decides to roll and widen his position by selling his current options and buying a $40 call option and a $55 put option. This allows John to take advantage of any potential upward movement while also managing risk.

In conclusion, adjusting an iron condor trade can be a useful strategy for managing risk and maximizing profits. By considering the current market and selecting the appropriate adjustment strategy, traders can navigate potential challenges and capitalize on opportunities in the options market. As always, it is important to remember to manage risk and have a solid plan in place before making any adjustments to a trade. With the right approach and a bit of practice, traders can use iron condor adjustments to enhance their options trading strategies and improve their overall performance in the market.

Chapter 77: What is a Dynamic Iron Condor?

A dynamic iron condor is a type of options trading strategy that aims to generate profits while also limiting potential losses. The strategy involves selling a call option and a put option at different strike prices while also buying a call option and a put option at even further out-of-the-money strike prices. The goal of the dynamic iron condor is to capture the premium from selling the options while also limiting potential losses if the underlying asset moves in an unexpected direction.

Definition of a dynamic iron condor

A dynamic iron condor is a type of options trading strategy that combines elements of both the traditional iron condor and the dynamic hedging strategy. The traditional iron condor involves selling a call option and a put option at different strike prices while also buying a call option and a put option at even further out-of-the-money strike prices. The goal of the

440

traditional iron condor is to capture the premium from selling the options while also limiting potential losses if the underlying asset moves in an unexpected direction.

A dynamic iron condor, on the other hand, involves adjusting the strike prices of the options as the underlying asset moves in order to limit potential losses. This is done by adjusting the strike prices of the options to be closer to the current price of the underlying asset. This is known as dynamic hedging.

How a dynamic iron condor differs from a traditional iron condor

The main difference between a traditional iron condor and a dynamic iron condor is the way in which the options are adjusted as the underlying asset moves. In a traditional iron condor, the strike prices of the options are fixed and do not change as the underlying asset moves. In a dynamic iron condor, the strike prices of the options are adjusted as the underlying asset moves in order to limit potential losses.

Another difference between the two strategies is that a traditional iron condor has a limited profit potential while a dynamic iron condor can have unlimited profit potential. This is because a traditional iron condor is a neutral strategy that profits when the underlying asset stays within a certain range, while a dynamic iron condor can profit from both bullish and bearish movements in the underlying asset.

Importance of using a dynamic iron condor in options trading

A dynamic iron condor is a useful strategy for traders who are looking to generate profits while also limiting potential losses. The strategy is particularly useful for traders who are uncertain about the direction of the underlying asset, as it allows them to profit from both bullish and bearish movements.

Additionally, a dynamic iron condor can also be a useful strategy for traders who are looking to generate income from their portfolio, as the strategy involves selling options, which can generate a steady stream of income.

Strategies for trading a dynamic iron condor, including when to enter and exit the trade, and how to adjust the trade as needed

When trading a dynamic iron condor, it is important to choose the right underlying asset and strike prices. The underlying asset should be one that is expected to stay within a certain range, as this will maximize the chances of the strategy being successful.

It is also important to choose the right strike prices for the options. The strike prices should be chosen so that they are out-of-the-money, as this will maximize the chances of the options expiring worthless and generating a profit.

When entering the trade, it is important to set a stop-loss to limit potential losses. This can be done by setting a stop-loss at the level at which the options will be adjusted.

To adjust the trade, the trader can either roll the options to a later expiration date or widen the spread by selling a further OTM option and buying a further ITM option. This helps to adjust for changes in the underlying asset's price and volatility, and can potentially increase the chances of a profitable trade.

Strategies for trading a dynamic iron condor

One strategy for trading a dynamic iron condor is to keep a close eye on the underlying asset's price and volatility. If the price and volatility are both increasing, the trader may want to adjust the trade by rolling to a later expiration date or widening the spread. On the other hand, if the price and volatility are both decreasing, the trader may want to adjust the trade by rolling to an earlier expiration date or narrowing the spread.

Another strategy for trading a dynamic iron condor is to use a combination of technical and fundamental analysis. Technical analysis can help the trader identify trends and patterns in the underlying asset's price, while fundamental analysis can help the trader understand the underlying asset's underlying value and potential for future growth. By combining these two types of analysis, the trader can make more informed decisions about when to enter and exit the trade, and how to adjust the trade as needed.

Example of a Dynamic Iron Condor Case Study

Let's consider a trader named John, who is interested in trading a dynamic iron condor. John is bullish on ABC stock and believes that the price of ABC stock will stay within a certain range over the next month. He decides to sell a $70 call option and buy a $75 call option, while also selling a $60 put option and buying a $55 put option. The spread between the call and put options is $5, which John believes is a reasonable amount of risk for the potential reward.

However, as the month goes on, John notices that the price of ABC stock is starting to rise and the volatility is also increasing. In order to adjust for these changes, John decides to roll the options to a later expiration date and widen the spread by selling a $75 call option and buying a $80 call option, while also selling a $55 put option and buying a $50 put option. By doing this, John is able to adjust the trade and potentially increase the chances of a profitable trade.

In conclusion, a dynamic iron condor can be a useful strategy for managing risk and maximizing profits in options trading. By keeping a close eye on the underlying asset's price and volatility, and adjusting the trade as needed, traders can potentially increase their chances of a profitable trade. It's important to use a combination of technical and fundamental analysis to make informed decisions about when to enter and exit the trade, and how to adjust the trade as needed.

Chapter 78: Different Types of Iron Condors

Iron condors are a popular options trading strategy that can be used to generate income and manage risk. However, not all iron condors are created equal. In this chapter, we will explore different types of iron condors, including the traditional iron condor, the chicken iron condor, and the dynamic iron condor. We will also discuss the pros and cons of each type, as well as strategies for adjusting and managing different types of iron condors.

Comparison of different types of iron condors

The traditional iron condor is the most well-known type of iron condor. It involves selling a call option and a put option at different strike prices, while also buying a call option and a put option at different strike prices. The goal of the traditional iron condor is to generate income from the options premium, while also managing risk by limiting the potential loss.

The chicken iron condor is a variation of the traditional iron condor. It involves selling a call option and a put option at the same strike price, while also buying a call option and a put option at different strike prices. The goal of the chicken iron condor is to generate income from the options premium, while also managing risk by limiting the potential loss.

The dynamic iron condor is another variation of the traditional iron condor. It involves selling a call option and a put option at different strike prices, while also buying a call option and a put option at different strike prices. The difference with the dynamic iron condor is that it can be adjusted as the market conditions change. The goal of the dynamic iron condor is to generate income from the options premium, while also managing risk by limiting the potential loss.

Pros and cons of each type, and when to use each one

The traditional iron condor is the most well-known and widely used type of iron condor. It is a simple and straightforward strategy that can be used to generate income and manage risk. However, it can be challenging to adjust the trade as market conditions change.

The chicken iron condor is a more advanced type of iron condor that can be used to generate income and manage risk. It is a great strategy for traders who are bullish on a particular underlying asset. However, it can be challenging to adjust the trade as market conditions change.

The dynamic iron condor is a more advanced type of iron condor that can be used to generate income and manage risk. It is a great strategy for traders who are looking to adjust their trades as market conditions change. However, it can be challenging to adjust the trade as market conditions change.

Strategies for adjusting and managing different types of iron condors

When adjusting a traditional iron condor, it is important to consider the current market conditions and the underlying asset's price movements. If the underlying asset's price is moving in a particular direction, it may be necessary to adjust the trade by rolling the options to a different strike price.

When adjusting a chicken iron condor, it is important to consider the current market conditions and the underlying asset's price movements. If the underlying asset's price is moving in a particular direction, it may be necessary to adjust the trade by rolling the options to a different strike price.

When adjusting a dynamic iron condor, it is important to consider the current market conditions and the underlying asset's price movements. If the underlying asset's price is moving in a particular direction, it may be necessary to adjust the trade by rolling the options to a different strike price.

Example of a Dynamic Iron Condor Case Study

Let's consider a trader named John, who is interested in trading different types of iron condors. John is bullish on XYZ stock and believes that the price of XYZ stock will stay within a certain range over the next month. He decides to use a traditional iron condor strategy, which involves selling a call option and a put option at a certain strike price, and buying a call option and a put option at a higher and lower strike price, respectively.

This creates a "condor" shape on the options chain, with the call and put options creating a range for the stock price to stay within. John chooses the strike prices and expiration dates based on his expectations for the stock price. However, after a few days, the stock price starts to move outside of John's expected range, and he realizes that he needs to adjust his trade.

This is where the chicken iron condor and dynamic iron condor come into play. The chicken iron condor strategy involves selling a call option and a put option at a strike price closer to the current stock price, which reduces the potential profit but also reduces the potential loss. The dynamic iron condor strategy involves actively adjusting the trade as the stock price moves, by either rolling the options to different strike prices or narrowing/widening the range.

In John's case, he decides to adjust his traditional iron condor trade to a chicken iron condor, which reduces his potential loss but also reduces his potential profit. He also decides to use a dynamic iron condor strategy, which involves actively monitoring the stock price and adjusting the trade as needed. This way, he is able to manage his risk and maximize his profits.

In conclusion, different types of iron condors can be used for different market conditions and personal risk tolerance. The traditional iron condor is a good option for traders who expect the stock price to stay within a certain range, while the chicken iron condor and dynamic iron condor are better options for traders who want to manage risk and adjust their trades as needed. It is important for traders to understand the pros and cons of each type of iron condor and choose the one that best aligns with their expectations and risk tolerance.

Chapter 79: What is a Broken Wing Butterfly?

A broken wing butterfly, also known as a BWB, is a type of options trading strategy that combines elements of both a butterfly spread and a broken wing collar. This strategy is often used by traders who are looking to take advantage of a stock's movement within a certain range, while also limiting their risk.

Definition of a broken wing butterfly

A broken wing butterfly is a type of options trading strategy that involves the simultaneous purchase of a call option and a put option, with the same expiration date, at different strike prices. The call option is typically purchased at a strike price that is higher than the current market price, while the put option is typically purchased at a strike price that is lower than the current market price.

How a broken wing butterfly differs from a traditional butterfly

A traditional butterfly spread involves the purchase of two call options and two put options, with the same expiration date, at different strike prices. The goal of a traditional butterfly spread is to profit from a stock's movement within a certain range. In contrast, a broken wing butterfly is designed to be more flexible and allows for more adjustments as the market moves.

Importance of using a broken wing butterfly in options trading

One of the main advantages of using a broken wing butterfly is that it can be a more cost-effective way to take advantage of a stock's movement within a certain range. This is because the broken wing butterfly typically requires less capital than a traditional butterfly spread. Additionally, the broken wing butterfly allows for more flexibility in adjusting the trade as the market moves.

Strategies for trading a broken wing butterfly, including when to enter and exit the trade, and how to adjust the trade as needed

When trading a broken wing butterfly, it is important to enter the trade when the stock is trading near the strike price of the call option. This will allow for the greatest potential for profit. To exit the trade, it is important to watch for signs of a trend change in the stock's price. Additionally, it is important to adjust the trade as needed, by either rolling the options or adjusting the strike prices.

Example of a Broken Wing Butterfly Case Study

Let's consider a trader named Jack, who is interested in trading a broken wing butterfly. Jack is bullish on XYZ stock and believes that the price of XYZ stock will stay within a certain range over the next month. He decides to enter a broken wing butterfly by purchasing a call option with a strike price of $100 and a put option with a strike price of $90. Jack sets his profit target at $5 per share and his stop loss at $2 per share.

As the market moves, Jack realizes that XYZ stock is trending higher and decides to adjust his trade by rolling his call option to a higher strike price of $110. This allows him to lock in profits and still remain in the trade. As the market continues to move in his favor, Jack eventually exits the trade at a profit of $7 per share.

This case study illustrates how a broken wing butterfly can be a useful strategy for taking advantage of a stock's movement within a certain range, while also allowing for flexibility in adjusting the trade as the market moves. It also highlights the importance of being able to recognize a trend change in the stock's price and adjusting the trade accordingly to maximize profits.

In conclusion, a broken wing butterfly can be a useful strategy for options traders looking to take advantage of a stock's movement within a certain range, while also limiting their risk. By understanding the differences between a traditional butterfly spread and a broken wing butterfly, and by using strategies for entering and exiting the trade, as well as adjusting the trade as needed, traders can increase their chances of success when using this strategy. In the next case study, we will take a look at how a trader named Jane used a broken wing butterfly to profit from a stock's movement within a certain range.

Example of a Broken Wing Butterfly Case Study

Jane is an options trader who is bullish on XYZ stock and believes that the stock will stay within a certain range over the next month. She decides to use a broken wing butterfly strategy to take advantage of this expected movement. Jane sells a call option at a strike price of $100 and buys a call option at a strike price of $110. She also sells a put option at a strike price of $90 and buys a put option at a strike price of $80. By selling the call option at a higher strike price and the put option at a lower strike price, Jane is able to collect more premium than she would with a traditional butterfly spread.

As the stock price moves within the expected range, Jane's trade becomes profitable. However, if the stock price moves outside of the expected range, Jane's trade will start to lose money. To manage this risk, Jane sets a stop loss at a certain point where she will exit the trade if the stock price moves outside of the expected range.

In this case, Jane's trade was successful and she was able to profit from the stock's movement within the expected range. By using a broken wing butterfly strategy, Jane was able to collect more premium and limit her risk compared to a traditional butterfly spread.

In conclusion, a broken wing butterfly can be a useful strategy for options traders looking to take advantage of a stock's movement within a certain range, while also limiting their risk. It is important for traders to understand the differences between a traditional butterfly spread and a broken wing butterfly, and to use strategies for entering and exiting the trade, as well as adjusting the trade as needed, in order to increase their chances of success.

Chapter 80: How to Close a Broken Wing Butterfly

In options trading, closing a trade is just as important as opening it. One of the most popular options strategies is the broken wing butterfly, which is a variation of the traditional butterfly spread. However, closing a broken wing butterfly can be tricky, and it's important to understand the different strategies available and how to choose the right one for different market conditions. In this chapter, we will explore various strategies for closing a broken wing butterfly, including rolling, rolling and widening, and rolling and narrowing. We will also discuss strategies for managing risk and maximizing profits when closing a broken wing butterfly.

Definition of a Broken Wing Butterfly

A broken wing butterfly is a type of options strategy that involves selling a call and a put option, while also buying two other call and put options with different strike prices. The key difference between a broken wing butterfly and a traditional butterfly spread is that the strike prices of the options are not equidistant from the underlying stock's current price. Instead, the strike prices are closer to the current price, which makes the strategy more flexible and allows traders to take advantage of a stock's movement within a certain range.

How a Broken Wing Butterfly Differs from a Traditional Butterfly

A traditional butterfly spread involves selling two call options and two put options with the same expiration date, but with different strike prices. The strike prices are equidistant from the current price of the underlying stock, which means that the strategy is designed to profit if the stock remains within a certain range.

A broken wing butterfly, on the other hand, is more flexible and can be used to profit if the stock moves in either direction, as long as it stays within a certain range. The strike prices of the options in a broken wing butterfly are closer to the current price of the underlying stock, which means that the strategy can be adjusted to take advantage of different market conditions.

Importance of Using a Broken Wing Butterfly in Options Trading

One of the main advantages of using a broken wing butterfly is that it allows traders to take advantage of a stock's movement within a certain range, while also limiting their risk. The strategy is designed to profit if the stock remains within a certain range, but it can also be adjusted to take advantage of a stock's movement in either direction.

Another advantage of using a broken wing butterfly is that it is a relatively low-risk strategy compared to other options strategies, such as buying call or put options. The strategy involves selling options, which means that the trader is collecting premium, and can reduce the risk of losing money if the stock moves in the wrong direction.

Strategies for Trading a Broken Wing Butterfly

When trading a broken wing butterfly, it's important to choose the right strike prices and expiration dates to align with your expectations for the stock's movement. It's also important to adjust the trade as needed, depending on the market conditions.

One strategy for trading a broken wing butterfly is to enter the trade when the stock is trading at or near the strike price of the options. This allows the trader to collect premium and take advantage of the stock's movement within a certain range.

Another strategy is to enter the trade when the stock is trading at or near the middle strike price of the options. This allows the trader to take advantage of a stock's movement in either direction, as long as it stays within a certain range.

It's also important to exit the trade when the stock reaches the strike price of the options, or when the expiration date of the options is approaching.

Case Study: Closing a Broken Wing Butterfly

Let's consider a trader named Jane, who is interested in closing her broken wing butterfly trade on XYZ stock. Jane has been holding the trade for a few weeks, and has noticed that the stock has been trading in a tight range. She is now looking to close the trade and take her profits.

Jane has several options when it comes to closing her broken wing butterfly trade. She could roll the trade, which involves closing her current position and opening a new one with a different strike price and expiration date. This can be a useful strategy if she believes that the stock will continue to trade in a tight range, and she wants to take advantage of that by adjusting her strike prices.

Another option for Jane would be to roll and widen the trade. This involves closing her current position and opening a new one with the same strike price but a longer expiration date. This strategy can be useful if she believes that the stock will continue to trade in a tight range for a longer period of time, and she wants to take advantage of that by extending her expiration date.

Finally, Jane could also choose to roll and narrow the trade. This involves closing her current position and opening a new one with the same expiration date but a tighter strike price range. This strategy can be useful if she believes that the stock will begin to trade in a tighter range, and she wants to take advantage of that by adjusting her strike prices.

In order to choose the right strategy for closing her broken wing butterfly trade, Jane must consider the current market conditions and her expectations for the stock. She must also be aware of the risks and rewards associated with each strategy, and must be prepared to adjust her trade as needed.

To manage risk and maximize profits when closing her broken wing butterfly trade, Jane must also consider factors such as the stock's volatility, implied volatility, and the time remaining until expiration. She must also be prepared to adjust her stop-loss levels and take profits at the right time.

In conclusion, closing a broken wing butterfly trade can be a complex and challenging task, but with the right strategies and a solid understanding of the market conditions, it is possible to manage risk and maximize profits. By using strategies such as rolling, rolling and widening, and rolling and narrowing, and by carefully considering the current market conditions and your expectations for the stock, you can close your broken wing butterfly trade successfully.

Chapter 81: Broken Wing Put Butterfly Tutorial

A broken wing put butterfly is a complex options trading strategy that can be used to take advantage of a stock's movement within a certain range, while also limiting risk. Unlike a traditional put butterfly, which involves selling two at-the-money puts and buying one out-of-the-money put and one in-the-money put, a broken wing put butterfly involves selling one at-the-money put and buying one out-of-the-money put and one in-the-money put at a strike price that is farther out-of-the-money.

One of the main benefits of using a broken wing put butterfly is that it allows traders to enter the trade with a higher probability of success. This is because the trade is positioned further out-of-the-money, which means that the stock has a greater chance of remaining within the desired range. Additionally, the broken wing put butterfly also allows traders to enter the trade with a smaller initial investment, as the trade is positioned further out-of-the-money and therefore requires less capital.

However, it's important to note that the broken wing put butterfly does come with some risks. One of the main risks is that if the stock moves too far out-of-the-money, the trade can become unprofitable. Additionally, if the stock moves too far in-the-money, the trade can also become unprofitable. Therefore, it's important for traders to have a plan in place for adjusting the trade as needed.

In order to trade a broken wing put butterfly successfully, traders should have a good understanding of the stock they are trading, as well as the current market conditions. They should also be familiar with the various strategies for adjusting the trade, including rolling, rolling and widening, and rolling and narrowing. Additionally, traders should have a plan in place for managing risk and maximizing profits.

Case Study: Trading a Broken Wing Put Butterfly

Let's consider a trader named John, who is interested in trading a broken wing put butterfly on XYZ stock. John is bullish on the stock and believes that it will remain within a certain range over the next few months. He decides to enter the trade by selling one at-the-money put and buying one out-of-the-money put and one in-the-money put at a strike price that is farther out-of-the-money.

John's trade is successful and the stock remains within the desired range. However, as the expiration date approaches, the stock starts to move out-of-the-money. John quickly realizes that his trade is becoming unprofitable and decides to adjust the trade by rolling the at-the-money put to a higher strike price. By rolling the put, John is able to minimize his losses and continue to participate in the trade.

In conclusion, a broken wing put butterfly can be a useful strategy for options traders looking to take advantage of a stock's movement within a certain range, while also limiting their risk. By understanding the differences between a traditional put butterfly and a broken wing put butterfly, and by using strategies for adjusting the trade as needed, traders can successfully trade a broken wing put butterfly. It's important to have a plan in place for managing risk and maximizing profits, and to be familiar with the current market conditions.

Chapter 82: What is a Poor Man's Covered Put?

A poor man's covered put is a type of options trading strategy that is used to generate income while also limiting risk. It is similar to a traditional covered put, but it involves the use of options contracts rather than stocks to achieve the same result. In this chapter, we will discuss the definition of a poor man's covered put, how it differs from a traditional covered put, and why it is important to use this strategy in options trading. We will also explore strategies for trading a poor man's covered put, including when to enter and exit the trade and how to adjust the trade as needed.

1. Definition of a poor man's covered put

A poor man's covered put is a type of options trading strategy that involves selling a put option on a stock that the trader already owns. The trader receives a premium for selling the put option, which can be used to generate income. If the stock price falls below the strike price of the put option, the trader may be obligated to sell the stock at the strike price, but the premium received for selling the put option can help to offset any potential losses.

2. How a poor man's covered put differs from a traditional covered put

A traditional covered put involves selling a put option on a stock that the trader does not own. The trader must purchase the stock in order to sell the put option, which increases the risk of the trade. A poor man's covered put, on the other hand, involves selling a put option on a stock that the trader already owns. This reduces the risk of the trade, as the trader has already invested in the stock and is therefore less likely to suffer a significant loss.

3. Importance of using a poor man's covered put in options trading

A poor man's covered put is an important strategy to use in options trading because it allows traders to generate income while also limiting risk. By selling a put option on a stock that the trader already owns, the trader can receive a premium that can be used to offset any potential losses if the stock price falls below the strike price of the put option. Additionally, using a poor man's covered put can also help to reduce the overall volatility of a stock portfolio, making it a valuable tool for risk management.

4. Strategies for trading a poor man's covered put

When trading a poor man's covered put, it is important to carefully consider the strike price of the put option, as well as the expiration date. The strike price should be set at a level that is below the current stock price, but not so low that the stock is likely to fall below it. The expiration date should be chosen based on the trader's expectations for the stock price, as well as the amount of premium received for selling the put option.

To enter a poor man's covered put trade, a trader would first purchase a stock they believe will stay relatively stable or increase in value. Next, they would sell a put option on that stock with a strike price that is below the current stock price and a expiration date that aligns with their expectations for the stock. For example, if a trader owns 100 shares of XYZ stock that is currently trading at $50 per share, they may sell a put option with a strike price of $45 and an expiration date of one month.

To adjust the trade, a trader may choose to roll the put option to a later expiration date or to a different strike price. This can be done to take advantage of changes in the stock price or to increase the amount of premium received for selling the put option.

Another strategy for adjusting the trade is to close the trade early and take the profit before the expiration date if the stock price has moved significantly in the desired direction. This strategy is known as "taking profits early" and can be a great way to lock in gains while minimizing risk. In conclusion, a poor man's covered put can be a useful strategy for options traders looking to generate income and manage risk. By understanding the differences between a traditional covered put and a poor man's covered put, and by using strategies for entering, exiting, and adjusting the trade, traders can increase their chances of success and achieve their financial goals.

Case Study: Trading a Poor Man's Covered Put

Let's consider a trader named Jack, who is interested in trading a poor man's covered put on XYZ stock. Jack is bullish on XYZ stock and believes that the stock price will rise in the near future. He decides to sell a put option with a strike price of $50 and buy a call option with a strike price of $55 to offset the risk of the put option. Jack enters into this trade with a net credit, which means that he receives a cash payment when he enters into the trade.

As the expiration date approaches, the stock price of XYZ moves above $55, and Jack decides to close the trade early and take the profit. He buys back the put option and sells the call option, locking in a profit of $200. By using a poor man's covered put, Jack was able to generate income and manage his risk by offsetting the risk of the put option with the long call option. This strategy allowed him to take advantage of his bullish outlook on XYZ stock while limiting his risk.

In conclusion, the poor man's covered put is a great strategy for options traders looking to generate income and manage risk. By understanding the differences between a traditional covered put and a poor man's covered put, and by using strategies for entering, exiting, and adjusting the trade, traders can increase their chances of success and achieve their financial goals. It is important to consider the current market conditions and the volatility of the underlying stock before entering into a poor man's covered put trade. Additionally, it is important to have a plan for exiting the trade and taking profits early if the stock price moves in the desired direction. By following these strategies and guidelines, traders can use the poor man's covered put to achieve their financial goals and reach their full potential as options traders.

Chapter 83: How to Trade a Poor Man's Covered Put

The poor man's covered put is a strategy that involves selling a put option on a stock that you do not own. The goal of this strategy is to benefit from a potential decline in the stock's value, while also limiting your potential losses. The strategy is called "poor man's" because it allows traders to participate in the market without having to have a large amount of capital to invest in the stock itself.

To trade a poor man's covered put, the first step is to choose the right strike price. The strike price is the price at which the option can be exercised. It is important to choose a strike price that is below the current market price of the stock, as this will increase the chances of the option being exercised.

The next step is to choose the right expiration date. The expiration date is the date on which the option expires. It is important to choose an expiration date that is far enough in the future to give the stock enough time to move in the direction you anticipate, but not so far in the future that the option will expire worthless.

Once you have chosen the strike price and expiration date, you can sell the put option. This will generate income for you, but it also puts you at risk of having to buy the stock at the strike price if the option is exercised. To manage this risk, you can use stop-loss orders or other risk management strategies.

One example of a poor man's covered put trade is a trader who believes that the stock of XYZ company will decline in value. The trader does not have the capital to purchase the stock, so they sell a put option with a strike price of $50 and an expiration date of three months from now. If the stock does decline in value and the option is exercised, the trader will be forced to purchase the stock at $50. However, if the stock does not decline in value, the trader will keep the income generated from selling the put option.

Another example is a trader who believes that the stock of ABC company will remain relatively stable, but may experience a slight decline in value. The trader sells a put option with a strike price of $40 and an expiration date of six months from now. If the stock does decline in value and the option is exercised, the trader will be forced to purchase the stock at $40. However, if the stock remains stable or even increases in value, the trader will keep the income generated from selling the put option.

In conclusion, the poor man's covered put is a valuable strategy for traders who do not have the capital to purchase a stock but still want to benefit from potential declines in its value. By choosing the right strike price and expiration date, managing risk, and monitoring market conditions, traders can successfully trade a poor man's covered put. It is important to remember that the potential for profit is limited by the strike price of the option and that this strategy should be used as part of a larger, diversified trading plan. With practice and discipline, traders can use the poor man's covered put to enhance their options trading portfolio and potentially generate significant profits.

How a poor man's covered put differs from a traditional covered put

A traditional covered put involves selling a put option on a stock that the trader does not own. The trader must purchase the stock in order to sell the put option, which increases the risk of the trade. A poor man's covered put, on the other hand, involves selling a put option on a stock that the trader already owns. This reduces the risk of the trade, as the trader has already invested in the stock and is therefore less likely to suffer a significant loss.

Importance of using a poor man's covered put in options trading

A poor man's covered put is an important strategy to use in options trading because it allows traders to generate income while also limiting risk. By selling a put option on a stock that the trader already owns, the trader can receive a premium that can be used to offset any potential losses if the stock price falls below the strike price of the put option. Additionally, using a poor man's covered put can also help to reduce the overall volatility of a stock portfolio, making it a valuable tool for risk management.

Strategies for trading a poor man's covered put

When trading a poor man's covered put, it is important to carefully consider the strike price of the put option, as well as the expiration date. The strike price should be set at a level that is below the current stock price, but not so low that the stock is likely to fall below it. The expiration date should be chosen based on the trader's expectations for the stock price, as well as the amount of premium received for selling the put option.

To enter a poor man's covered put trade, a trader would first purchase a stock they believe will stay relatively stable or increase in value. Next, they would sell a put option on that stock with a strike price that is below the current stock price and a expiration date that aligns with their expectations for the stock. For example, if a trader owns 100 shares of XYZ stock that is currently trading at $50 per share, they may sell a put option with a strike price of $45 and an expiration date of one month.

To adjust the trade, a trader may choose to roll the put option to a later expiration date or to a different strike price. This can be done to take advantage of changes in the stock price or to increase the amount of premium received for selling the put option.

Another strategy for adjusting the trade is to close the trade early and take the profit before the expiration date if the stock price has moved significantly in the desired direction. This strategy is known as "taking profits early" and can be a great way to lock in gains while minimizing risk. In conclusion, a poor man's covered put can be a useful strategy for options traders looking to generate income and manage risk. By understanding the differences between a traditional covered put and a poor man's covered put, and by using strategies for entering, exiting, and adjusting the trade, traders can increase their chances of success and achieve their financial goals.

Case Study: Trading a Poor Man's Covered Put

Let's consider a trader named Jack, who is interested in trading a poor man's covered put on XYZ stock. Jack is bullish on XYZ stock and believes that the stock price will rise in the near future. He decides to sell a put option with a strike price of $50 and buy a call option with a strike price of $55 to offset the risk of the put option. Jack enters into this trade with a net credit, which means that he receives a cash payment when he enters into the trade.

As the expiration date approaches, the stock price of XYZ moves above $55, and Jack decides to close the trade early and take the profit. He buys back the put option and sells the call option, locking in a profit of $200. By using a poor man's covered put, Jack was able to generate income and manage his risk by offsetting the risk of the put option with the long call option. This strategy allowed him to take advantage of his bullish outlook on XYZ stock while limiting his risk.

In conclusion, the poor man's covered put is a great strategy for options traders looking to generate income and manage risk. By understanding the differences between a traditional covered put and a poor man's covered put, and by using strategies for entering, exiting, and adjusting the trade, traders can increase their chances of success and achieve their financial goals. It is important to consider the current market conditions and the volatility of the underlying stock before entering into a poor man's covered put trade. Additionally, it is important to have a plan for exiting the trade and taking profits early if the stock price moves in the desired direction. By following these strategies and guidelines, traders can use the poor man's covered put to achieve their financial goals and reach their full potential as options traders.

Chapter 84: What are Calendar Spread Strategies?

Calendar spread strategies, also known as time spread strategies, are a popular method for options traders to take advantage of the time decay of options. These strategies involve buying and selling options with different expiration dates, but with the same strike price. The goal of these strategies is to profit from the difference in time decay between the options, and to make a profit even if the stock price does not move much.

Definition of Calendar Spread Strategies

Calendar spread strategies involve buying a call or put option with a longer expiration date and selling a call or put option with a shorter expiration date. The goal of this strategy is to take advantage of the time decay of options, as the option with the shorter expiration date will lose value faster than the option with the longer expiration date. This can lead to a profit, even if the stock price does not move much.

How Calendar Spread Strategies Affect Options Trading

Calendar spread strategies can have a significant impact on options trading. These strategies allow traders to take advantage of the time decay of options, and to make a profit even if the stock price does not move much. Additionally, calendar spread strategies can help traders to manage risk by limiting the amount of capital that is exposed to the market at any given time.

Importance of Using Calendar Spread Strategies in Options Trading

Calendar spread strategies are an important tool for options traders, as they allow traders to take advantage of the time decay of options and to make a profit even if the stock price does not move much. Additionally, these strategies can help traders to manage risk by limiting the amount of capital that is exposed to the market at any given time.

Strategies for Using Calendar Spread Strategies

When using calendar spread strategies, traders must choose the right strike prices and expiration dates for the options. The best strike price is typically the current stock price, as this gives the options the best chance of being in the money at expiration. The best expiration date is the one that gives the options the most time to expire, as this allows the options to experience the most time decay.

Traders must also manage risk when using calendar spread strategies. This can be done by using stop-loss orders, or by closing the trade early if the stock price moves in an unexpected direction. Additionally, traders must be aware of the potential for volatility, and must adjust the trade as needed to account for this volatility.

Case Study: Calendar Spread Strategies

Let's consider a trader named John, who is interested in using calendar spread strategies to take advantage of the time decay of options. John decides to buy a call option with a strike price of $50 and an expiration date of six months from now, and to sell a call option with a strike price of $50 and an expiration date of three months from now. By doing this, John is able to take advantage of the difference in time decay between the options, and to make a profit even if the stock price does not move much.

However, John must also be aware of the potential for volatility, and must adjust the trade as needed to account for this volatility. For example, if the stock price moves unexpectedly, John may choose to close the trade early, or to use a stop-loss order to limit his risk. Additionally, John must be aware of the expiration dates of the options, and must adjust the trade as needed to account for the changing expiration dates.

In conclusion, calendar spread strategies can be a useful tool for options traders looking to take advantage of the time decay of options and to make a profit even if the stock price does not move much. By understanding the importance of choosing the right strike prices and expiration dates, and by utilizing strategies for managing risk, traders can use calendar spread strategies to maximize their profits and minimize their losses.

Chapter 85: How to Create a Put Calendar Spread

A put calendar spread, also known as a horizontal calendar spread, is a popular strategy among options traders looking to take advantage of the time decay of options. This strategy involves selling a near-term put option and simultaneously buying a longer-term put option with the same strike price. By selling the near-term option, the trader is able to collect a premium and potentially make a profit even if the stock price remains unchanged or even increases.

A step-by-step guide for creating a put calendar spread:

1. When creating a put calendar spread, there are several key factors to consider in order to maximize your chances of success. First, it is important to choose

the right strike prices for both the near-term and longer-term options. The strike price should be below the current stock price and in a range that you believe the stock is likely to remain within in the near future.

Next, it is important to choose the right expiration dates for both options. The near-term option should have a shorter expiration date than the longer-term option, typically one to two months. This allows you to collect a premium on the near-term option while also giving you more time for the stock price to move in your favor.

Finally, it is important to manage your risk when creating a put calendar spread. This can be done by setting stop-losses and adjusting the trade as needed.

Real-world examples of put calendar spread trades and their outcomes:

2. One example of a successful put calendar spread trade is a trader who sold a

near-term put option with a strike price of $50 and expiration date of one month, and simultaneously purchased a longer-term put option with a strike price of $50 and expiration date of three months. The stock price remained unchanged and the trader was able to collect a premium on the near-term option, resulting in a profit.

Another example is a trader who sold a near-term put option with a strike price of $60 and expiration date of two months, and simultaneously purchased a longer-term put option with a strike price of $60 and expiration date of six months. The stock price decreased to $55 within the two months, allowing the trader to exercise their long-term option and make a profit.

Tips and tricks for successful put calendar spread trading:

> 3. One tip for successful put calendar spread trading is to choose the right strike prices and expiration dates that

align with your expectations for the stock price. It is also important to keep an eye on market conditions and adjust your trade as needed.

Another tip is to use a risk management strategy, such as setting stop-losses, to limit your potential losses.

Case Study: Creating a Put Calendar Spread

Let's consider a trader named Michael, who is interested in creating a put calendar spread on XYZ stock. Michael believes that the stock is likely to remain within a certain range in the near future and wants to take advantage of the time decay of options.

First, Michael chooses a strike price of $70, which is below the current stock price and in a range that he believes the stock will remain within. He then chooses a near-term option with an expiration date of one month and a longer-term option with an expiration date of three months.

Next, Michael sells the near-term put option and simultaneously buys the longer-term put option. He is able to collect a premium on the near-term option and waits for the stock price to move in his favor.

Michael also sets a stop-loss at $65, to limit his potential losses if the stock price were to increase unexpectedly.

Case Study: Creating a Put Calendar Spread

In this example, we will walk through the steps of creating a put calendar spread trade using the stock ABC. The current stock price of ABC is $70 and the trader, Michael, believes that the stock will not go above $75 in the next month. He also believes that the stock may decrease slightly in the next three months. To take advantage of this, he decides to create a put calendar spread using the following options:

1. Buy a put option with a strike price of $75 and expiration date of one month
2. Sell a put option with a strike price of $75 and expiration date of three months

This creates a put calendar spread, where Michael is betting that the stock price will decrease in the next three months, but will not go below $75. By selling the put option with the later expiration date, Michael is able to collect a premium, which helps to offset the cost of buying the put option with the earlier expiration date.

As the stock price decreases, the value of the put option with the one month expiration date increases, while the value of the put option with the three month expiration date decreases. This allows Michael to make a profit, even if the stock price does not go below $75.

However, if the stock price does go below $75, Michael can exercise his put option and sell the stock at a higher price than the market value. This results in a larger profit, but it also means that Michael must have the cash on hand to buy the stock if the option is exercised.

To manage risk, Michael sets a stop-loss at $65. This means that if the stock price increases unexpectedly and goes above $65, he will close the trade to limit his potential losses. This strategy also allows him to lock in his profits if the stock price decreases as expected.

In conclusion, put calendar spread strategies can be a useful tool for options traders looking to take advantage of the time decay of options and to make a profit even if the stock price does not move much. By understanding the importance of choosing the right strike prices and expiration dates, managing risk and using stop-losses, traders can successfully create and execute a put calendar spread tradc.

Chapter 86: How to Trade Call Calendar Spreads

Call calendar spreads are a popular strategy among options traders, as they allow traders to take advantage of the time decay of options while also potentially profiting from a stock price increase. In this chapter, we will explore how to trade call calendar spreads, including the steps involved in creating a call calendar spread, the importance of choosing the right strike prices and expiration dates, and strategies for managing risk.

1. A step-by-step guide for trading call calendar spreads

To create a call calendar spread, traders typically purchase a call option with a near-term expiration date, and then sell a call option with a longer-term expiration date. The difference in the expiration dates is known as the "spread" and is the key factor in creating a calendar spread.

The first step in creating a call calendar spread is to select the underlying stock or index that you want to trade. It's important to choose a stock that has a history of volatility and a significant options market.

Next, choose the strike prices for the call options. The strike price is the price at which the option can be exercised. It's important to choose strike prices that are close to the current stock price, as this will maximize the potential for profit.

Once you've chosen the strike prices, select the expiration dates for the call options. The near-term option should have an expiration date that is less than 30 days away, while the longer-term option should have an expiration date that is at least 60 days away.

Finally, place your trade by purchasing the near-term call option and selling the longer-term call option. Be sure to set a stop-loss, which will limit your potential losses if the stock price moves against you.

2. Real-world examples of call calendar spread trades and their outcomes

One example of a successful call calendar spread trade was on the stock XYZ. The trader, John, purchased a call option with a strike price of $50 and an expiration date of 15 days out. He also sold a call option with a strike price of $50 and an expiration date of 60 days out.

The stock price of XYZ ended up increasing to $55 within the 15 days, resulting in John's near-term call option being in the money. He was able to exercise his option and sell the longer-term call option for a profit.

Another example of a successful call calendar spread trade was on the stock ABC. The trader, Jane, purchased a call option with a strike price of $75 and an expiration date of 30 days out. She also sold a call option with a strike price of $75 and an expiration date of 90 days out.

The stock price of ABC remained relatively stagnant, resulting in both call options expiring out of the money. However, the near-term option had a higher time decay, resulting in a net profit for Jane.

3. Tips and tricks for successful call calendar spread trading

One important tip for successful call calendar spread trading is to be mindful of the implied volatility of the underlying stock. Implied volatility is a measure of how volatile the stock is expected to be in the future. Options with higher implied volatility will have higher premiums, making them more expensive to trade.

Another tip is to pay attention to upcoming events that may affect the stock price, such as earnings reports or product announcements. These events can cause the stock price to fluctuate, which can impact your calendar spread trade.

Finally, it's important to have a plan for managing risk. This can include setting stop-losses, adjusting the trade as needed, and having an exit strategy in place. One strategy for managing risk is to use a combination of technical and fundamental analysis to determine when to enter and exit the trade. By using a combination of these two types of analysis, traders can make more informed decisions about when to buy and sell options.

In conclusion, call calendar spreads can be a powerful tool for options traders looking to take advantage of the time decay of options and make a profit even if the stock price does not move much. By understanding the importance of choosing the right strike prices and expiration dates, and by using strategies for managing risk, traders can increase their chances of success when trading call calendar spreads.

Chapter 87: How to Manage Calendar Spreads

Calendar spreads, also known as horizontal spreads, are a popular strategy among options traders. These spreads involve buying and selling options with the same strike price but different expiration dates. They are used to take advantage of the time decay of options and to make a profit even if the stock price does not move much. However, managing calendar spreads can be tricky and requires careful planning. In this chapter, we will discuss various strategies for managing calendar spreads, including rolling, rolling and widening, and rolling and narrowing, as well as how to choose the right strategy for different market conditions.

1. Various strategies for managing calendar spreads

2. How to choose the right strategy for different market conditions
3. Strategies for managing risk and maximizing profits when managing calendar spreads

When it comes to managing calendar spreads, there are a few different strategies traders can use. One of the most popular strategies is rolling. Rolling involves closing out one option and opening a new option with a different expiration date. This can be done to take advantage of a change in market conditions or to lock in profits. Rolling can also be used to avoid the risk of the option expiring worthless.

Another popular strategy for managing calendar spreads is rolling and widening. This involves closing out one option and opening a new option with a different expiration date and a wider strike price range. This can be done to take advantage of a change in market conditions or to lock in profits. Rolling and widening can also be used to avoid the risk of the option expiring worthless.

A third strategy for managing calendar spreads is rolling and narrowing. This involves closing out one option and opening a new option with a different expiration date and a narrower strike price range. This can be done to take advantage of a change in market conditions or to lock in profits. Rolling and narrowing can also be used to avoid the risk of the option expiring worthless.

When choosing the right strategy for managing calendar spreads, it is important to consider the current market conditions. For example, if the market is trending upward, rolling and widening may be the best strategy. If the market is trending downward, rolling and narrowing may be the best strategy. It is also important to consider the expiration date of the options and the strike price range.

In addition to choosing the right strategy, it is also important to have a plan for managing risk. This can include setting stop-losses, adjusting the trade as needed, and having an exit strategy in place. For example, a trader may set a stop-loss at a certain price point to limit their potential losses if the stock price were to move against them. They may also adjust the trade as needed if the market conditions change.

Case Study: Managing a Calendar Spread on ABC Company

Let's consider a trader named Michael, who has a calendar spread on ABC Company. He bought a call option with a strike price of $70 and an expiration date of June, and sold a call option with a strike price of $70 and an expiration date of July. The market has been trending downward, and Michael is worried that the June option will expire worthless. He decides to roll the June option to a July option. He closes out the June option and buys a July option with a strike price of $75. By doing this, he is able to lock in some of his profits and avoid the risk of the option expiring worthless.

In conclusion, managing calendar spreads can be a tricky but profitable strategy for options traders. By understanding the various strategies available and choosing the right one for the current market conditions, traders can maximize their profits and minimize their risk. Additionally, by setting stop-losses, adjusting the trade as needed, and having a well thought-out exit strategy, traders can greatly reduce the risk of losing money on a calendar spread trade. It's also important to remember that managing calendar spreads is not a one-size-fits-all approach and traders should always be willing to adapt to changing market conditions. With a solid understanding of the different strategies and risk management techniques, traders can successfully navigate the world of calendar spreads and potentially reap significant rewards.

Chapter 88: What is a Butterfly Spread?

A butterfly spread is a type of options strategy that involves the simultaneous purchase and sale of options with different strike prices, but the same expiration date. This strategy is often used to take advantage of the volatility of a stock or index and to potentially make a profit even if the stock price does not move much. In this chapter, we will explore the definition of a butterfly spread, how it affects options trading, the importance of using a butterfly spread in options trading, and strategies for using a butterfly spread.

Definition of a Butterfly Spread

A butterfly spread is an options trading strategy that involves buying and selling options with different strike prices, but the same expiration date. The strategy is typically made up of three options: one call option and two put options. The call option is bought at the highest strike price, while the two put options are sold at the middle and lower strike prices. The goal of the butterfly spread is to make a profit if the stock price remains within a certain range, while limiting potential losses if the stock price moves outside of that range.

How a Butterfly Spread Affects Options Trading

A butterfly spread can affect options trading in several ways. One of the main benefits of this strategy is that it allows traders to take advantage of the volatility of a stock or index. If the stock price remains within a certain range, traders can make a profit. However, if the stock price moves outside of that range, traders can limit their potential losses. Additionally, a butterfly spread can also be used to generate income from options trading. By selling the middle and lower strike options, traders can earn a premium, which can be used to offset the cost of buying the call option.

Importance of Using a Butterfly Spread in Options Trading

The importance of using a butterfly spread in options trading cannot be overstated. This strategy allows traders to take advantage of the volatility of a stock or index and to potentially make a profit even if the stock price does not move much. Additionally, a butterfly spread can also be used to generate income from options trading. By selling the middle and lower strike options, traders can earn a premium, which can be used to offset the cost of buying the call option. Furthermore, a butterfly spread also allows traders to limit their potential losses if the stock price moves outside of a certain range.

Strategies for Using a Butterfly Spread

There are several strategies for using a butterfly spread, including when to enter and exit the trade, and how to adjust the trade as needed. One strategy is to enter the trade when the stock price is at or near the middle strike price. By doing this, traders can take advantage of the volatility of the stock and potentially make a profit if the stock price remains within a certain range. Additionally, traders should set a stop-loss at the lower strike price to limit potential losses if the stock price moves outside of that range. Another strategy for adjusting the trade is to close the trade early if the stock price starts to move outside of the expected range.

Real-world Example:

For example, let's say that John is interested in trading a butterfly spread on XYZ stock, which is currently trading at $70. He believes that the stock will remain within a range of $68-$72 for the next month. He decides to buy a call option with a strike price of $72, and sell two put options with strike prices of $68 and $70. The call option costs $2, while the put options bring in $1 each. John's total investment is $1, which is the difference between the cost of the call option and the premium earned from selling the put options.

One strategy for using a butterfly spread is to enter the trade when the stock price is at or near the middle strike price. In this case, John would enter the trade when XYZ stock is trading at or near $70. This allows for the best chance for the stock price to move in either direction and for the options to expire in-the-money. Another strategy is to exit the trade early if the stock price starts to move too far away from the middle strike price. For example, if XYZ stock starts to trade above $72 or below $68, John may choose to close the trade early to minimize potential losses.

Another strategy for adjusting the trade is to roll the options. This involves closing the current options and opening new options with different strike prices and expiration dates. For example, if John sees that the stock price is trending upward and he believes it will continue to do so, he may choose to roll the $68 put option to a higher strike price, such as $70. This can increase the potential for the options to expire in-the-money and increase profits.

In conclusion, a butterfly spread is a versatile strategy for options traders. By understanding the mechanics of the trade and using strategies such as entering and exiting at the right time, adjusting the trade as needed, and managing risk, traders can potentially earn a profit even if the stock price does not move much. It is important to note, however, that as with any options trading strategy, it is important to do research and fully understand the potential risks and rewards before entering into a butterfly spread trade.

Chapter 89: How to Trade a Butterfly Spread

A butterfly spread is a type of options strategy that involves buying and selling options at different strike prices. This strategy is designed to take advantage of the volatility of the underlying asset and to make a profit even if the stock price does not move much. In this chapter, we will discuss how to trade a butterfly spread, including how to choose the right strike prices, expiration dates, and manage risk.

A step-by-step guide for trading a butterfly spread:

The first step in trading a butterfly spread is to choose the underlying asset. This can be any stock, index, or commodity that is traded on an exchange. Once you have chosen the underlying asset, you need to decide on the strike prices and expiration dates for the options.

The next step is to buy a call option with a strike price that is higher than the current stock price, and sell two put options with strike prices that are lower than the current stock price. The call option should have the same expiration date as the put options. This will create a butterfly spread.

The final step is to manage the trade. This includes setting stop-losses, adjusting the trade as needed, and having an exit strategy in place. It is also important to monitor the underlying asset and adjust the trade if the stock price moves outside of the expected range.

Real-world examples of butterfly spread trades and their outcomes:

One example of a successful butterfly spread trade was in 2017, when a trader decided to trade a butterfly spread on the S&P 500 index. The trader bought a call option with a strike price of 2,500 and sold two put options with strike prices of 2,450 and 2,475. The trader's total investment was $50, which was the difference between the cost of the call option and the premium earned from selling the put options.

The S&P 500 index remained within the expected range of 2,450-2,500 for the next month, and the trader was able to make a profit of $200. This is a 400% return on investment.

Tips and tricks for successful butterfly spread trading:

One tip for successful butterfly spread trading is to choose the right underlying asset. This means selecting an asset that has a high level of volatility and is expected to remain within a certain range. It is also important to choose the right strike prices and expiration dates, as well as to have a plan for managing risk.

Another tip is to monitor the underlying asset and adjust the trade as needed. This includes adjusting the strike prices or expiration dates, or even closing the trade if the stock price moves outside of the expected range.

In conclusion, a butterfly spread is a powerful options strategy that can help traders make a profit even if the stock price does not move much. By understanding how to choose the right strike prices, expiration dates, and manage risk, traders can maximize their profits and minimize their risk. Additionally, by monitoring the underlying asset and adjusting the trade as needed, traders can maximize their chances of success.

Chapter 90: How to Manage Butterfly Spreads

Butterfly spreads are a popular options trading strategy that can be used to profit from a stock's price staying within a certain range. However, managing these spreads can be tricky and requires a good understanding of the different strategies available. In this chapter, we will explore various strategies for managing butterfly spreads, including rolling, rolling and widening, and rolling and narrowing. We will also discuss how to choose the right strategy for different market conditions and strategies for managing risk and maximizing profits when managing butterfly spreads.

Various strategies for managing butterfly spreads

There are several strategies that traders can use to manage butterfly spreads, including rolling, rolling and widening, and rolling and narrowing. Rolling is a strategy that is used to adjust the expiration date of the options in a butterfly spread. This can be done by closing the current position and opening a new one with a different expiration date. Rolling and widening is a strategy that is used to increase the width of the range in which the stock is expected to trade. This can be done by buying a new call option with a higher strike price and selling a new put option with a lower strike price. Rolling and narrowing is a strategy that is used to decrease the width of the range in which the stock is expected to trade. This can be done by buying a new call option with a lower strike price and selling a new put option with a higher strike price.

How to choose the right strategy for different market conditions

Choosing the right strategy for managing butterfly spreads is crucial for maximizing profits and minimizing risk. The key is to understand the current market conditions and the direction in which the stock is likely to move. For example, if the stock is expected to trade within a narrow range, a rolling and narrowing strategy may be the best choice. If the stock is expected to trade within a wider range, a rolling and widening strategy may be more appropriate. Additionally, if the stock is expected to move in a certain direction, a rolling strategy may be the best choice. It's important to note that these strategies should be used in conjunction with proper risk management techniques.

Strategies for managing risk and maximizing profits when managing butterfly spreads

Managing risk is an important part of successfully trading butterfly spreads. One way to do this is by setting stop-losses. A stop-loss is a predetermined point at which a trader will close their position to limit their potential losses. Another way to manage risk is by adjusting the trade as needed. For example, if the stock is trading outside of the expected range, the trader may choose to close their position and open a new one with a different strike price or expiration date. Additionally, having an exit strategy in place is crucial for maximizing profits. This can include taking profits at a certain point, or waiting for the stock to reach a certain price before closing the position.

Example of a Case Study:

In this case study, we will look at how a trader named Michael used a rolling and narrowing strategy to manage a butterfly spread on XYZ stock. Michael had originally entered into a butterfly spread on XYZ stock, which was trading at $70. He believed that the stock would remain within a range of $68-$72 for the next month. However, after a few weeks, the stock began to trade outside of this range. Michael decided to close his original position and open a new one with a different expiration date and strike prices. He bought a new call option with a strike price of $71 and sold two put options with strike prices of $69 and $70. By rolling and narrowing his position, Michael was able to reduce his risk and increase his chances of profit. In the end, Michael's strategy paid off as XYZ stock remained within his predicted range and he was able to close his position with a profit.

It's important to note that while rolling and narrowing worked well in this scenario, it may not always be the best strategy. Market conditions are constantly changing, and it's crucial to assess the current market and choose the appropriate strategy for managing your butterfly spread.

Another strategy for managing butterfly spreads is rolling and widening. This strategy involves closing the original position and opening a new one with a wider range of strike prices. This can be useful in a market where the stock is expected to make a large move in either direction. However, it's important to keep in mind that this strategy also increases risk, as the trader is now exposed to a larger range of possible outcomes.

Managing risk is crucial when trading butterfly spreads. One way to do this is by setting stop-losses and taking profit at predetermined levels. This can help limit potential losses and lock in profits. Additionally, it's important to have a plan for adjusting the trade as needed, whether that's rolling, widening, or narrowing the position.

In conclusion, butterfly spreads can be a valuable tool for options traders, but it's important to have a plan for managing the trade.

By understanding the different strategies available, choosing the right one for the current market conditions, and managing risk, traders can maximize their profits and minimize their losses. As always, it's important to do your own research and be aware of the potential risks involved in any trade.

Chapter 91: What is a Condor Spread?

A condor spread is a type of options trading strategy that involves buying and selling four different options contracts with the same expiration date but different strike prices. The goal of a condor spread is to profit from a neutral market where the price of the underlying asset remains within a certain range.

To create a condor spread, a trader will typically buy a call option at the highest strike price and sell a call option at the next strike price. They will also buy a put option at the lowest strike price and sell a put option at the next strike price. This creates a spread where the trader has both a long and short position, and can profit as long as the underlying asset remains within the range of the strike prices.

The condor spread is considered a neutral strategy because it profits from a lack of movement in the underlying asset. This makes it a popular strategy for traders who believe that the market will remain relatively stable and that the underlying asset will not experience a significant price change.

One of the key benefits of a condor spread is that it can be used to generate income while also managing risk. Because the spread involves both long and short positions, the trader can profit even if the underlying asset's price moves slightly in either direction. Additionally, because the spread is created using options contracts with different strike prices, the trader is able to limit their potential losses if the underlying asset's price moves outside of the range.

However, it's important to note that a condor spread is not without its risks. If the underlying asset's price moves outside of the range of the strike prices, the trader can experience significant losses. Additionally, if the underlying asset's price moves too far in either direction, the trader may be forced to close the position at a loss.

Despite these risks, many traders find that the condor spread can be a valuable tool for managing risk and generating income in a neutral market. One example of this is a case study of a trader named Sarah who used a condor spread to profit from a neutral market.

Sarah believed that the price of XYZ stock would remain within a range of $75-$80 for the next month. She decided to create a condor spread by buying a call option with a strike price of $80 and selling a call option with a strike price of $78. She also bought a put option with a strike price of $75 and sold a put option with a strike price of $77.

By creating this spread, Sarah was able to limit her potential losses if the price of XYZ stock moved outside of the range. Additionally, she was able to generate income as long as the price of XYZ stock remained within the range. In the end, Sarah was able to profit from the neutral market and manage her risk effectively.

In conclusion, a condor spread is a valuable tool for options traders looking to profit from a neutral market while also managing risk. By understanding how to create and manage a condor spread, traders can increase their chances of success and minimize their potential losses. It's important to understand the risks involved, but with proper knowledge and strategy, a condor spread can be a powerful tool for options trading.

Chapter 92: How to Trade a Condor Spread

A condor spread is a type of options trading strategy that involves buying and selling options with different strike prices and expiration dates. This strategy is often used by traders who believe that the underlying asset will remain within a certain price range for a specific period of time. In this chapter, we will discuss the steps involved in trading a condor spread, as well as real-world examples of how this strategy can be used.

A step-by-step guide for trading a condor spread

Trading a condor spread can be a bit tricky, so it's important to have a clear understanding of the steps involved before you begin. Here's a step-by-step guide to help you get started:

Step 1: Choose the underlying asset. Before you can trade a condor spread, you need to choose an underlying asset to trade. This could be a stock, commodity, currency, or other financial instrument.

Step 2: Determine your price range. Once you've chosen your underlying asset, you need to determine the price range within which you believe the asset will remain for the duration of the trade. This will help you choose the strike prices for your options.

Step 3: Choose your strike prices. A condor spread requires buying and selling options with four different strike prices. It is important to choose strike prices that are within the determined price range and have expiration dates that match the time frame of the trade.

Step 4: Buy and sell options. Once you've chosen your strike prices, you can buy and sell options. The exact number of options you buy and sell will depend on your risk tolerance and the size of your trading account.

Step 5: Monitor the trade. Once you've entered into the condor spread, it's important to monitor the trade closely. This will help you identify any potential problems and make adjustments as needed.

Step 6: Exit the trade. When the expiration date of the options approaches, it is important to evaluate the trade and decide whether to close the position or roll it over to the next expiration date.

Real-world examples of condor spread trades and their outcomes

Now that we've gone over the steps involved in trading a condor spread, let's take a look at a few real-world examples of how this strategy can be used.

Example 1: Trading a condor spread on XYZ stock

In this example, we'll look at how a trader named John used a condor spread to trade XYZ stock. John believed that the stock would remain within a range of $68-$72 for the next month. He decided to buy a call option with a strike price of $72, and sell a call option with a strike price of $74, a put option with a strike price of $68, and a put option with a strike price of $66. The call options cost $2 each, while the put options brought in $1 each. John's total investment was $2, which was the difference between the cost of the call options and the premium earned from selling the put options. In the end, John was able to make a profit of $3 when the stock closed at $71 at expiration.

Example 2: Trading a condor spread on Gold

In this example, we'll look at how a trader named Michael used a condor spread to trade gold. Michael believed that the price of gold would remain within a range of $1,300-$1,350 for the next month. He decided to enter into a condor spread by buying a call option with a strike price of $1,350 and selling two put options with strike prices of $1,325 and $1,300. He also sold a call option with a strike price of $1,325 and bought a put option with a strike price of $1,300.

To enter this trade, Michael paid $2 for the call option at $1,350, received $1 for each of the put options at $1,325 and $1,300, and received $3 for the call option at $1,325 and paid $2 for the put option at $1,300. His total investment for this trade was $1, which is the difference between the cost of the call option at $1,350 and the premium earned from selling the put options at $1,325 and $1,300, and the call option at $1,325 and the premium paid for the put option at $1,300.

During the next month, the price of gold remained within the expected range of $1,300-$1,350. As a result, Michael was able to earn a profit of $150 from this trade, which is the difference between the premium earned from selling the call and put options and the cost of the call option at $1,350. This profit represents a return on investment of 15,000%, which is a significant return for a relatively small investment.

In this example, Michael was able to successfully use a condor spread to trade gold and earn a significant return on his investment. By carefully choosing the right strike prices and expiration dates, and managing his risk through the use of stop-losses, Michael was able to maximize his profits and minimize his risk. This example illustrates the potential of using a condor spread in options trading and the importance of understanding the various strategies and tools available for managing these types of trades.

Tips and Tricks for Successful Condor Spread Trading

1. Choose the right strike prices: To maximize your chances of success, it is important to choose strike prices that are within the expected range of the underlying asset.
2. Manage your risk: Use stop-losses and other risk management tools to minimize the potential for loss.
3. Be prepared to adjust the trade as needed: If the market conditions change, be prepared to adjust your trade to take advantage of the new situation.

4. Keep an eye on volatility: High volatility can increase the potential for profit, but it can also increase the potential for loss.
5. Monitor your trade: Keep a close eye on your trade and be prepared to exit if the market conditions change.

In conclusion, a condor spread is a powerful trading strategy that can be used to earn significant returns on investment. By understanding the various strategies and tools available for managing these types of trades, and by carefully choosing the right strike prices and expiration dates, traders can maximize their profits and minimize their risk. Additionally, by setting stop-losses, adjusting the trade as needed, and monitoring the trade closely, traders can increase their chances of success in the fast-paced world of options trading.

Chapter 93: How to Manage Condor Spreads

A condor spread is a type of options trading strategy that involves selling two options with different strike prices and buying two options with different strike prices. The goal of this strategy is to profit from a market that remains within a certain price range. However, as with any options trading strategy, managing a condor spread can be challenging. In this chapter, we will explore various strategies for managing condor spreads, including rolling, rolling and widening, and rolling and narrowing. We will also discuss how to choose the right strategy for different market conditions and strategies for managing risk and maximizing profits when managing condor spreads.

- Definition of a condor spread

- Various strategies for managing condor spreads, including rolling, rolling and widening, and rolling and narrowing
- How to choose the right strategy for different market conditions
- Strategies for managing risk and maximizing profits when managing condor spreads

A condor spread is a type of options trading strategy that involves selling two options with different strike prices and buying two options with different strike prices. The goal of this strategy is to profit from a market that remains within a certain price range. However, as with any options trading strategy, managing a condor spread can be challenging. In this chapter, we will explore various strategies for managing condor spreads, including rolling, rolling and widening, and rolling and narrowing. We will also discuss how to choose the right strategy for different market conditions and strategies for managing risk and maximizing profits when managing condor spreads.

One strategy for managing a condor spread is rolling. Rolling involves closing your current position and opening a new one with a different expiration date and strike prices. This strategy can be used to reduce risk and increase profits, but it also requires you to have a good understanding of the market conditions and the direction that the market is likely to move.

Another strategy for managing a condor spread is rolling and widening. This strategy involves closing your current position and opening a new one with a different expiration date and strike prices, but with a wider range. This strategy can be used to reduce risk and increase profits, but it also requires you to have a good understanding of the market conditions and the direction that the market is likely to move.

Finally, rolling and narrowing is a strategy for managing a condor spread that involves closing your current position and opening a new one with a different expiration date and strike prices, but with a narrower range. This strategy can be used to reduce risk and increase profits, but it also requires you to have a good understanding of the market conditions and the direction that the market is likely to move.

The key to managing a condor spread is to have a good understanding of the market conditions and the direction that the market is likely to move. This requires you to have a good understanding of the market conditions and the direction that the market is likely to move. Additionally, it's important to choose the right strategy for different market conditions, as well as strategies for managing risk and maximizing profits when managing condor spreads.

Case Study: Managing a Condor Spread on XYZ Stock

In this case study, we will look at how a trader named Michael used a rolling and narrowing strategy to manage a condor spread on XYZ stock. Michael had originally entered into a condor spread on XYZ stock, which was trading at $70. He believed that the stock would remain within a range of $68-$72 for the next month. However, after a few weeks, the stock began to trade outside of this range. Michael decided to close his original position and open a new one with a different expiration date and strike prices. He bought a new call option with a strike price of $71 and sold two put options with strike prices of $69 and $70, as well as two call options with strike prices of $73 and $74. By rolling and narrowing his position, Michael was able to reduce his risk and increase his chances of profit. In the end, the stock did indeed stay within the desired range, and Michael was able to make a substantial profit on his trade.

It is important to note that while this strategy worked well for Michael, it may not work for every trader in every market condition. This is why it is crucial to carefully evaluate the market and choose the right strategy for managing a condor spread. In addition, it is essential to have a solid understanding of the underlying asset and its volatility, as well as the expiration date and strike prices of the options involved in the trade.

Another strategy for managing a condor spread is to roll the trade. This involves closing the current position and opening a new one with a different expiration date and strike prices. This can be done to adjust for changes in the market or to take advantage of new opportunities. For example, if a trader believes that the market is going to become more volatile, they may choose to roll their trade to a later expiration date, giving them more time to profit from the increased volatility.

Additionally, it is important to have a solid risk management plan in place when managing a condor spread. This can include setting stop-loss orders and adjusting the trade as needed to limit potential losses. It is also important to have a clear exit strategy in place, so that the trader knows when to take profits or cut losses.

In conclusion, a condor spread is a complex and powerful trading strategy that can be used to take advantage of market conditions and maximize profits. However, it is important to have a solid understanding of the underlying asset and its volatility, as well as the expiration date and strike prices of the options involved in the trade. It is also crucial to choose the right strategy for managing the trade, and to have a solid risk management plan in place. By following these guidelines, traders can successfully use a condor spread to profit in the options market.

Chapter 94: What is a Diagonal Spread?

A diagonal spread is an options trading strategy that involves buying or selling a call or put option at one strike price and expiration date, and then simultaneously selling or buying a call or put option at a different strike price and expiration date. The goal of a diagonal spread is to take advantage of the time decay of options and the potential for price movement in the underlying asset.

Diagonal spreads can be created using both call and put options, and can be either bullish or bearish depending on the combination of options used. A bullish diagonal spread involves buying a longer-term call option and selling a shorter-term call option with a higher strike price, while a bearish diagonal spread involves buying a longer-term put option and selling a shorter-term put option with a lower strike price.

The key to successfully using a diagonal spread is to choose the right strike prices and expiration dates for both options. The strike price of the option that is sold should be closer to the current price of the underlying asset, while the strike price of the option that is bought should be farther away from the current price of the underlying asset. Additionally, the expiration date of the option that is sold should be sooner than the expiration date of the option that is bought.

Diagonal spreads can be a useful tool for options traders looking to hedge their positions or take advantage of a potential price movement in the underlying asset. However, it is important to keep in mind that these spreads involve a significant amount of risk, and should only be used by experienced traders who are comfortable with the potential risks and rewards of this type of trade.

Example: Trading a Diagonal Spread on XYZ Stock

In this example, we'll look at how a trader named Michael used a diagonal spread to trade

XYZ stock. Michael believed that the stock would remain within a range of $70-$75 for the next month. However, he also believed that there was a good chance that the stock would rise above $75 in the next three months.

To take advantage of this potential price movement, Michael decided to enter into a bullish diagonal spread. He bought a call option with a strike price of $75 and an expiration date of 3 months from now, and simultaneously sold a call option with a strike price of $72 and an expiration date of 1 month from now.

By selling the shorter-term option, Michael was able to collect a premium that would help offset the cost of buying the longer-term option. Additionally, by selling the call option with a strike price of $72, he was able to limit his potential losses if the stock did not rise above $75 in the next three months.

In the end, Michael's trade was successful. The stock rose above $75 in the next three months, and he was able to sell his long call option for a profit. Additionally, the short call option expired worthless, resulting in a net profit for Michael.

It is important to note that diagonal spreads require a good understanding of the underlying asset and its potential price movements, as well as the ability to manage risk effectively. Traders who are not comfortable with the level of risk involved in diagonal spreads should consider other options trading strategies. Additionally, it is essential to have a clear exit strategy in place before entering into a diagonal spread. This will help to protect against potential losses and maximize profits.

In conclusion, diagonal spreads can be an effective options trading strategy for those with a good understanding of the underlying asset and the ability to manage risk. However, it is important to have a clear exit strategy in place and to be comfortable with the level of risk involved. By following these guidelines, traders can use diagonal spreads to potentially increase profits and manage risk in their options trading portfolio.

Case Study: Trading a Diagonal Spread on XYZ Stock

In this case study, we will look at how a trader named Michael used a diagonal spread to trade XYZ stock. Michael had been following XYZ stock for several months and believed that it had the potential for a significant price increase in the next six months. However, he also believed that there was a chance that the stock could experience a short-term dip in price. To take advantage of this potential price increase while also managing risk, Michael decided to enter into a diagonal spread.

Michael bought a call option with a strike price of $80 and an expiration date of six months in the future. He also sold a call option with a strike price of $75 and an expiration date of three months in the future. This created a diagonal spread with a potential profit of $5 per share if XYZ stock was trading above $80 at the six-month expiration date.

As it turned out, XYZ stock did experience a short-term dip in price and was trading at $72 at the three-month expiration date. However,

Michael had also placed a stop loss order at $70, which protected him from significant losses. By the six-month expiration date, XYZ stock had recovered and was trading at $85. Michael was able to close out his diagonal spread for a profit of $5 per share, as originally planned.

This case study illustrates how a diagonal spread can be an effective way to take advantage of potential price increases in the underlying asset while also managing risk. By choosing the right strike prices and expiration dates, and by implementing a stop loss order, Michael was able to successfully trade a diagonal spread on XYZ stock.

In conclusion, diagonal spreads can be an effective options trading strategy for those with a good understanding of the underlying asset and the ability to manage risk. Traders should choose the right strike prices and expiration dates, and implement a stop loss order to protect against potential losses. By following these guidelines, traders can use diagonal spreads to potentially increase profits and manage risk in their options trading portfolio.

Chapter 95: How to Trade a Diagonal Spread

A diagonal spread is a type of options trading strategy that involves buying or selling options with different strike prices and expiration dates. This allows traders to take advantage of different market conditions and price movements in order to maximize profits and minimize risk. In this chapter, we will provide a step-by-step guide for trading a diagonal spread, as well as real-world examples of successful trades and tips for making the most of this strategy.

Step-by-Step Guide for Trading a Diagonal Spread

1. Choose the underlying asset: The first step in trading a diagonal spread is to choose the underlying asset that you want to trade. This could be a stock, commodity, currency, or other financial instrument. It is important to choose an

asset that you have a good understanding of and that you believe will experience price movements in the near future.
2. Choose the strike prices and expiration dates: The next step is to choose the strike prices and expiration dates for the options that you will be buying or selling. In a diagonal spread, you will typically choose one option with a longer expiration date and another option with a shorter expiration date. The strike prices should also be different, with the option with the longer expiration date having a higher strike price than the option with the shorter expiration date.
3. Decide on a direction: Before entering into a diagonal spread, it is important to decide on a direction for the trade. Will you be buying a call option and selling a put option, or will you be selling a call option and buying a put option? This decision will depend on your outlook for the underlying asset and your risk tolerance.
4. Execute the trade: Once you have chosen the underlying asset, strike prices, expiration dates, and direction for the

547

trade, it is time to execute the trade. You can do this by placing an order with your broker or trading platform.
5. Manage risk: One of the most important aspects of trading a diagonal spread is managing risk. This means setting stop-loss orders and monitoring the trade closely to ensure that you are not exposed to excessive risk. It is also important to have a clear exit strategy in place before entering into a diagonal spread. This will help to protect against potential losses and maximize profits.

Real-World Examples of Diagonal Spread Trades

Example 1: Trading a diagonal spread on XYZ stock

In this example, a trader named Michael used a diagonal spread to trade XYZ stock. Michael believed that the stock would experience price movements in the near future, but was unsure of the direction of these movements. He decided to enter into a diagonal spread, buying a call option with a strike price of $70 and an expiration date of 3 months, and selling a put option with a strike price of $65 and an expiration date of 1 month. Michael was able to take advantage of different market conditions and price movements, and ultimately made a profit on the trade.

Example 2: Trading a diagonal spread on Gold

In this example, a trader named Sarah used a diagonal spread to trade gold. Sarah believed that the price of gold would experience price movements in the near future, but was unsure of the direction of these movements. She decided to enter into a diagonal spread, buying a call option with a strike price of $1,500 and an expiration date of 6 months, and selling a put option with a strike price of $1,450 and an expiration date of 3 months. By doing this, Sarah was able to take advantage of the potential price movements in gold, while also limiting her risk.

The trade paid off for Sarah as the price of gold did indeed experience significant price movements over the next few months. The call option that Sarah bought increased in value, while the put option she sold decreased in value. In total, Sarah made a profit of $2,000 on the trade.

One of the key factors in this trade's success was Sarah's ability to choose the right strike prices and expiration dates. By selecting a call option with a strike price of $1,500 and an expiration date of 6 months, Sarah was able to take advantage of a potential increase in the price of gold over the longer term. At the same time, by selling a put option with a strike price of $1,450 and an expiration date of 3 months, Sarah was able to limit her risk and lock in a profit if the price of gold fell in the short term.

Sarah's trade also highlights the importance of having a clear exit strategy in place when trading diagonal spreads. She was able to manage her risk effectively by exiting the trade at the right time, which ultimately led to a successful outcome.

In conclusion, diagonal spreads can be a powerful tool for options traders looking to take advantage of potential price movements in the underlying asset. However, they do require a good understanding of the underlying asset and the ability to manage risk effectively. By following a step-by-step guide, choosing the right strike prices and expiration dates, and having a clear exit strategy in place, traders can successfully trade diagonal spreads and potentially earn a profit.

Chapter 96: How to Manage Diagonal Spreads

Diagonal spreads are a popular options trading strategy that can be used to take advantage of price movements in the underlying asset. However, managing a diagonal spread can be challenging, as it requires a good understanding of the market and the ability to adjust the trade as needed. In this chapter, we will explore various strategies for managing diagonal spreads and provide tips and tricks for maximizing profits and minimizing risk.

- Various strategies for managing diagonal spreads, including rolling, rolling and widening, and rolling and narrowing
- How to choose the right strategy for different market conditions
- Strategies for managing risk and maximizing profits when managing diagonal spreads

One strategy for managing a diagonal spread is to roll it. Rolling a diagonal spread involves closing the existing position and opening a new one with different strike prices and expiration dates. This can be done to take advantage of a change in market conditions or to lock in profits. For example, if the underlying asset has moved in the trader's favor, they may choose to roll the spread to a higher strike price to lock in profits. Similarly, if the underlying asset has moved against the trader, they may choose to roll the spread to a lower strike price to minimize losses.

Another strategy for managing a diagonal spread is to roll and widen it. This involves closing the existing position and opening a new one with a wider range of strike prices and expiration dates. This can be done to take advantage of increased volatility in the market. For example, if the trader believes that the underlying asset will experience significant price movements in the near future, they may choose to roll and widen the spread to capture these movements.

A third strategy for managing a diagonal spread is to roll and narrow it. This involves closing the existing position and opening a new one with a narrower range of strike prices and expiration dates. This can be done to take advantage of reduced volatility in the market. For example, if the trader believes that the underlying asset will experience minimal price movements in the near future, they may choose to roll and narrow the spread to minimize risk.

When choosing which strategy to use for managing a diagonal spread, it is important to consider the current market conditions and the trader's outlook on the underlying asset. For example, if the trader believes that the underlying asset will experience significant price movements, they may choose to roll and widen the spread. However, if they believe that the underlying asset will experience minimal price movements, they may choose to roll and narrow the spread.

In addition to choosing the right strategy for managing a diagonal spread, it is also important to manage risk effectively. This can be done by setting stop-loss orders and using risk management tools such as options Greeks. For example, using the delta of an option can help a trader to determine the likelihood of the option expiring in the money. Additionally, using the vega of an option can help a trader to determine the sensitivity of the option to changes in volatility.

Case Study: Managing a Diagonal Spread on XYZ Stock

In this case study, we will look at how a trader named Michael used a rolling and narrowing strategy to manage a diagonal spread on XYZ stock. Michael had originally entered into a diagonal spread on XYZ stock, which was trading at $70. He believed that the stock would experience price movements within a range of $68-$72 for the next month. However, after a few weeks, the stock began to trade outside of this range. Michael decided to close his original position and open a new one with a different expiration date and strike prices. He bought a new call option with a strike price of $75 and an expiration date of 3 months, and sold a new put option with a strike price of $65 and an expiration date of 2 months. By narrowing the strike prices and expiration dates, Michael was able to reduce his risk and increase his potential profits.

It is important to note that when managing diagonal spreads, it is crucial to have a clear exit strategy in place. This means having a plan for when to close the trade, whether it is because the stock has reached a certain price or because the expiration date is approaching. Additionally, it is important to monitor the market conditions and adjust the trade as needed. For example, if the market is showing signs of volatility, it may be wise to roll the trade to a later expiration date to give the stock more time to move in the desired direction.

Another important strategy for managing diagonal spreads is to diversify your portfolio. This means not putting all of your eggs in one basket by only trading one stock or commodity. Instead, consider spreading your investments across multiple assets to reduce risk and increase potential profits.

In conclusion, diagonal spreads can be a powerful tool for options trading, but they require a good understanding of the underlying asset and the market conditions. By having a clear exit strategy, monitoring the market, and diversifying your portfolio, traders can effectively manage diagonal spreads and maximize their profits.

Chapter 97: How to Trade Options on Volatility

Options trading is a popular way to make money in the stock market, but it can also be a risky endeavor. One of the most important factors to consider when trading options is volatility. Volatility refers to the degree of uncertainty or risk associated with the size of price changes in an asset. In this chapter, we will explore how to trade options on volatility and how to use volatility to make trades that are profitable and low-risk.

Definition of trading options on volatility

Trading options on volatility is a strategy that involves buying or selling options based on the volatility of the underlying asset. The underlying asset can be a stock, commodity, currency, or index. Volatility is a measure of the degree of uncertainty or risk associated with the size of price changes in an asset. When the volatility of an asset is high, it means that the price of the asset is likely to change significantly in a short period of time. When the volatility of an asset is low, it means that the price of the asset is likely to change only slightly in a short period of time.

How volatility affects options trading

Volatility affects options trading in several ways. When volatility is high, the price of options contracts will be higher, as the likelihood of large price movements in the underlying asset is greater. This means that traders who buy options contracts when volatility is high will have to pay more for the contracts, but they will also have the potential to make larger profits. When volatility is low, the price of options contracts will be lower, as the likelihood of large price movements in the underlying asset is smaller. This means that traders who buy options contracts when volatility is low will have to pay less for the contracts, but they will also have the potential to make smaller profits.

Importance of understanding volatility in options trading

Understanding volatility is crucial for options trading because it allows traders to make informed decisions about when to buy and sell options contracts. By understanding the volatility of an underlying asset, traders can predict the likelihood of large price movements in the asset, and make trades that are more profitable and low-risk. Additionally, volatility can be used as a tool to manage risk. For example, traders can use options contracts with expiration dates that are further out when volatility is high, and options contracts with expiration dates that are closer when volatility is low.

Strategies for using volatility to make trades

There are several strategies for using volatility to make trades. One strategy is to buy options contracts when volatility is high, and sell options contracts when volatility is low. This is known as volatility trading. Traders can also use options contracts with different expiration dates to manage risk. For example, when volatility is high, traders can use options contracts with expiration dates that are further out, and when volatility is low, traders can use options contracts with expiration dates that are closer. Additionally, traders can use options contracts with different strike prices to manage risk. For example, when volatility is high, traders can use options contracts with strike prices that are further out, and when volatility is low, traders can use options contracts with strike prices that are closer.

Case Study: Trading Options on Volatility on Apple Stock

In this case study, we will look at how a trader named John used volatility trading to make trades on Apple stock. John believed that the volatility of Apple stock would increase in the near future. He decided to buy call options contracts with expiration dates that were further out and strike prices that were further out. As the volatility of Apple stock increased, the price of the options contracts also increased, and John was able to make a large profit on his trade.

In conclusion, trading options on volatility can be a powerful tool for options traders. By understanding the impact of volatility on options prices and using strategies like purchasing longer-term options contracts with higher strike prices, traders can potentially capitalize on market movements and make profitable trades. However, it is important to remember that volatility can be unpredictable, and traders should always be mindful of the risks involved and have a solid risk management plan in place. With the right understanding and strategies, trading options on volatility can be a valuable addition to any options trading arsenal.

Chapter 98: Risk Management for Options Trading

Options trading can be a high-risk, high-reward endeavor. In order to be successful in options trading, it is essential to have a solid risk management plan in place. This chapter will explore various strategies for managing risk in options trading, including diversification, position sizing, and stop-loss orders. We will also look at how to create a risk management plan for options trading and provide tips and tricks for successful risk management.

Definition of Risk Management

Risk management is the process of identifying, assessing, and prioritizing potential risks to an investment portfolio. The goal of risk management is to minimize the potential for losses and maximize the potential for gains. This is achieved by implementing strategies that reduce the likelihood of losing money and increase the chances of making money.

Diversification

Diversification is one of the most important strategies for managing risk in options trading. Diversification involves investing in a variety of assets, such as stocks, bonds, and commodities, to spread out the risk. This helps to reduce the impact of any one investment on the overall portfolio. For example, if one stock in a portfolio experiences a significant loss, the other stocks in the portfolio will help to offset the loss.

Position Sizing

Position sizing is another important strategy for managing risk in options trading. Position sizing involves determining the appropriate amount of money to invest in a particular trade. This helps to ensure that the potential for losses is kept to a minimum. For example, if a trader has a risk tolerance of $1,000 and is considering a trade that has a potential loss of $500, it would be appropriate to invest $500 in that trade.

Stop-Loss Orders

Stop-loss orders are another important strategy for managing risk in options trading. A stop-loss order is an order placed with a broker to sell a security at a certain price in order to limit potential losses. For example, if a trader buys a stock for $100 and places a stop-loss order at $90, the stock will be sold automatically if the price drops to $90. This helps to ensure that the potential for losses is kept to a minimum.

Creating a Risk Management Plan

Creating a risk management plan is essential for successful options trading. A risk management plan should include a clear definition of the trader's risk tolerance, as well as strategies for managing risk. For example, the plan may include diversification, position sizing, and stop-loss orders. The plan should also include a clear exit strategy for each trade, as well as a plan for adjusting the trade as needed.

Tips and Tricks for Successful Risk Management

- Set clear risk management goals and strategies before entering into a trade
- Have a clear exit strategy in place before entering into a trade
- Be willing to adjust trades as needed in order to manage risk effectively
- Diversify your portfolio to spread out risk
- Use stop-loss orders to limit potential losses
- Continuously monitor and adjust your risk management plan as needed

Case Study: Risk Management for Options Trading

In this case study, we will look at how a trader named Sarah used risk management strategies to successfully trade options. Sarah had a clear risk management plan in place, which included diversification, position sizing, and stop-loss orders. She also had a clear exit strategy in place for each trade.

Sarah began by diversifying her portfolio, investing in a variety of stocks, bonds, and commodities. She also used position sizing to determine the appropriate amount of money to invest in each trade. For example, if a trade had a potential loss of $500, she would only invest $500 in that trade. This helped her to minimize her potential losses and maximize her potential profits.

In addition to diversifying her portfolio and using position sizing, Sarah also implemented stop-loss orders into her trading strategy. A stop-loss order is a type of order that automatically closes a trade when the price of the underlying asset reaches a certain level. This helped her to limit her potential losses and protect her capital.

Case Study: Risk Management for Options Trading on XYZ Stock

In this case study, we will look at how a trader named Michael used risk management strategies to trade options on XYZ stock. Michael had a strong belief that XYZ stock would experience price movements in the near future, but was unsure of the direction of these movements. He decided to enter into a long straddle options trade, buying a call option and a put option with the same strike price and expiration date. However, he knew that this type of trade carried a high level of risk and decided to implement risk management strategies to protect his capital.

Michael began by diversifying his portfolio, investing in a variety of stocks, bonds, and commodities. He also used position sizing to determine the appropriate amount of money to invest in each trade. He then implemented stop-loss orders on his long straddle options trade, setting a stop-loss order at a level that would limit his potential losses and protect his capital.

In conclusion, risk management is an essential aspect of options trading. By diversifying your portfolio, using position sizing, and implementing stop-loss orders, you can minimize your potential losses and maximize your potential profits. It is important to have a clear and well-defined risk management plan in place before entering into any options trade. By following these strategies, traders can increase their chances of success in the options market.

Chapter 99: How to Create a Trading Plan

A trading plan is a comprehensive document that outlines your trading strategy, goals, risk management plan, and other important details. It serves as a roadmap for your trading journey, helping you to stay focused and on track. A well-crafted trading plan can help you to achieve your goals, minimize risk, and make better trading decisions. In this chapter, we will discuss the importance of creating a trading plan and provide a step-by-step guide for creating one.

1. Definition of a trading plan

A trading plan is a detailed document that outlines your trading strategy, goals, risk management plan, and other important details. It is a roadmap that guides your trading journey and helps you to stay focused and on track. A trading plan should be tailored to your individual trading style and goals. It should also be flexible enough to adapt to changing market conditions.

2. Why creating a trading plan is important

Creating a trading plan is essential for several reasons. First, it helps you to set clear and achievable goals for your trading journey. This can help you to stay focused and motivated. Second, a trading plan can help you to minimize risk by outlining a risk management plan that is tailored to your individual risk tolerance. Third, a trading plan can help you to make better trading decisions by providing a framework for analyzing market conditions and choosing trades.

3. Steps for creating a trading plan

Creating a trading plan is a process that takes time and effort. It is important to be thorough and to take your time. Here are the steps for creating a trading plan:

Step 1: Set your goals

The first step in creating a trading plan is to set clear and achievable goals. These goals should be specific, measurable, and time-bound. For example, "I want to make a 20% return on my investment within the next year."

Step 2: Identify market conditions

The next step is to identify the market conditions that you will be trading in. This includes analyzing the overall market conditions, as well as specific conditions for the assets that you will be trading. This analysis should include an examination of economic indicators, technical indicators, and other relevant data.

Step 3: Create a risk management plan

The third step is to create a risk management plan. This plan should outline the steps that you will take to minimize risk and protect your capital. This may include using stop-loss orders, diversifying your portfolio, and using position sizing.

Step 4: Develop a trading strategy

The fourth step is to develop a trading strategy. This strategy should be tailored to your individual trading style and goals. It should also be flexible enough to adapt to changing market conditions.

Step 5: Implement and monitor your plan

The final step is to implement and monitor your plan. This includes setting up a system for tracking your progress and making adjustments as needed.

4. Tips and tricks for successful trading plan creation
- Be realistic: Set goals that are achievable and realistic.
- Be flexible: Your plan should be flexible enough to adapt to changing market conditions.
- Be thorough: Take your time and be thorough when creating your plan.

- Be consistent: Stick to your plan and be consistent in your trading.
- Keep learning: Keep learning about the markets and new trading strategies.

Case Study: Creating a Trading Plan for Jane

Jane is a new trader who wants to create a trading plan to guide her journey. She begins by setting a goal of making a 10% return on her investment within the next year. Next, she conducts research on market conditions and identifies that she wants to trade in Jane is a new trader who wants to create a trading plan to guide her journey. She begins by setting a goal of making a 10% return on her investment within the next year. Next, she conducts research on market conditions and identifies that she wants to trade in
the technology sector, as it has been growing consistently in recent years.

To achieve her goal, Jane decides to create a risk management plan. She begins by diversifying her portfolio and investing in a variety of technology companies. She also sets a stop-loss order for each trade to limit her potential losses. Additionally, she sets a limit on the amount of money she will invest in each trade, based on her overall portfolio size and risk tolerance.

Jane also creates a plan for monitoring her trades and making adjustments as needed. She sets aside time each day to review her portfolio and make any necessary adjustments. She also conducts research on the companies she is invested in, keeping an eye out for any news or events that may affect their stock prices.

Finally, Jane creates a plan for exiting trades. She sets a target profit for each trade and exits when that target is reached. She also has a plan in place for cutting her losses if a trade is not going in her favor.

By following these steps and sticking to her trading plan, Jane is able to achieve her goal of making a 10% return on her investment within the year. She also gains confidence and experience as a trader, setting her up for success in the future.

In conclusion, creating a trading plan is crucial for success in options trading. It helps traders set clear goals, identify market conditions, manage risk, and make informed decisions. By following the steps outlined in this chapter and using the example of Jane as a guide, traders can create a comprehensive and effective trading plan to guide their journey.

Chapter 100: Conclusion

Options trading can be a challenging and complex topic, but with the right education and practice, it can also be a highly profitable one. Throughout this book, we've covered a wide range of topics and strategies that can help traders of all levels to become successful in the options market.

Summary of key takeaways:

- The importance of understanding the basics of options trading, including the types of options, the mechanics of options trading, and the key terms and concepts involved.
- The importance of having a clear understanding of market trends and conditions, as well as how to use technical and fundamental analysis to make informed trading decisions.

- The importance of developing a solid trading plan and risk management strategy, including how to set goals, identify market conditions, and manage risk effectively.

The importance of ongoing education and practice:

- The options market is constantly changing, so it's essential for traders to stay up-to-date on the latest market trends and developments.
- Regular practice is key to building the skills and discipline necessary for successful options trading.
- Ongoing education can be achieved through self-study, online courses, and mentorship programs.

Final tips for successful options trading:

- Start small and gradually increase your position size as your confidence and experience grow.
- Don't be afraid to take losses and adjust your trading plan accordingly.
- Stay disciplined and stick to your trading plan, even when faced with market volatility or unexpected events.

Common mistakes to avoid:

- Over-leveraging or risking too much capital on a single trade.
- Chasing after hot tips or jumping into trades without conducting proper research.
- Not having a solid risk management strategy in place.
- Failing to stay up-to-date on market trends and developments.

Resources for further learning:

- Websites such as Investopedia and the Options Industry Council offer a wealth of information and resources on options trading.
- Online courses and mentorship programs can provide traders with the opportunity to learn from experienced professionals.
- Stay informed by reading financial news and following market trends and developments.

A reminder of the importance of discipline, patience, and consistency:

- Successful options trading requires discipline, patience, and consistency.
- Traders must be willing to take losses, adjust their trading plan, and stay disciplined in order to achieve long-term success.
- Consistency is key to building the skills and discipline necessary for successful options trading.

In conclusion, options trading is a challenging and complex topic, but with the right education, practice, and discipline, it can be a highly profitable endeavor. We hope that this book has provided you with the knowledge and resources you need to become a successful options trader. Remember to stay up-to-date on market trends and developments, stay disciplined and consistent, and never stop learning and practicing. Good luck on your options trading journey!

Printed in Great Britain
by Amazon